Church Revitalization in Rural America: Restoring Churches in America's Heartland

By Tom Cheyney

with

John Kimball, Jim Grant, Rob Hurtgen, & Chris Irving

RENOVATE
Publishing Group

First published by Renovate Publishing Group in 9/5/2018.

ISBN-13: **9780998738468**

ISBN-10: **0998738468**

Printed in the United States of America

Dedication (Tom)
To Cheryl, my beloved!

My best friend, life companion, and one who challenges me every day to be the best I can for my Lord. You mean the world to me. There are so many things I truly admire about you as a person, as my best friend and as my wife. Your smile lights up my soul. As a church revitalizer's wife, you have been courageous to go even when the path seemed unclear and yet the hand of God was certain. You have given much and sacrificed more so others might see Jesus. To all of those Church Revitalizers serving in local churches asking God to do great things once more and revive their church once more. The course is not easy, but the need is great and our Master longs to see the church restored for future generations.

"For God has not given us a spirit of fearfulness, but one of power, love, and sound judgment"

2 Timothy 1:7 HCSB

To God be the glory forever and ever.

To the more than 350 rural pastors and laity who shared their hearts and their souls for the sake of the rural American church! Thank you.

What Others Are Saying About *Church Revitalization in Rural America!*

Tom Cheyney knows churches. As a church leader himself and as an advisor to countless pastors, Tom has developed insights about church life and health which are valuable resources for all of us. In particular, Tom has a heart for church revitalization, which is one of the most pressing issues of our day. I am thankful for the investment Tom has made in helping pastors and other leaders breathe new life into dying and declining congregations.

Michael Duduit, Executive Editor of Preaching Magazine and founding Dean of the Clamp Divinity School at Anderson University in Anderson, SC)

During the years I spent as an Organizational Change Consultant, I observed first-hand the kind of impact that leaders can have when they embrace the role of change agent. In *Church Revitalization in Rural America: Restoring Churches in America's Heartland*, Tom Cheyney gives church leaders tools to take on that critical role. This book will help to increase your confidence to become the kind of catalyst leader needed to lead your church into the future.

Lee Kricher, Author
For a New Generation: A Practical Guide for Revitalizing Your Church

I am convinced that nobody and I mean nobody in America understands Church Revitalization like my friend, Dr. Tom Cheyney, founder of the Renovate National Church Revitalization Conference. He not only understands the intricacies of the revitalization process itself, but the dynamics required of the leaders who attempt this important work. Tom Cheyney is the seminal leader in the Church Revitalization Movement in America today. His vast experience as a church planter and revitalizer, coupled with his ability to communicate within both academia and to the church, uniquely qualifies him to write the official playbook of revitalization strategies. In *Church Revitalization in Rural America: Restoring Churches in America's Heartland*, Cheyney has comprehensively identified and described the contemporary strategies for addressing rural church revitalization. Church leaders, looking for guidance as they lead their churches into a revitalization process, will find this work to be an essential and invaluable tool to guide them in the strategy that best fits their settings.

Terry Rials
Church Revitalizer & Pastor of Crestview Baptist Church
Co-Author of *The Nuts and Bolts of Church Revitalization*

I don't know anyone who is more well-versed or written on church revitalization than Tom Cheyney. His advice is solid, practical, and helpful. This is one for your tool chest pastors.

Ron Edmondson, Blogger
CEO Leadership Network
ron.edmondson@gmail.com

Tom Cheyney does it again! He addresses a critical need in Church Revitalization in a way that is both insightful and practical. In *Church Revitalization in Rural America: Restoring Churches in America's Heartland*, Dr. Cheyney, who is quickly becoming known as the father of the church revitalization movement, writes about this crucial role for church revitalizers. Let us never forget the obvious- that church revitalization requires significant change. Readers will discover that much more is being done in the area of church revitalization than previously realized. This book is for and about those whose job it is to lead churches to do what they are reluctant to do. Inspiring and hopeful, this is a must read for anyone who is concerned about the state of rural churches in North America.

Mark Weible, Director of Church Planting Greater Orlando Baptist Association

Tom Cheyney understands Church Revitalization like few others. He realizes the local pastor of the church in search of revitalization is the key. If my rural church was struggling and in need of revitalization than I would want to first read *Church Revitalization in Rural America: Restoring Churches in America's Heartland*. Tom leads a growing multi-denominational church revitalization movement that impacts thousands of churches and pastors. He is the leader in the field and the voice that so many turn to when it comes to church revitalization and renewal. This book, will be a valuable asset to any rural pastor desiring to lead his church through the process of Revitalization. This is a book you want to read and what to read it now.

Larry Wynn, Co-author
Preaching Towards Church Revitalization and Renewal

Buy this book, the cost is small in dollars but large in impact. *Church Revitalization in Rural America: Restoring Churches in America's Heartland*, is about new paradigms for the rural church. Tom trains revitalization pastors who take action and bring about healthy change. Cheyney is like few in this world on Church Revitalization. Tom helps me consistently become a more effective leader personally and with churches. He will do the same with you here. It is important to understand that there, are specific "skill sets" that are either learned or acquired by Pastors as they walk down the paths of their ministries. Everybody brings something to the table when they arrive to pastor a rural church. However, if they arrive at the table with an inability to analyze, create and adapt, they are going to be in for a rough "Pastor-Life," experience. I have known Dr. Tom Cheyney for over forty years. *Church Revitalization in Rural America: Restoring Churches in America's Heartland*, is packed with valuable insights that he has gleaned through the "School of Hard Ministry Knocks." Tired of watching others succeed in changing their situations where you are too scared to lead? Read this book! Don't know how to move your rural church past an entrenched establishment that hasn't changed in years? Read this book! Starting out in ministry and looking to not have to "learn the hard way?" Read this book!

Greg Kappas
President, Grace Global Network
Vice President, The Timothy Initiative
Author *Five Stages for Multiplying Healthy Churches*

No one has researched and trained more church leaders in the area of church revitalization than Dr. Tom Cheyney. As you peruse the pages of this book, you will discover how God is calling you to help bring necessary change to your church. Both pastors and lay leaders will benefit greatly from the challenges here. May the Lord use this tool in your church's life as it moves toward life!

Joel Breidenbaugh
Author, *Preaching for Body Building*
Senior Pastor and Church Planter

Leading change is one of the most difficult disciplines in rural church revitalization, yet one that cannot be overlooked. In Tom Cheyney's most recent book, *Church Revitalization in Rural America: Restoring Churches in America's Heartland*, he is going to help you understand those necessary principles that will help you be an effective rural pastor in your church setting. If you find yourself in a place where change is so desperately needed, this is a must have book for you. Through Cheyney's expertise and experience, you will develop an appreciation for the many ways that God can bring about health and vitality in the church. The stakes are high and the challenge is big, but with the perils of wisdom you find within this book, as a rural leader you will gain confidence and understanding for how you can see revitalization in your church, for the glory of God.

Dr. Michael Atherton, Author of *The Revitalized Church*

Acknowledgements

Tom: I am blessed to serve each day the Greater Orlando Baptist Association (GOBA). This is a network of churches which is changing the way we have done associational work across Southern Baptist. No longer bound by geography, GOBA has raised the bar by working with churches, networks, and partners to plant healthy churches, to revitalize those churches in need of renewal, and to develop leaders equipped for the ministry through the GOAL Leadership Development Training. The Renovate National Church Revitalization Conference is one of these new things, which have impacted Christianity cross denominationally. Spearheaded by the wonderful pastors and laity who have partnered with us for the work of the Lord may I say thank you.

To my many committed Church Revitalization Practioners who join with me annually to make the Renovate National Church Revitalization Conference the largest conference focused on helping declining churches, I thank you. Your gifts and your passion for hurting churches make my heart leap with such godly compassion. To those just beginning the journey seeks God's best and become the best daily so you become a vessel fully developed for the work of a church revitalize

Church Revitalization in Rural America: Restoring Churches in America's Heartland

TABLE OF CONTENTS

Introduction

It is with great appreciation to the Greater Orlando Baptist Association that I was able to spend my 2017 study sabbatical researching rural church revitalization. That time made it possible for me to study 250 rural churches in five different states. These five states were Florida - my home state -, Georgia, Missouri, Kansas, and Kentucky. Since that time, I have had conversations with another one hundred rural pastors from various denominations. These pastors have been from Illinois, Alabama, North Carolina, and Tennessee. Nine different areas but each and every one while different in some aspects all had three distinct types of churches in the field of rural church revitalization. These there were: churches led by pastors who have given up and embraced maintaining the status quo, churches led by pastors which are stuck and doing little, and churches led by forward thinking pastors designing ways to embrace rural community and its population.

There are four gentlemen, rural church revitalizers in their own right I wish to thank. John Kimball who is a church planter and part of the 4C denomination, Jim Grant who is part of the national Renovate Steering Committee and pastors a rural church in Illinois, Rob Hurtgen who has been the Book Reviewer for the Church Revitalizer Magazine since its conception over seven years go and a rural pastor in Missouri, and Chris Irving who has been part of the Renovate Revitalization team for the last five years and pastors a rural church in Texas. These men have been a great help and their contribution to the cause is appreciated more than they will ever know. All of these men are authors in the field of revitalization and great trainers of pastors desiring to turn their churches around.

I would also wish to thank the one hundred plus rural churches which are part of the Greater Orlando Baptist

Association Family. While most of you are our Bivocational hero's, never let it be said that you are not acknowledged and appreciated. All around central Florida are rural communities where the cause of Christ is being honored by these godly men and their families.

If you are pastoring a rural church in North America you understand the numerous obstacles to growing and renewing a rural church. Many a rural pastor I interviewed or spoke with appeared overworked and overwhelmed. It can be very demanding for many rural pastors to stay encouraged and not lose heart. A growing number of rural pastors have lost hope in their rural ministries and have moved on to greener pastures. Some have become so disheartened they have left the ministry all together. There is a feeling of isolation in many rural pastorates. In 1920, most Americans lived on farms or in small, rural communities. By 1990, the population had shifted to the point that only about one in every four Americans lived in rural areas. Denominations have moved their emphasis from rural churches to urban or suburban churches. Feeling isolated and lacking in resources, pastors may find it difficult to maintain intellectual stimulation as they wrestle through difficult Bible passages and message preparation. A declining population can bring about feelings of isolation for pastors and their families. Smaller populations often translate into fewer resources and conveniences. Schools, community services, and entertainment may be further away from home.

A challenge we discovered all across the rural American landscape was the influx of Walmartization church plants. While I will always be a vocal voice for the planting of healthy New Testament churches, we are seeing these plants drawing the younger families and generations away from remote rural churches in favor of the seemingly more vibrant ministries taking place in a new plant in an adjoining town. Rural pastors need to speak up, get writing on the subject of rural, and challenge the masses to return to revitalizing rural churches. In a seminary I teach for, there was a doctorial seminar in revitalization which gave one full day to rural revitalization only to be replaced with discussion times currently about other topics. Today most Bible Schools and Seminaries offer very little training on rural ministry. Far too many who are called believe that a small rural pastorate is only a stepping stone for a larger suburban church after a few years of experience. My tribe, the Southern Baptist Convention, estimates that as many as 20,000, or roughly 65% of their pastors are bi-vocational; pastors who receive at least part of their income from a non-church source, which might include their spouse's employment. In fact, many pastors prefer to be bi-vocational viewing it as an opportunity for additional ministry.

The rural church in the heartlands of North America is still an important part of the Christian community and needs to be assisted, developed, and honored. There are obstacles and challenges as you will see within this work. Small town America is thriving in some places and struggling in other places. Weather you pastor in a prosperous rural area or a challenged rural area, there is still a great need for the local church in those areas. Jesus is alive in the rural heartland just like He is alive in the urban area and everywhere in between. The rural pastor must be honored. The rural pastor must be encouraged. The rural pastor must be loved on and encouraged until Jesus comes. We love rural pastors and want to see the best things happen in the rural areas where they pastor. Hold on dear rural pastor. There is a crown in heaven for you and your family as you seek to revitalize the heartlands.

Tom Cheyney, Founder & Directional Leader
The Renovate National Church Revitalization Conference
2 Timothy 1:7

Chapter 1
Church Revitalization in Rural America

Use your heads as you live and work among outsiders. Don't miss a trick. Make the most of every opportunity. Be gracious in your speech. The goal is to bring out the best in others in a conversation, not put them down, not cut them out.[1]

The church in rural America is undergoing large economic, demographic, and environmental changes. For some areas where they are fortunate to have abundant amenities, the Baby Boomer population, which is choosing to retire in these communities, is different than other areas where there is abundant poverty. Despite a popular perception, rural America is not a single community of homogenous farmers struggling to make a living. The communities of rural America are arguably far more diverse than their urban counterparts. Economically, socially, and culturally, rural America is at the forefront of adaptive change. Migration into and out of rural communities plays an important role in determining the demographic characteristics of rural America.

Rural America is a highly conservative set of communities, which are mostly, resistant towards any type of change. These occupants are locked in the thinking of the past and are out of touch with the postmodern beliefs and actions of our current world. As such there is a huge resistance towards any change, which will upset the status quo. The rural church pastor more often than not serves a particular congregation on a part-time base. Some will even minister to two or more congregations allowing a shared pooling of limited resources to support the work of the preacher. These ministers operate more as a chaplain to the

---

[1] Eugene H. Peterson, *The Message: The Bible in Contemporary Language* (Colorado Springs, CO: NavPress, 2005), Col 4:5–6.

community and are seen as the local parson who looks out for the needs of those are less fortunate. They face local dysfunctionality as the community addictions; abuses and gossips add to the struggles the minister faces as he tries to reach those who are not believers in the area.

There are a few things, which should be understood relating to becoming a Church Revitalizer in a rural community. It will be your most challenging calling to minister. It will take a deep skinned individual to bring about revitalization in an area which might say they desire such but in reality it will be a hard sell and take much time and work. People will talk about you and those of the community you so desperately want to reach will listen. You will need to be willing to anchor your soul and your life into the area as you work towards renewal. Your family must be rock solid and your spouse must be committed to you and the family. Those who initially call you to be their pastor might become your largest enemies because you are making changes, which will lead to the revitalization of their church. If you are called to revitalize a rural church you must love small town America and seek to adapt one's life in order to minister in such a place. Jesus loved all types of places and so should we.

For the Church Revitalizer seeking to revitalize a rural church there are some best practices or sage advice, which should be offered. It is always preferred to have the efforts towards renewal initiated by those within the church over the leader who has come to serve the church. Even if you are loved by your congregants, as the new leader you will still be seen as an outsider and your ideas or opinions will often be resisted. Therefore it is more wise to work with a team and allow them to bring about the ideas which could be considered. Another recommendation would be that any changes or modifications to program and structure should be taken gradually and with care. This will allow your membership to adapt to the modifications of existing and new ministries. Understand that the rural landscape is changing. Many have labeled this change as the new impact on rural or "nurural." The impetus for change comes both from within and without. Those leading the revitalization effort must become adapt of the telling of stories. Those who attend these churches and those who they are most effective with, tend to be "oral" learners as contrasted with "literary" individuals. The Gospel truth is best communicated by the church revitalizer through moving stories that touch the heart over the head. Another best practice is focusing your revitalization efforts towards the older rural dweller since they will most often make up the majority of the residents within these communities. Remember that the Church Revitalizer operates more often in the rural community as the social navigator of key needs and issues and becomes the influencer for the betterment of the community. Helping those who are impoverished is a great cause for the local rural church. Renewal is focused on care of community residents, conversionism, social services, social issues of the community, and serving as a leadership voice into the community for the residents. If a rural church has individuals, which can host and lead various educational programs in order to assist those with the acquiring of new skill sets, it will prove helpful. An often-overlooked best practice is that of developing great skill sets in the marrying and burying of those within the community. It is during these events that the church revitalizer becomes more of the community chaplain that the local churches pastor. A final practice, which has been found useful, is to push your churches outreach and ministry focus from six miles to a thirty-mile emphasis.

The Rural Church Revitalizer

What does the rural church revitalizer look like and function as? Being a rural church revitalizer is perhaps the hardest calling there is. Yet if you are called to it, it can be the most enjoyable ministry a preacher of the gospel can have.

He is part church planting catalyst, part entrepreneur, part pastor teach, part watcher for the lowly, and part community chaplain. What he is not is a big city pastor and if he operates within that ideology, he will not only hurt his family but could further destroy the church he has been called to revitalize. The church revitalizers vision must match the rural climate and harmonize the goals of the church with his own goals for the church to be successful. The rural revitalizer must see the work of the ministry in a fashion which paces the ministry with the pace of the climate of the community. He cannot expect huge budgets to do the work of the ministry. He will need to learn how to do a lot with very little. He must understand that everyone is related to some extent and if you tick off one individual you might be alienating a large part of the community and congregation.

Many a rural revitalization effort has centered around the re-opening of a church which had become dormant. Often reasons for this was a mismatch of pastor and church and the church leaders simply closed the church. Time passed and there became a new desire to reopen the church. These type of re-openings often tem from an urban pastor coming to a rural locale and trying to force feed a city structure and profile on a rural field. The nurural may have former city dwellers returning to their rural roots but the rural church in America is still a church with rural tendencies and the church revitalizer must identify with such mentality if he is going to be successful.

The Rural Church Revitalizer is Often Bi-vocational

Church revitalizers working in the rural landscape will often need to have outside employment in order to sustain their families livelihood. Money is tight in a rural church and ministers which do well have discovered outside employment to support the family while ministering in a rural church. If outside employment can be discovered and the work is enjoyable, then the minister and the church have a greater chance to succeed than one where the ministers dislikes outside employment and begrudges having to find an outside source for income. There is a growing willingness by pastors today to actually embrace bi-vocationalism. What was previously the elephant in the room type of thing, many pastors have realized that their quality of life is much better if they select to be a pastor who has one calling but two vocations. Many a church wants a full time minister but cannot afford one so they should be willing to embrace bi-vocationalism. The rural revitalizer must also live a modestly debt free life due to the rarity that they will ever be provided with additional resourcing from the church they lead. Church Revitalizers which have a high degree of indebtedness find it difficult to maintain the financial discipline required for them to serve a declining rural church.

The Rural Church Revitalizer is Often a Retired Minister

In the nurural church is it likely that a retired minister who longs for a simpler life will often serve a church. These wonderful servants of the Lord are not seeking to keep up the hectic pace that some many churches in other areas demand and they are happy to love on God's children and reach out to the unchurched in a rural assignment. Because they have provided for their retirement during their earlier days of ministry, they are able to assist a rural church in an area where they have retired. It is my prayerful wish that as all of us move into retirement, we would be open to such an assignment and send the last few years of full-time ministry learning everything possible about church revitalization so we could give assistance to a rural church in decline and be a blessing to them and not burden their smaller resources available. It is my repetitive prayer that when retirement comes my way, the Lord will show me a small declining rural church in which I might bless the people and keep a New Testament Church open on the rural landscape. The

Renovate National Church Revitalization Conference group is working hard at trying to connect such ministers and churches together. Rural communities need a gospel witness and there are a large number of retired ministers who could fill the need if they could be connected with one another.

The Rural Church Revitalizer is Often Sponsored by Another Church

God is beginning to raise up an army of concerned churches and pastors for the declining rural churches of north America. These churches work towards providing leadership assistance to these communities and churches. Such church revitalization leaders will utilize individuals from within its membership to take on the declining rural church as a preaching point each week. Men who have been called to ministry can be a tremendous opportunity for the rural church to have a pastor. Often in our churches there are men who are also learning to preach and need to be given a regular opportunity to preach the gospel. Such a church willing to sponsor the costs involved for a member to drive out weekly from the suburbs to a smaller community and preach for a town and country church is a blessing to both parties. The future preacher is learning how to minister to god's people and to preach, while the rural church is learning how to partner with a revitalizing church who wants to help. There are tens of thousands of thee preaching points all over North America and we need to connect the church in need with the revitalization church which is willing and move towards keeping these nurural churches open and functioning.

The Rural Church Revitalizer Lives in the Community

One of the best practices for rural revitalization is when a church revitalizer is able to live within the community where he is trying to revitalize the church. Living where those who worship in the church makes a strong statement that roots are being developed and that the minister has a heart for the community. While he may still be viewed as an outsider unless the minister is returning home to where he grew up, it does demonstrate the level of commitment he is willing to make.

The Rural Church Revitalizer is Content with Pastoring a Small Congregation

There are many benefits and blessings of leading a smaller rural church. A minister must not fall victim to the bigger is better craze of that was so prevalent in the church growth movement of the 1980's and 1990's. For almost twenty years proponents espoused the bigger is better theory for growing churches. Yet what we are left with after these twenty years of preachers and denominational leaders giving the clarion call of bigness is a western Christianity with huge percentages of decline and shrinking baptisms. If the bigger is better mentality was so successful, then why are we left with such high numbers of rapidly declining or dying churches. Bigness was embraced for a time but it did not impact the western culture the way the proponents hoped it would. So if you are trying to climb the ladder as a pastor over the true call to minister and meet individual needs, then you will struggle with a calling to consider pastoring a small rural church. The rural revitalizer must be content with pastoring people who have chosen a simpler lifestyle. Those who look at big as be blessed and those who are small as those who are not blessed, might have to take some serious re-evaluation of the true calling for the Lord's service. Ministry in the rural landscape is about serving people and ministering to their needs. Work as a church revitalizer to reconstruct what it means to be called to ministry and that begins with loving people no matter where god places you. There is great contentment in rural living so do not opt out of the blessings, which might come your way to revitalize a rural church. Rural living is fun so do not count it out.

The Rural Church Revitalizer prepare the young as missionaries for when they leave rural

Operating as a mission-sending center is also a great way for the rural church revitalizer to function. Rural churches will lose a certain number of young people annually as a result of them leaving the area for urban fringe and city life. Operating as a missionary training center for young adults between the ages of thirteen and eighteen will be a tremendous way to grow deep Christian young people who will be faithful as they go to the more urbanized area. Rural areas have children and young people. Working to lead them to Jesus, grow them in Jesus, and deploying them for Jesus is a great goal for the rural pastor. Nurturing young people who will eventually become servants in churches all over the world is something, which a rural church revitalizer could take a great sense of accomplishment. Preparing these young adults for the work of ministry is a tremendous way to impact future lives as they leave the rural communities all across our country. I see a day when these rural church revitalizers stand before our great and mighty Lord and He declares the mighty works of them ministers of God

The Rural Church Revitalizer Thinks Memorial Stones, Not Stepping Stones

Closely related to above the rural church revitalizer is more interested in creating memorial stones over that of developing stepping-stones. Rural revitalization is dignified work and the memories that can be made for the Lord in such areas are immeasurable. Those who want to renew a church are given an opportunity to make long lasting memorial stones for the rural church and the community it is called to serve. Such church revitalizers need to drive down stakes in the community and become a voice of compassion for those residents. Here are the most basic of stakes to anchor as a rural revitalization pastor. Remember you are:

Sent by God
Tireless in your effort
Always prayerful for community
Keeps the Church united
Encouraging to other community leaders
Secure in calling and ministry

Such a positive persona will assist you in task that when times of challenge, doubt, or discouragement come, you will stay firmly rooted in the surety that this is where the Lord wants you and you will find your heart and life fulfilled through the ministry to His rural people. Anything less then driving down firmly rooted stakes will lead you to flight once the troubles which come with revitalizing a rural church present themselves.

The Rural Church Revitalizer knows people, knows names, knows kindred, and orchestrates no problems

It goes without saying that in most rural revitalization efforts the church revitalizer must come to understand the people of the community first. H needs to take the time, make the time, and spend the time getting to know who lives there and how they are connected. He need to work on the family trees and the names of those patriarchal and matriarchal family leaders and how to minister to their families. If he will work diligently at this, there will be less problems that surface from alienating the family leasers and how they guide their families. Spending time with these family leaders hearing their ideas, praying with them, and sensing their heart for the rural church will give you much historical information as to why the church is the way that it is and what might be done to bring about a rebirth. It should be no surprise that these are the individuals, which bring the big actions to the church and not the rural church revitalizer.

The Rural Church Revitalizer becomes a watcher and chaplain for the larger region

Rural Church Revitalizers understand the climate of the small town community. They operate as a chaplain for the entire region over merely being the pastor of a single church. Yes they lead one congregation but the work of the ministry in a rural region is larger than just preaching on Sunday. Being at the big events is just as critical and the high school football, basketball, or baseball game on Friday night. The watcher in the rural revitalizer goes to town meetings and is a voice for the down and outs and those who are struggling over those who are comfortable. The rural landscape has huge needs and you need to be a voice for those who are unable to speak. One's daily schedule, as a rural revitalizer is much larger at times due to the other things he should be part of. Developing community events, thinking of ways to assist the young, attending to the elderly, and so much more make up the day for the rural revitalization leader.

The Rural Church Revitalizer might share his time between two churches

Small rural communities might have a building but are unable to have a full time minister lead their church. Several options are available to this church. One way for such a church is to have an early service in one community and a later service in another. Other rural areas have a church which meets every other week and share a minister that way. A third example is what is often called a quarter time church. This is a church, which has a worship service once every four weeks. A church revitalizer who shares his time between two or more churches is displaying his heart for the rural landscape and people. Rural people need churches and church revitalizers are individuals who have the heart for re-opening, re-cultivating, re-growing, and revitalizing the rural church.

The Rural Church Revitalizer desires to make the church better, not go to another one

Making a church better is much preferred over running from one church to another. Rural church revitalizers settle into an area and stop looking for the bigger is better next place and grow confident in God's calling of them to reach rural people. Investment of one's life in the rural area become enough rather than seeking greener pastures over the horizon. Greener pastures are often sitting on top of broken and leaking septic tanks. Stop climbing the rungs of success and become successful right where God wants you. Dedication to the rural landscape and investment of one's life towards reaching the lost in these communities is a great and worthy ministry.

The Rural Church Revitalizer concentrates on the numbers that really matter over those that do not

There is an old saying often overused by church practioners is that what really matters for the local church are nickels, numbers, and noses. For the name it and claim it group that is probably still the case. Yet, for the Rural Church Revitalizer, there are some other barometers that are more important to the revitalization of the rural church. Here are the ones, which are useful for the rural leaders of revitalization:

Increase Your Church's Visitor Flow - New faces and families in a rural church enable members to believe again in a brighter future and invest again in their buildings, their witness, and their efforts to please God.

Develop New Units – Arthur Flake's formula is still for real! This basic formula was: Know the possibilities, Enlarge the organization, Enlist and train the workers, Provide space and then go get them.

Increase Your Number of Volunteers – Every rural church has, at some time or another, complained about a lack of volunteers. Excuses are given as to why volunteers aren't showing up and a mad scramble usually ensues to figure out how to get the work of the church done. But most of the conceptions that we have about volunteers are misconceptions. Some of the reasons our churches give for not making great strides in recruiting volunteers are not good reasons they are myths. ☐

Work on Increasing Your Adult Attenders - According to Albert Einstein, the definition of insanity is "doing the same thing over and over again and expecting different results." This can directly apply to many situations, including attendance at your small church. If you are not satisfied with the number of attendees at your church, you cannot remain stagnant and expect to draw the masses. Instead, you may have to think strategically in order to increase attendance at your small church.

Increase the number of individuals being discipled - All Christians are disciples, but not all disciples are Christians. Jesus had many disciples who left Him in John 6:64-71 because of His teaching being hard to understand. Why? Because it was spiritual sayings about himself. What it was not about is things they must practice. Whenever people were stumbled over his words 9 out of 10 times it was about his person. These enormous numbers of people leaving can't be explained away as all fall a ways, those who could not continue being disciples and endure to the end. When they left Jesus it was because they did not understand spiritually who he was. When they leave your Church they can't keep up or cope with the strain of living on the edge of being discipled by another.

Outreach visits made - It is not likely that a church will grow or decline for one reason alone. It takes a combination of factors (what we call the growth mix) to cause church growth. The simplest concept in church growth is this; No visitors–no growth! The most influential thing in your growth mix is the friendship factor. If a person does not perceive they have made seven friends in the first year, it is unlikely they will be there at the end of the second year.

How many are you passing on the baton - A relay race is run by a team of four runners. The first runner carries a baton. After running a specified distance, called a "leg" the runner hands the baton to the next team member. The exchange must occur within a zone a few meters long. Timing is crucial. If the runners do not exchange the baton within this zone, the team is disqualified. The length of the race varies from four hundred to six thousand meters. The relay race is not necessarily won by the team that runs the fastest, but by successfully passing the baton in the exchange zone. That's right; races are won or lost in the passing of the baton. Teams can be disqualified by a bad pass. Passing the baton is essential to win the race. A lesson to be learned throughout the Bible is the importance of passing the baton from one generation to another. This is clearly seen (to give a few examples) in Moses passing the baton to Joshua, David to Solomon, Elijah to Elisha, Jesus to His disciples, and Paul to Timothy. It is not enough to run the race. We also pass our mission to the next generation. We must hand off the baton, at the right time, and must do it well. Jesus handed the baton to His disciples. They ran a good race and passed the baton to the next generation.

Timothy received the baton from Paul, and was instructed to pass it on to others (2 Timothy 2:2). It is so sad when we read about ministers who was not worried about the next generation. They are only worried about himself. Some are so selfish and "me" centered. They are more worried about his own pleasures over raising up a next generation of leaders to carry on the work of the ministry.

The Rural Church Revitalizer Cultivates His Talent To Lead a Rural Church

The Lord could do everything without us if we pause for a moment and reflect. If God selects you for the work of being a rural church revitalizer, it is a great work. Regardless of your prior training, you will still need to cultivate your talents to lead a rural church.

The Rural Church Revitalizer looks through the sands of the hourglass and finds it enough.

Remember the old daytime soap opera *Day of Our Lives?* It was one of the longest-running scripted television programs in the world, airing nearly every weekday since November 8, 1965. It focused of a few families and the lives in which they lived and the challenges they were facing. For the rural church revitalizer he looks through similar hourglasses to a time, which is a slight pace different than the hustle of the urban landscape. The days of his life are spent focusing on those who live work and play within a specific geographical location. While many church revitalizers are expanding their target of outreach from six miles to thirty, still there is a small area in which they focus and minister. This smaller area becomes much more than a target for ministry, it becomes the minister's life ministry and he finds it enough. No need for moving to the city for a rural church revitalizer. The quality of life fits well with their make up and wiring. Being a rural church revitalizer is a rewarding vocation. If you are lucky to serve such a rural community you have a quality of life, which other ministers might long to have themselves. Your influence will grow locally and you will be viewed in respectable ways that few city preachers ever achieve. You will have knowledge of individuals and families from the church and community you serve. Your depth of ministry will be most rewarding unlike many urban pastors, which are only afforded a lesser depth due to the size and location of the church. Your impact will be much more significant than you ever expected. While you may never have a reputation outside of a county or two, it will be a life worthy of the investment and the influence given.

The Rural Church Revitalizer knows how to do media and marketing from the back forty

Even in rural areas the need to let residents know what is going on at your church is essential. How you go about it is usually a little different. While the printed brochure is often overlooked in more rural contexts, it is a useful tool of dropping one off it the rural revitalizer finds no one home. Additionally flyers and posters put up in the local high traffic stores with the permission of the owner is still a great way to promote what is going on at your church. Since there is usually a local place where occupants gather for morning coffee or breakfast and lunch, dropping by to say hello and hand out a small card promoting the event you want them to know about is wise. Rural church revitalizers can capitalize upon hosting events in their sanctuary or fellowship hall for the community. Thus allowing those who are not yet comfortable with attending the church to feel welcomed in a non-threatening format. Also many smaller rural areas will allow pastors to do a daily devotional thought on the radio or newspaper. Creativity in this effort will often be rewarded by new prospects checking you and your church revitalization efforts out.

The Rural Church Revitalizer has learned that repetition reduces resistance

I had a history professor in college who would continually drill into us as students an array of facts and dates.

He would share them over and over in many and various ways. One day a young lady asked him why he had shared these bits of information that day at least four times during his lecture. He smiled and said, "Lassie, repetition reduces resistance!" I have never forgotten that day and his sly remark. What the professor was declaring was that if he continued to drill it in more than once we as students were more likely to learn it and be able to recall it when we needed it for the final exam. Those were the days when professors relished in see students learn the material and make it part of their memories. For the church revitalizer if you begin the work of making disciples and growing deep Christian character into your church members, you will discover that this repetition will be a well-loved friend. You will have the chance to build character and integrity into those you disciple one on one. Deepening a believer comes naturally as time is spent together and rural church revitalizers have a great chance to do that in the lives of the residents of a rural community. Take the long view and build church members, which are deep and developed through the Word of God.

Wrapping it up!

The lasting solutions to rural America's churches challenges will be found in rural America. The rural church in America in the twenty-first century must develop new relationships and new ways of doing things to ensure prosperous and socially healthy future. But we should not delude ourselves into thinking that the rural American church has so many unique issues. In fact, most of the challenges facing the rural American church today are often the same challenges for the declining rural, urban fringe, and extreme urban church seeking renewal and revitalization. Yet, while the challenges are similar, the solutions are more unique. The rural church in America in this century, must develop new relationships and new ways of doing things to ensure a prosperous, and healthy future while tapping into the resourcefulness and creativity of rural people.

There are a few things which should be stated about rural church revitalization are:
This will be the most challenging ministry assignment you will ever face! Stay at your post.

Your initial friends in the rural church will often become your biggest enemies due to your calling to revitalize a dying rural church.

Some of those who take flight will talk about you forever in that community so you must be toughed skinned.

Your marriage must be strong if you are to survive.

Often you will feel like you are the sacrificial lamb being led to the slaughter.
JESUS loves the little communities as much as he loves the big ones!

There is a higher sense of closeness in rural churches. Your skills as the under-shepherd will become further developed as a result of revitalizing a rural church. The pace of the rural church revitalizer is less rapid than that of the urban church revitalizer. You will grow to feel that your life is counting for something vital and enjoyable. There is a concern growing in the rural American community. This concern is how long will their churches actually be able to hold on. Many community leaders which previously looked at the denominational churches in their community in favor, are now highly suspect due to the high achy shifting their focus. Some denominations which were previously committed to the rural landscape of America are now moving their concern and resources to the suburbs and causing some of the decline in the religious landscape in small town America.

Business leaders and rural ministers hope that these previously committed denominations will realize the strong roots they had as part of growing such denominations. We live in a sad day when Christian organizations leave their rural roots in hope of becoming something they are not and that is a citified urban denomination. The Rural church needs to be revitalized and it will take church revitalizers committed from many and all types of denominational faith to refocus on the rural landscape. The smaller towns, villages, townships, ranches, farms, open spaces, and counties across America need rural church revitalizers to commit to rebirthing the heartland. It is estimated that there are more than 200,000 local congregations doing the work of ministry in rural America today. These churches have over seven million church members. For instance within my denomination of Southern Baptist there are 20,227 rural churches as reported during the last Church Membership Survey.

Tapping into the resourcefulness and creativity of the new rural (nu-rural) people will be essential in addressing this challenge. However, those returning to the rural landscape cannot do it alone. Those who have remained in the rural communities all of their lives must be open to new ideas and innovative opportunities while becoming a receptor of the new people coming to rural America.

CHAPTER 2
Developing Vision for Rural Revitalization

So, let God work his will in you. Yell a loud no to the Devil and watch him scamper. Say a quiet yes to God and he'll be there in no time. Quit dabbling in sin. Purify your inner life. Quit playing the field. Hit bottom and cry your eyes out. The fun and games are over. Get serious, really serious. Get down on your knees before the Master; it's the only way you'll get on your feet.[2]

Vision. It's absolutely essential for a healthy church ministry, and yet there is so much written on it that many congregations may be more-or-less inoculated against its intended impact. Just the term "vision" elicits a negative reaction in some circles from folks who have not seen vision development and deployment done well. This is particularly true in rural church settings where, with good intentions, a pastor or lay leader reads a book or attends a seminar and then tries to implement what they've learned without proper groundwork and contextualization. Simply put: cookie-cutter approaches to vision casting don't work.

So what exactly is a ministry vision, and how is one discerned and cast in a rural congregation? It must be done within the uniqueness of that particular rural ministry. That's the topic of this chapter.

Decision Making in the Rural Church

Having been a rural church pastor, I (John) had to learn the hard way that every congregation has its own decision-making process. The best, most biblical vision in the world will fall flat if it is developed and executed outside of the decision-making custom of that congregation. And the

---

[2] Eugene H. Peterson, *The Message: The Bible in Contemporary Language* (Colorado Springs, CO: NavPress, 2005), Jas 4:7–10.

culture of rural America has a huge impact on the way rural congregations make decisions. I am indebted to my friend Jason McConnell on this point.3 Jason has extensive experience in rural and small town ministry, and he beautifully explains some of the special considerations one must make when serving there.

1. Rural churches are usually driven by history

For pastors and leaders raised in city or suburban churches, this is often a tough lesson to learn. The history of a church (and of its community for that matter) is of high importance for rural church people. It is not unusual for church members to be able to articulate their congregation's story in terms of key events and people going all the way back to the founding of the church. Most will remember the pastors who have served during their lifetime – both the good and bad memories – and will be quick to relate the ministry of the current pastor to one or more of his predecessors. This passion for the church's history provides a very important anchor for the congregation – and woe to the pastor or leader who does not pay attention to this anchor when instituting change or articulating vision. But when vision honors and builds on that history, the result can be incredible.

2. Rural churches don't want to take risks

While it's true that most churches don't like risk, one will find less risk takers in rural congregations than in their city counterparts. Life in the rural setting is about consistency. The more agrarian the congregation, the more they will value that consistency. Farming families literally follow the seasons

---

3 Jason McConnell, *Principles for Effective Rural Ministry*, Franklin VT, 2014. Jason's seminar on rural ministry digs deep into rural culture, pastoral ministry and other key considerations for a successful pastorate in a rural setting.

like clockwork. They plant and harvest at the same time, every year, their whole lives. This predictable cycle provides great stability and simplifies planning. Vision requires change, and change is risky. So it is important to remember that most rural congregants will respond differently to vision casting simply because they respond to change and risk differently.

3. Rural churches come on board one leader at a time

Family ties and key relationships are very powerful in rural congregations. Because of this, change, vision casting and decision-making happen through those channels. Many a well-meaning pastor has tried a top-down approach when casting vision or instituting needed change only to come up against the strength of the decision makers. Too often, those decision makers have been labeled as "faithless" or "obstinate" when they are only instinctively resisting change and risk. But when time is taken to build good relationships with these leaders, and they begin to understand the need for change and are impassioned for the vision, change not only happens more smoothly but takes on solid roots as well. Every church – every organization – has people who will simply refuse to change and will thereby reject a new vision, but they are never the majority. More will be said below about communicating vision to various personality types, but just know it is worth the time and effort to communicate vision and ideas well to and through one decision-making leader at a time.

4. Rural churches make decisions differently

The culture of rural congregations usually changes the way they approach major decisions. McConnell points out that decision-making is often emotional, subjective, popular, informal and family-oriented. Change in a rural church setting is rarely objective; it usually requires emotional equity. Altering any component of the congregation's life together that has long historical roots will always invoke an emotional response. The people will look to those who maintain the stability for leadership, so the more those decision makers (especially matriarchs/patriarchs) are on board, the more readily popular opinion will sway. And it is essential to remember that decisions in rural churches are almost always made informally well before any formal vote is taken – what happens in dialogue around kitchen tables, while servicing combine harvesters and in the parking lot of the church will have more power than the number of hands raised in a business meeting.

Before any significant vision work can be done in a rural congregation, the pastor and leaders must take the necessary time and make the necessary effort to understand the change culture of their church and then build good relationships with the key players who will influence vision decisions. Too many pastors pigeonhole "the opposition" early in their pastoral tenure, essentially defining enemies. This destroys any hope of leading the congregation in a new direction for the kingdom and effectively undermines the pastor's ministry with well-established members. The time it takes to develop loving alliances with influential leaders (both official and unofficial) is time and difficulty saved later on.

Leading Change and the Four Personalities

God was gracious to me (John) in my first senior pastorate. I was green and the church to which I was called was nearly 250 years old. The five founding families were still well represented in the pews every Sunday. For a headstrong young pastor from Detroit serving in the peanut fields of southern Virginia, it could have been a disastrous combination. But I remained there 15 years and was blessed with much kingdom fruit.

When it came time to cast a renewed vision for this historic congregation, I had already learned much of the needed church and community history. I wish I could say I implemented all the principles we're providing in this book, but that would be a lie. It was a long and difficult process – one that frustrated me greatly at times because I did not then understand the dynamics of change in a rural community. After preaching through the new vision and working it out with several leaders, we held a Vision Banquet and celebrated the new direction God was taking us. The banquet itself was exciting and truly was a success. But we planned something that night that showed me I had not really done my homework. We had commitment cards at each place setting and asked folks after a time of prayer and dedication to bring the cards forward and place them in a wooden box as a step of faith. The idea was fine, but we had not prepared the congregation well. While the majority of the congregation gave an enthusiastic "Yes" that night, there was another phenomenon also at work: many folks deposited blank cards! They went forward because of peer pressure, but did not make a commitment. Most of these were simply not ready. But some were also not in favor of the changes we were prayerfully suggesting.

There is no doubt that it pays prepare. Taking the time to know your congregation pays big dividends when it comes to casting vision for a new ministry direction. Different personalities will respond to change and vision in different ways. And knowing these differences can greatly increase the likelihood of successfully leading the congregation in that direction.

Many people are familiar with the work of Everett M. Rogers from the 1960s, which shows the various personalities related to innovation on a typical bell curve.4 Rogers uses five categories to describe these responses: Innovators, Early Adopters, Early Majority, Late Majority and Laggards, giving percentages for where people typically fall into the curve (see graphic on next page).

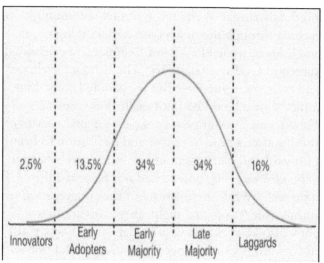

Such classifications are helpful for understanding how and even when to approach each personality as the vision process unfolds. Dr. Ken Priddy, Executive Director of the GO Center, a ministry of the Evangelical Presbyterian Church Presbytery of the Mid-Atlantic, has taken the work of Rogers and applied it to the local church setting. Priddy has masterfully identified four key personalities in the church – and his work helps to clarify both the way they respond to change and how church leaders should approach them.5

4 Everett M. Rogers, *Diffusion of Innovators*, New York: The Free Press, 1962.

5 Kenneth Priddy, *G.O.2: Expanding Your Church's Great Commission Matrix - The Narrative*, 2012.

Theorists

Theorists are people who catch the vision immediately and jump in proverbially with both feet to make it happen. Their quick and passionate response is both a blessing and a bane, however, because Theorists are easily frustrated when things do not change fast enough. In fact, a word of caution here, church leadership may need to keep lovingly tight reins on the Theorists so that they do not get ahead of the planned, healthy pace of implementation. In their zeal, Theorists can unwittingly harm the vision process. Communicate with them regularly and help them to respond with patience to the rest of the congregation as they wait for change.

Realists

The Realists in a church tend to catch the vision rather quickly, but will often ask the leadership to implement it in stages or even to experiment with vision components to make sure they will bear the intended fruit before fully instituting them. Realists appreciate "trial balloons" when it comes to vision, and their innate caution can help identify issues that the pastor and other leaders may otherwise have missed. In addition, I have found over the years that Realists garner a lot of trust because of their caution. This becomes important when wooing the next group, Pragmatists, who will need to see the vision adopted by those they trust before they will make the move to follow.

To win Realists to the new vision, involve them directly in the change process and allow them to take part in designing the vision experiments that will ultimately prove the vision's authenticity. Bring them into the vision conversation ask them about their concerns. Their wisdom and insights will be a blessing. And when they become convinced, they

41

will make excellent spokespersons for the vision to the rest of the congregation.

Pragmatists

The Pragmatists will usually make up the majority of a congregation. Pragmatists, by definition, do not like change. They can be a very resistant group when it comes to a new or renewed vision; however, it is a mistake to assume that this resistance is to the vision itself. Often, Pragmatists will be very taken with the vision and will even acknowledge the need for it – they are just uncomfortable with the changes necessary to make that vision a reality.

It is also a mistake to assume that all Pragmatists are older individuals. Discomfort with change increases with age; but resistance to change is a matter of personality. They are not the same! Pastors are often surprised that a large percentage of their Pragmatists are under the age of 50. In fact, in the churches I have served, I've known Pragmatists in their teens and twenties.

A final caution when it comes to Pragmatists is to confuse them with the next group -- Preservationists. They are not at all the same, but they are often allies by default. We'll address that in a moment.

Winning Pragmatists to the new vision takes time and patience – and it is important not to rush this part of the process, which in some cases can take a year or more. Pragmatists will often respond better to vision conversations conducted one-on-one or in couples. Some of the greatest impact with Pragmatists about the vision will happen in their own family rooms. Visiting them in their own homes to answer their questions and lovingly address their concerns is huge. Praying *with* them about the vision is critical. Involve Realists in these conversations (once they are convinced of the vision) and then allow the Holy Spirit to initiate a change of heart. When Pragmatists catch the vision and come on board, they will often become the vision's most ardent supporters. Be patient and allow the Spirit to do His work.

Preservationists

Preservationists have a vested interest in keeping things the way they are. These folks are often the loudest opponents and are usually very proficient with church politics, policies, the constitution, and parliamentary procedure (e.g., Roberts' Rules of Order). As such, they are also very influential. Preservationists are not necessarily evil people (although narcissistic, manipulative and intimidating people are often Preservationists), they are just closed to new vision and change. Their opposition can be in protection of their own power or position, or it may emanate from wounds they have received in life. The bottom line is that they will dig in their heels and remain immovable.

The reason Pragmatists are often lumped in with Preservationists is because Preservationists are experts at influencing them. Remember, Pragmatists do not like change. Preservationists use that resistance to their benefit. And because Pragmatists are often the largest personality group in the congregation, Preservationists learn quickly how to swing the power where they want it by promising Pragmatists that they can prevent those changes by working together. This influence tends to make the Preservationist camp appear much larger than it really is. In a church of 100 people, usually only 2 or 3 are actually Preservationists (remember, most pastors who leave churches under duress typically do so because of only one or two influential people in the church).

While Preservationists, by definition, are closed to change, I (John) have seen God change a Preservationist's heart! It's not common, but it *does* happen. The key to winning a Preservationist to the new vision is combining intercessory prayer and a gentle, loving relationship with them. Only the Holy Spirit can change a heart, but you can be a willing instrument in His hands.

Shifting the Personalities

Building on Priddy's work, I have found the following illustration helpful over the years in coaching pastors ·on how to bring about change. Think about all of these personalities residing on the right side of a teeter-totter (see diagram below). They may be there because they've not been recently challenged with vision, or they may be held there by powerful people-centered agendas in the church – but the point is that all the "weight" is on the historic side of the fulcrum. However, as each group is lovingly won to the new vision (the left side of the fulcrum), the "weight" shifts toward the new vision. The balance of power in the church moves toward adopting the singular Immanuel Agenda, and the new vision is empowered.

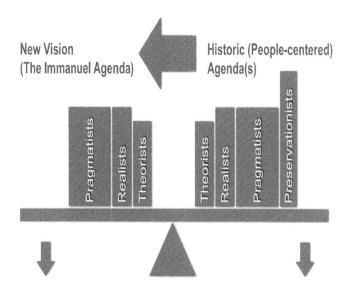

As noted above, this shift takes time and intentionality as you work with each group, but it is worth it! As a pastor begins to witness the Pragmatists slowly adopt the new vision, the inertia of human agendas diminishes and even immovable Preservationists are unable to prevent it. I'm reminded here of the wisdom of Paul's teacher, Gamaliel in Acts 5:33-39:

> [33] When [the religious leaders] heard this, they were furious and wanted to put [Peter and the other apostles] to death. [34] But a Pharisee named Gamaliel, a teacher of the law, who was honored by all the people, stood up in the Sanhedrin and ordered that the men be put outside for a little while. [35] Then he addressed them: "Men of Israel, consider carefully what you intend to do to these men. [36] Some time ago Theudas appeared, claiming to be somebody, and about four hundred men rallied to him. He was killed, all his followers were dispersed, and it all came to nothing. [37] After him, Judas the Galilean appeared in the days of the census and led a band of people in revolt. He too was killed, and all his followers were scattered. [38] Therefore, in the present case I advise you: Leave these men alone! Let them go! For if their purpose or activity is of human origin, it will fail. [39] But if it is from God, you will not be able to stop these men; you will only find yourselves fighting against God." [6]

Take the necessary time to work through your church's membership directory and identify which of the four personalities each person falls into (and remember to look at individuals and not families: a Pragmatist can be married to a Theorist!). Then, begin with the Theorists and slowly work your way through the Realists and then the Pragmatists. When blanketed in prayer and practiced with love and grace, this practical process can be very fruitful to develop an

---

[6] *The Holy Bible: New International Version.* 1984 (Ac 5:33–39). Grand Rapids, MI: Zondervan.

understanding and passion for the new vision in the hearts of your congregants.

Understanding Vision

He was an extremely gifted young pastor. He had a background in business but had pursued the ministry with a passionate calling. He loved the church to which he was called, likening it to a "dream job" for a first assignment. And his ministry there began with much excitement and expectation. He was a natural teacher, had musical talent, and was very personable. But within the first year, things were not going well and by the second he was praying about leaving. What happened? Like so many others before him, he broke the first cardinal rule of rural ministry. He saw this little pastorate as a stepping stone to bigger and better ministries later in his career. This "dream job" was only the first wrung in a very tall ladder – and while he never actually said so, it became clear in everything he did including vision development.

It may seem odd to talk about this in a chapter on vision, but it's important. A pastor (or other church leaders for that matter) will not be able to lead a congregation into a new vision and ministry direction if he ultimately has his sites set elsewhere. Much damage has been done to rural churches by the "stepping stone" mentality. There is no doubt that God will use small and rural congregations to hone the ministry skills and character of pastors. And God does increase pastors' capacity and influence, sometimes taking them to larger ministries. But for the local pastor, significance is a matter of calling and obedience, not congregational size, budget or influence! Unless God is specifically leading a pastor to a larger ministry venue, then it behooves that pastor to put down permanent roots with that church family and to choose to live among them.

Vision deployment in a rural congregation can be a very fickle thing. If the pastor gives the people any reason to think he is only "passing through," vision work is dead before it begins. A good rule of thumb is that vision work should only be done by a pastor who knows he is called to and passionate about ministry in that church for the long haul (like planning to retire from that pulpit). God may one day lead the pastor elsewhere, but that conclusion should be as much a surprise to the pastor as to the rest of the congregation.

When it comes to vision there are several important considerations for pastors and church leaders. First, vision is always specific to a congregation, impacting that church's particular community. The vision of one church can certainly influence the vision of another, but vision cannot be transplanted. Some pastors start developing a vision before they know what church they will serve. This is a huge mistake! God may call a pastor to a particular ministry emphasis – but then that pastor must seek out a church that already shares that passion. Vision work must be completed in conjunction with the church leadership after the pastor has had adequate time to put down some roots (6 months to a year).

Secondly, vision is from God, not from a pastor's own mind, a book or other resources. As such, the primary tool to use in vision development is prayer (we'll talk about this more in the next section). There are many good processes one can implement to help develop a workable vision statement, but it must always be remembered that the Source of the vision is God Himself. And because vision is from God, it will always be God-sized – requiring significant faith and dependence on Him to become reality.

Thirdly, vision encompasses what I (John) call the Four Arenas of Mission. Taken from Acts 1:8, we learn that the church brings the love and gospel ministry of Jesus to Jerusalem, Judea, Samaria and the ends of the earth. This passage can be tactically interpreted as our immediate ministry context (church and community), our regional ministry context (the larger region around us with a similar culture), our regional ministry context that crosses cultural lines (other ethnicities within our larger region) and global, cross-cultural missions. A local church should be intentionally impacting each of these four arenas simultaneously. Depending on God's particular calling upon that congregation, one of these may be more emphasized than the others – but all four must be part of the vision planning.

Fourth, vision sees God's preferred future, but is led by the people who are there and those who join them. In other words, it is certainly God-sized, but it is unpacked in doable steps as people are stretched by walking in faith. Vision is always attainable over time, even if it is currently out of reach.

A final word: when it comes to understanding vision in the local church, vision always transforms existing systems and structures. It does not do an "end run" around them. We've already talked about this above, but it's a good reminder. Vision work requires addressing inadequate, obsolete and dysfunctional systems, structures and traditions that have become obstacles to faithful obedience as a congregation. When part of a loving approach to vision implementation, such work can set the congregation free to bear significantly more kingdom fruit.

Discerning Vision

If vision is from God Himself, then exactly how does one go about discovering it? This is where vision work in the local church separates from vision work in corporate America (and why much of the material on vision today is simply not helpful to our purpose). The first and single most-important answer to our question is prayer. Simply put: pastors and congregations that do not make prayer and intercession a consistently high priority are unlikely to discern God's preferred future for them. Vision will often come out of a season of prayer and fasting (e.g. see Acts 13) – specifically intercessory prayer and fasting for the congregation's four arenas of mission (see the last section). If your congregation is not regularly gathering together for concerted prayer and intercession, start there. God prepares the heart of the congregation as they pray together. God releases the resources to fulfill His vision because the congregation prays together. God calls laborers forth to fulfill His vision as fruit of the congregation's prayer together (Luke 10:2). The bottom line is this: if you are not birthing your vision work from a congregational prayer movement, then you have already lost the battle. The vision process will only bring frustration.

One of the ministries with which I (John) work, The Praxis Center for Church Development,7 provides a very helpful process for discerning and articulating vision for a local congregation. When it comes to the revitalization of a local church, this process is part of a larger, all-encompassing experience called *LifeFlow* which strives to reorient the church's values, vision, corporate divine design and mission around identifying and meeting the needs of its community in authentic, biblical love. One of the keys we teach is that a church must truly know its community. Often, people only truly know those in the community with which they already have relationship; therefore, many important trends and opportunities are overlooked. Vision – especially for local ministry – must meet the needs and answer the questions of the local community. As indications of vision emerge through prayer, they can be clarified through prayer mapping

---

7 The Praxis Center for Church Development works to help transform the lives and ministries of pastors, leaders and congregations to align them with Jesus' kingdom priorities of loving God, loving others and making disciples. www.praxiscenter.org.

and prayer walking. Vision will become very personal as church members increase their intentional intercession for their immediate neighbors and their needs. Vision gaps can then be filled in with good demographic data8 and information from the local governments. When vision rests on the church's core values, and applies the congregation's corporate personality, gift mix, skill set, ministry passions and resources to the community needs identified, a very practical mission statement can be produced that guides the whole congregation toward fulfilling that vision.

Communicating Vision

Communicating vision within any church, and especially within a rural congregation, is only effective when it's is consistent and multi-faceted. Communication must begin within the leadership itself. Vision casting must first bring the church's leadership team on board and then should also focus on other key "players" in the church (remember, not all leaders are on official boards and committees). Once the leaders of the church begin adopting and walking out the vision, then these people are the ones who should start communicating the vision with (not to) others. Pay attention to the four personalities mentioned above and systematically draw in theorists and realists first. Take the time and make the effort to communicate well with (again, not to – this is more like a dance than a PowerPoint presentation) pragmatists. And then as the vision begins to get traction, implement it incrementally with small "experiments" at first and then larger changes once the church has experienced some immediate successes.

---

8 MissionInsite has one of the best demographic systems available for ministry purposes. www.missioninsite.com

Developing a biblical vision in a rural congregation has its challenges, but when it is done well, the fruit and transformation are often nothing short of miraculous. Rural churches make decisions differently, but that doesn't make a new vision impossible. Rural congregations are culturally more resistant to change, but that doesn't mean they can't change. When vision – God's preferred future – is envisioned through prayer, is focused on all four arenas of mission, is rooted in the church's real values and is walked out using the church's divine design, the impact of the vision's fulfillment will be life-changing for many – both inside and outside the church. One cannot rush this process. It takes time, a lot of homework and a tremendous amount of effort. But the results are worth it.

Chapter 3
Assessment of the Rural Church's Potential

We who have run for our very lives to God have every reason to grab the promised hope with both hands and never let go. It's an unbreakable spiritual lifeline, reaching past all appearances right to the very presence of God where Jesus, running on ahead of us, has taken up his permanent post as high priest for us[9]

If you ask many individuals whom dwell in the cities, they often paint a bleak picture of the church in rural which is less than true. Many city dwellers believe that the rural church is in bad shape and in great decline. I would reply that it is in no worse decline then the churches in other demographic areas. During my study sabbatical of 2017, I actually interviewed 350 rural church pastors in five states[10] across this nation and found that in fact the rural church might be doing a little better than many urban churches. Every pastor I visited with desired to see their rural church grow. They wanted to bring a consistent level of health to not only their church but to their individual communities as well. Revitalizing a declining rural church does not happen quickly and it is never a given that the members of these churches actually desire for the church to become healthy and vibrant once more. But for those who want to seek renewal and develop new levels of rural church health, it will take the efforts of godly rural church members acting strategically and moving their congregation forward as thy seek to impact the

---

[9] Eugene H. Peterson, *The Message: The Bible in Contemporary Language* (Colorado Springs, CO: NavPress, 2005), Heb 6:18–20.

10 The five states in which I initially interviewed rural pastors were: Missouri, North Carolina, Florida, Kentucky, and Georgia. Further research is being conducted in an effort to discover what is working in rural church America and what is not. There was a clear difference between the growing rural church and those in decline. Recently, a sixth group of rural pastors were interviewed in the state of Tennessee.

rural community and culture. Assessing the rural churches potential is the place to begin.

Paul the apostle declares:

> *"And this is my prayer: that your love may abound more and more in knowledge and depth of insight, so that you may be able to discern what is best and may be pure and blameless until the day of Christ, filled with the fruit of righteousness that comes through Jesus Christ - to the glory and praise of God."*[11]

Is prayer a priority in a rural church for both the leaders and the congregation? A healthy rural church realizes that its ministries go forward through effective and consistent prayer. Assessing the rural landscape requires that the church revitalizer clearly understands and is able to convey to the congregation the churches mission and vision. One of the things I discovered in interviewing rural pastors is that those leading growing churches clearly understood why it exists and where it is going. They not only own the vision for reaching their rural community but the membership owns that same vision and are part of continually affirming such vision to community and church member.

Why Should a Rural Church Do an Assessment?

For the rural church to move off of either a declining or polarized state of existence, it is important to consider if the church and indeed the membership really want the church to grow or are they happy watching it decline. An assessment for a rural church is a necessary basic step towards understanding the needs of the church and developing an unbiased view of the current health and vitality of your rural church membership. Many a rural pastor and church leaders

---

11 C.f. Philippians 1:9-11.

wing it not very interested in discovering if they could be a growing and thriving church in the heartlands of our American culture. But for those who are interesting in discovering ways to impact such a key portion of our society, an assessment is helpful. Without the discipline to gather objective information about your rural church, you can end up miles down the road doing something that will not work. I found many churches which were "recovering fool's errand churches" that had actually done things which were keeping it from growing only to now have to make a 180 degree turn and rebound from doing things which perpetuated the status quo and decline. Periodic rural church evaluation and rural community evaluation is essential to informed decision-making and effective leadership for the pastor and lay church leaders. A key step toward Church Revitalization is the willingness to make an honest and well-rounded evaluation of the current state of the church's ministry, vision, attitudes, environment, and performance. Conducting a rural church assessment is an important tri-annual checkup to ensure that you and your church are doing the best things it can to bring growth and vitality to the local church. Possible issues will surface that need to be addressed and plans made to continue to try ideas which will enable you to reach the rural community. It is a proactive step rather than a reactive step and one that rural churches should consider taking every three to five years. A good assessment will enable rural church leaders to gain a clear and reliable picture of the rural church that means so much to them and their families. An assessment will also provide leaders with some benchmarks to use when determining priority actions. An assessment can provide a sense of consent from the church to address areas identified as needing attention.

Nine Quick Tips That Will Help the Rural Church Making an Assessment

Granted, for most rural churches they have never taken an assessment. Part of that is the wing it mentality because they are smaller congregations and do not have large infrastructures. But it is also due to their ability to exist without many rules and regulations for how they do church each week. That is the wonderful thing about rural churches. God shows up without a great deal of fan fair and simply blessed the people. But in the really growing rural church they have discovered that assessing what is working and what is not is an essential part of connecting the church to the rural community. Here are nine quick tips that will enable any rural church to make an assessment:

Let Everyone Know Why You are Leading an Assessment

A church assessment can sometimes be a difficult sell to the rural congregation. Take is often because it could bog the church down in some individual's opinion. Beginning with church leaders, pastors can use ideas within this chapter to present the value of an assessment. The Church Revitalizer should reassure members that the results of the assessment will not be used as a means of pushing a pre-determined agenda, attacking someone's ministry, or pointing guilt and blame at people within the rural church. People should be reminded that an assessment is a way of getting the most feedback from as many members as possible and that is a way of valuing everyone's perspective.

Commit to Developing Key Questions and Use Them for Everyone Taking the Assessment

Writing a set of key questions to be utilized in the assessment is a great way to keep everyone on the same page.

Be sure that everyone taking the assessment is answering the same set of questions. It is vital that the questions developed are not developed with any degree of bias. I have seen churches hurt themselves by trying to target areas with such biased questions that people are reluctant to take the assessment. Work to attain important insight from those taking the assessment by gathering key thought, feelings, and information.

Create an Assessment that Will Be Acceptable for Your Church

In many a rural church using something like survey monkey will be a great way to conduct your assessment. Yet, for some rural church efforts using a printed assessment will be the better choice due to older members fear of technology. Even in some rural churches doing a guided conversation is the best choice. The goal is to get the information you need and whatever the best format to gain the needed information ought to be utilized. The more specific your questions the better the responses will be to the assessment and more helpful to developing future ministry ideas and plans. There are assessments out there that are fee based but often the rural church will buck at such utilization and expenditure of resources for something that they could do themselves.

Provide Ample Time for the Rural Church Assessment

Never be in such a hurry when gathering information that could help your rural church develop ministries that will impact one's community and local church. Almost all of the churches I interviewed during my sabbatical spoke about treading slowly into uncharted territory. Some form of assessment launch should be utilized as the rural church leaders seek to gather momentum towards the assessment survey. Calendaring it during the time of year when most of your churches members are back in town. One church spoke of doing it in the summer which was a failure because they failed to take into account people being away. Their effort fizzled because of their desire to rush into the effort and by the time members returned from vacations there was little or no momentum remaining.

Make the Assessment Easy to Take by Offering Options

Your goal as the leaders of your rural church is to get the information and opinion from your membership so provide many ways and avenues to take the assessment. Allow groups such as Sunday School, Youth Groups, Parents of Children's Programs, and Seniors venues where they can take the assessment that is convenient. You might also want to provide the assessment questions via an email to the church at large in order to gain the largest number of participants possible. There could be a time at the close of a worship service for the assessment to be taken. Allowing for member's anonymity in the assessment will result in honest responses that might not surface if you are not given such privacy.

Consider Hosting Focus Group Meetings

Hosting focus groups is another way for the rural church to gather the information they are seeking. These group meetings are a way to receive information that you would be unable to obtain in the assessment. Assessments can miss a few questions and display gaps so hosting these group meetings is a good way to gather ideas and assure you have herd form as many parties as possible. The rural church revitalizer may want to conduct the guided conversations. Almost every denomination has some form of local church statistical data gathered annually which could be further assistance in your effort to develop future ministry plans. For instance, if you have a gap in the thirty to forty-year-old area in your church but the community has a large number of residents in that age group, then developing ministries to reach that demographic would be wise. It is an unexplored area for ministry for your church. Demographic trends may also shed light on possible explanations for why some assessment scores turned out the way that they did.

Pledge to Accept the Results

We live in a day where there is much scrubbing of information by mission agencies in an effort to present a more favorable picture of the findings. You as the rural church leader should pledge to accept the findings as they are. Leaders must promise in advance to accepting the results at face value and without reading into or explaining away the results. When an established assessment tool is used, accept the fact that the results are trustworthy and in all likelihood, correct in providing an accurate view of the congregation's perspective. Remember that any assessment cannot take into consideration every part of a church's impact in a community and in the lives of individual believers. While assessment data is reliable, it is not inspired or prophetic.

Promise to Utilize the Results in Only Positive Ways

I have seen many a church hurt by a passive aggressive church member trying to utilize an assessment as a tool to bring about harm to individuals and future plans. If you are doing a good job as the church leader there will be a few people who are not your biggest fans because you challenge their desire to maintain the status quo. Every assessment tool is designed to provide feedback while pointing out strengths and challenges for the local church. Many rural church leaders may tend to focus on what the assessment revealed as the difficulties that need to be corrected. However, a better starting point is to celebrate what the assessment reveals as areas of ministry that are valued and deemed effective by the rural church membership. Discover ways to celebrate the ministry of the church. Lead the church to give thanks to God for what He is doing through the identified areas. If an assessment comes back very negative it is best to utilize the findings as a means to create a new inspiring vision for the rural church as it begins developing plans for a new day.

Utilize the Assessment as a Means to Understand the Current Culture in Your Church

Once the assessment has been tabulated it is a good idea for it to be utilized in order to understand the current culture of one's rural church. By making it part of the churches culture, it serves as a launching point for presenting growth plans and a benchmark for future evaluation. As the church moves forward towards health and vitality such evaluation keeps the church from returning to polarization and the sense of felling stuck. Using the assessment also sets the bar for advancement challenging the membership to continually seek improvement in an effort to re-embrace the community and its changing culture. Not only will the membership need to keep up with changes in the community but the pastor leader will need to embrace the new culture that is emerging in one's rural community. It will often challenge the minister to re-sharpen various skill sets which have been allowed to coast for some time. Reinventing one's self was part of every church we interviewed that had shown renewal. Several commented that they were drifting until the revitalization process began and then they became inspired to get current and avoid staleness.

Assessment and evaluation should not be a cause of discomfort in the life of a rural church and its leadership. Those rural churches which sought to reconnect with community and culture had a great future. The utilization of assessment for acknowledging current reality is a good way to begin moving off of the plateau and advancing forward for the benefit of church and community. Assessments provide reliable data that can serve as the launching pad for future growth and reconnection of one's Jerusalem. Keep in mind that they are useful listening devices for effective leaders to gauge the barometer of one's church. Most members will revel in assessment things they would not tell the leadership one or one. The laity in a rural church is connected to community no matter how big or small the rural area. Valuing their thoughts, opinions, and reflections to a must for the rural pastor.

Does the Bible Speak to Assessments?

One does not need to go far to find examples of assessment and evaluations in scripture. Both the Old and New Testaments provide ample examples of admonishments to consider such appraisals. Here are some examples:

Proverbs 14:8

> *The wisdom of the prudent is to give thought to their ways, but the folly of fools is deception.*[12]

> *The wisdom of the prudent is to discern his way, but the folly of fools is deceiving.*[13]

> *The wisdom of the wise keeps life on track; the foolishness of fools lands them in the ditch.*[14]

---

12 *The Holy Bible: New International Version* (Grand Rapids, MI: Zondervan, 1984), Proverbs 14:8.

13 *The Holy Bible: English Standard Version* (Wheaton: Standard Bible Society, 2016), Proverbs 14:8.

14 Eugene H. Peterson, *The Message: The Bible in Contemporary Language* (Colorado Springs, CO: NavPress, 2005), Proverbs 14:8.

Proverbs 24:3-6

By wisdom a house is built, and through understanding it is established; through knowledge its rooms are filled with rare and beautiful treasures. A wise man has great power, and a man of knowledge increases strength; for waging war you need guidance, and for victory many advisers.[15]

By wisdom a house is built, And by understanding it is established; And by knowledge the rooms are filled, With all precious and pleasant riches. A wise man is strong, And a man of knowledge increases power. For by wise guidance you will wage war, And in abundance of counselors there is victory.[16]

A house is built by wisdom, and it is established by understanding; by knowledge the rooms are filled with every precious and beautiful treasure. A wise warrior is better than a strong one, and a man of knowledge than one of strength; for you should wage war with sound guidance victory comes with many counselors.[17]

Luke 14:28-32

Or can you imagine a king going into battle against another king without first deciding whether it is possible with his ten thousand troops to face the twenty thousand troops of the other?

---

15 *The Holy Bible: New International Version* (Grand Rapids, MI: Zondervan, 1984), Proverbs 24:3–6.

16 *New American Standard Bible: 1995 Update* (La Habra, CA: The Lockman Foundation, 1995), Proverbs 24:3–6.

17 *The Holy Bible: Holman Christian Standard Version.* (Nashville: Holman Bible Publishers, 2009), Proverbs 24:3–6.

And if he decides he can't, won't he send an emissary and work out a truce?[18]

"Suppose one of you wants to build a tower. Will he not first sit down and estimate the cost to see if he has enough money to complete it? For if he lays the foundation and is not able to finish it, everyone who sees it will ridicule him, saying, 'This fellow began to build and was not able to finish.' "Or suppose a king is about to go to war against another king. Will he not first sit down and consider whether he is able with ten thousand men to oppose the one coming against him with twenty thousand? If he is not able, he will send a delegation while the other is still a long way off and will ask for terms of peace.[19]

1 Corinthians 9:26

Therefore, I do not run like a man running aimlessly; I do not fight like a man beating the air.[20]

I don't know about you, but I'm running hard for the finish line. I'm giving it everything I've got. No sloppy living for me![21]

Eight Refocusing Summit Questions

Assessing the need for a new future will often begin by the rural church revitalizer convening a series of eight

---

18 Eugene H. Peterson, *The Message: The Bible in Contemporary Language* (Colorado Springs, CO: NavPress, 2005), Luke 14:28–32.

19 *The Holy Bible: New International Version* (Grand Rapids, MI: Zondervan, 1984), Luke 14:28–32.

20 *The Holy Bible: New International Version* (Grand Rapids, MI: Zondervan, 1984), 1 Co 9:26.

21 Eugene H. Peterson, *The Message: The Bible in Contemporary Language* (Colorado Springs, CO: NavPress, 2005), 1 Co 9:26.

summits with church members to consider a series of reflective questions that are critical for potential church advancement. While these summits are not difficult, taking the time to think on these things will help both the rural pastor and member to refocus and commit themselves towards the future of revitalization. These summits are often the highpoints that lead to breakthroughs for the stuck church. Let's look at these summits:

The Preparation Summit

It is always good to begin the summit with a reminder why the church exists and what is its Biblical purpose. Usually this can be accomplished by looking at various scriptures which encourage you as the leader and church members. Having everyone share a favorite passage is a good way to begin the summit. Additionally, most churches have a constitution and bylaws which share why the church exists and its purpose. On a white board, have those present, share their feelings relating to what was shared from church documents. Are the things revealed in paper documents relative to the current realities of the ministry area? Is there potential for other ideas to be added to the biblical purpose of the church. Spending time together praying for the church and thinking about the future of the church is a strong way to launch into the assessment of rural realities for the church. The preparation summit sets the mode for future summits so it is wise for the rural pastor to spend ample time in prayer asking the Lord for direction in leading such a summit.

The Honoring the Past Summit

If you do not honor the past as the rural church revitalizer it will cause great harm and could even derail any effort towards rural church revitalization. Impatient pastors often charge hard into the effort way before acknowledging that what has been done in the past is worthy of acknowledgement and thanks. If one does not realize that there were and are those who have been serving for a long time before the rural pastor arrived and that a lot of what they have done was incredibly awesome and blessed by the Lord. In one of my churches God called me to revitalize, I quickly understood the importance understanding that these dear members had been in the trenches actively working way before I ever arrived to be their leader. If I rushed in to destroy all that was dear towards their past, not only would it have been hurtful, but it would have done great harm towards my ability to lead these people. Honoring the past allows the rural church revitalizer to slowly move towards a future which will continue to honor the past but lead the church into an effective future.

The Historical Past Summit

The second summit necessary is that of holding the historical past discussion. Understanding where the rural church has been in the past, is a discussion worthy of the time necessary to understand how the Lord had walked upon His people within the church. Were there times when things were advancing steadily and if so what changed? Was the church impacted by the community or was the community impacted by the church? Often rural churches who are open change will find times in their past where they modeled the same behavior necessary for embracing a new culture today. Developing some sort of time line of the big events which impacted the church is a great way to begin. Lead participants to explore significant moments in the history of their church. Over the previous 20 years, what were the significant events, strategic actions, and defining moments that have shaped the rural church to be what it is today? Some will say go back thirty or forty years but in most of these churches twenty years will provide larger numbers for the discussions. Understanding past things such as: Why is the church situated where it is; Why is the present staff and leadership structured as such; Why do you have the ministries you have; Why do you not have certain ministries; Why does your constitution speak as it does; Why is your church timetable scheduled as it is; Why is your church governance shaped as it is; What were the moments in church history people recalled most; and What were the times in the past people would like to forget are all vital questions to consider? These are all important questions because they not only provide a historical time line but they present a series of lessons learned in the past that might help the rural church not to need to relearn them in the present or near future.

The Core Values Summit

As a church planter, I learned early in ministry the importance of core values. The Core Values Summit is a way for you to discuss present core values and determine if they need to be reworked in light of present realities and assessments. The rural pastors desired result of this summit is for those participating in the summit to be able to identify the various core values behind the functions found in scripture, the early church, and to understand their own core values or the need to revise these values to align with today's challenges and future ministry. Having a dialogue about what will become the rural church's core values. Read various passages in the Gospels and the Book of Acts as well as the Apostle Paul's epistles to understand how the early church developed and modeled core values. It is important for the rural church to understand that core values are either sacred centered on the scriptures or they are secular and centered on the world.

The Dream Big Summit

Another summit to hold is what I call the Dream Big Summit. This summit is a discussion on where it is that you as a rural church should go. Brainstorming and dreaming towards a preferred future is a healthy discussion that allows for participants to share ideas to be considered for ministry. This dialogue works to gather many ideas over a single idea. Idea gathering is a beginning place for reconnecting one's church to a changing rural community. New ideas are the lifeblood for a rural church revitalizer. New ideas help the renewal effort to get started. The inspiration gained from a group of church members sharing their dreams for the church is vital. Your church's process will usually be to collect as many ideas as possible, spend time working on the ones you think have potential, and then have a handful of ideas to work through in greater detail. There is no limit to where ideas and inspiration can come from. Inspiration can come from anywhere and everywhere. You have to be open to being inspired and pay attention to those things that inspire you and your church members. You have to cultivate the gift of looking for new ideas and be open to the process of collecting and generating new ideas. One way is to make sure you always have something at hand to record any ideas, thoughts, images that come to your conscious mind. Dreaming big takes practice and the ability to recall the ideas that begin to simmer is an art. Stay at it and you will be amazed how many times the Lord will lay it in your lap if you are a good note taker and not miss the moments when inspiration comes. People ask me how I know what the next book of mine will be and it is a simple answer, I listen to the inspiration of the Lord and when He flashes it before me I write it down and then get busy doing what He has asked me to do. Holding a summit designed for others to dream big is useful for the rural church.

The Outreach Summit

Another summit for another week is the outreach summit. Rural revitalization needs to include the action of outreach for the renewing church. Of the churches I interviewed, those which were growing all had a well-defined plan for how they were going about reaching individuals for the Lord and His church. Most of those present will offer the easier ideas so it is wise for the rural church revitalizer to be ready to discuss deeper ideas for outreach. Ask the participants whom the Lord has called them to reach and what is the mission focus for the renewing church.

The "Big Thing" Summit

Rural churches that are growing all have at least one "Big Thing" that connects the church to the changing culture and community. In the work of bringing renewal what is the big thing that the majority of those participating in the summits sense that the Lord might be presenting to the church as a means to reach the community? While there are times when doing something, almost anything is a good initial step in renewal, developing the "Big Thing" takes a full-blown commitment from almost everyone in the church. It is a driving force that impacts every person in the pew as well as every person that the rural church seeks to reach and present the message of salvation. The big thing is what the Lord is calling the church to accomplish in the future. It is wrapped in a new vision and delivered with a new vitality so that the victory is clearly that of the Lords at His due time.

The Journey Summit

Taking the journey towards the end result requires some clear thinking relating how one's church will get to the goal of the thing summit. To finish any great endeavor, you must first launch out. The purpose of this summit is to continue to develop ideas and begin making plans for carrying your member's ideas into action plans. This is where you begin to plot towards an end in mind. You begin to think sequentially one step at a time until the idea is completed. Once the first step is completed more on to the second and third all the way until you arrive at the end result. The journey summit is the process of working through each step to arrive at the next one. The beginning of any process is the most creative. The rural pastor and leader needs to become conscious of every single choice and action they make each day, so they can begin to make choices that fall in line with the direction of your church's dreams for tomorrow. When you and your church members are zealous about what it is that is to be achieved, nothing will stand in their way of getting it. This summit discusses how we will get there. Adding ministries is great but you must build strategy to reach one's community with your new offerings. This summit works on building strategic initiatives.

The Ministry Architecture Summit

As you have formalized your plan the Ministry Architecture Summit allows participants to begin to visualize how all of the ministries and actions plans that have been developed for all of these weeks come together. The rural church revitalizer should lead a discussion about how all of the new ministries and existing ministries will grow together to mold into the future ministry map for the renewing church. Once you have become aware of the steps you must take to do what you want to do, and are taking action, and are being accountable you will begin to produce the behavior you desire. You are moving towards realizing your desires and objectives. Are the ministries attractive to the new culture and community of your rural landscape? Will these ministries attract individuals which have a concern for the rural community they inhabit? Growing ministries draw growing individuals. They attract others who desire the same experiences.

The Summation Summit

This is the final summit where you officially launch the revitalization process of your church. All of the pre-renewal launch work has been accomplished and now begin the process of investing a thousand days towards the revitalization of your rural church. Everything should be in place and now begin the all-out effort to take the steps spoken of in previous summits. This is a great time for building momentum. The post summits time is the most exciting time because as the pastor you are seeking to get the church moving forward with great energy and excitement about the new things God could do in your church. Remember you are preparing to invest a minimum of one thousand days towards renewal so creating the enthusiasm required to launch out well is essential.

Wrapping it Up!

A constructive rural church assessment will fortify and form the body of Christ not condemn and divide. It will provide accountability and also a sense of ownership for those involved in the process. As a result of the needs assessment, you will identify strengths on which to build and weaknesses on which to work. A needs assessment will help you determine if new ministries should be initiated and/or if any existing ministries should be terminated. The rural church assessment is a means of discerning if the church's ministry is on track with God's purposes and design for the church and the community. How many people participate in the needs assessment could depend on the size of your church and also on how much effort you are willing to put into the assessment. The entire rural congregation could be involved in providing input or perhaps a cross-section of individuals from different areas of your church's life. The process could be coordinated by church leadership or an appointed committee. Doing the rural assessment internally would tend to build greater ownership in the implementation of results.

Rural churches matter so much to the cultural landscape. Far too many urban pastors dismiss rural pastors to their misfortune. Rural churches are a great place for ministers right out of Bible College or seminary to begin learning how to do ministry. Granted that some will fall in love with these wonderful communities while others might long for something else. But understand that rural congregations matter to the Lord because they are lighthouses in small communities that shine so the unchurched, unreached, un-discipled, and uncommitted. A pastor serving the Lord in a rural environment is on the front lines of ministry because he does not have a large army of volunteers to do the work and much rests on his shoulders. You are a great blessing and your work is a great blessing. You matter to your community and they need you. Preach the gospel each and every Sunday. God will bless your willingness and obedience as you creatively renew your church and reach your community. Doing a rural church assessment often works best during strategic times such as: a transition in church leadership, a change in community make up, a new focus for ministry, restructuring of staff both paid and volunteer, building expansion, annual goal setting, or discovering your churches individual strengths while seeking to amplify your opportunities.

CHAPTER 4
The Importance of Disciple-making in
Rural Renewal

*God is a safe place to hide, ready to help when we need him. We stand
fearless at the cliff-edge of doom, courageous in sea-storm and
earthquake, Before the rush and roar of oceans, the tremors that shift
mountains.*[22]

The priority of disciple making for every Christian
should indeed be a no-brainer. Unfortunately, many local
congregations in North America today have allowed Jesus'
Great Commission to be redefined. Some churches now
mistakenly believe this mandate to make disciples belongs to
pastors, missionaries and others with a credentialed "calling"
on their lives. Others have, in effect, removed the word
"obey" from the Commission and have made disciple making
all about the teaching task as if knowing truth and obeying
truth are the same thing. Still others have migrated so far
from Biblical truth that they simply no longer believe disciple
making is necessary. For most, this departure from faithful
obedience to Jesus' Prime Directive has been a slow process
over several generations. In many local churches today,
people simply do not know that they are missing the main
point and are thereby causing the churches they love to
plateau and decline. Rural congregations are no exception.

Disciple-making in the Rural Context

The making of disciples for Jesus is the same in every
context and culture to a limited extent. In each case there
must be an intentional, redemptive relationship. In each case,

---

[22] Eugene H. Peterson, *The Message: The Bible in Contemporary Language*
(Colorado Springs, CO: NavPress, 2005), Ps 46:1–3.

there is the conveying of biblical truth accompanied by a living, fruitful example to follow. In each case, the goal is to help the person be more like Jesus in his or her own cultural setting. And while there is so much that is shared across all believers around the world in disciple making, there are also unique considerations that make the process specialized to the disciple (think personal trainer rather than history teacher). This is why focusing discipleship strictly on teaching biblical truth falls short: helping a disciple to mature in Christ cannot be a standardized academic process. We're going to look at some of the unique aspects of discipling someone in a rural setting.

Disciple making in a rural congregation requires many things. First, it often requires a slower pace. This is not because people in rural settings are "uneducated" or "don't get it," but because the pace of life is slower and the demands of farming and related industries are unforgiving. I (John) remember pastors in my community who would become very frustrated with farmers in their congregations who worked the harvest on Sundays. Sometimes circumstances (like weather) require people who are otherwise faithful to miss Sunday worship and other activities so they don't lose some or all of their crop. Remember, this is their livelihood. There may be periods when rural folks simply cannot take time to meet for discipleship and mentoring. This is the nature of rural ministry. Be creative. Don't condemn.

Rural disciple making also often requires a deeper level of trust – meaning that the person being discipled needs to trust his or her discipler before true discipleship can begin. This is particularly true if the relationship between these two is new. A disciple is a follower, not just a learner. Following requires both an example and trust, and these are not easy in many rural communities. These people have seen pastors use churches and relationships as stepping stones to "bigger things." They may have experienced a level of church conflict most can't comprehend. And many have been victim to some of the harshest gossip and criticism imaginable (these are everywhere, but tend to have more impact in smaller, rural communities where everyone knows each other). Rural folks trust, but they don't do so quickly. They follow, but will only follow those they trust. Take time to build the relationship and be loyal to it. If something happens to damage the relationship, work for gospel restoration quickly. A steadfast, trusting relationship will almost always foster a level of discipleship rural folks have rarely experienced.

Rural discipleship requires a very personal investment. Cookie-cutter approaches and curricula simply will not bear the intended fruit. Rural communities operate in established relationships and transparency is rare. Do not simply offer your knowledge, but offer *yourself* in discipleship. Determine what you uniquely have to invest in the person being discipled and then provide it. As you do this, you'll find that you can only adequately disciple a few people at any given time. Gregarious pastors and leaders may be able to invest in 4 or 5 people as individuals and clusters, but most disciple-makers will max out around 3. The larger the group, the less actual discipling takes place. The key to reaching the church and community over time is to always make disciples who make disciples. This is why the multiplication principle of 2 Timothy 2:2 is so critical:
[2] And the things you have heard me say in the presence of many witnesses entrust to reliable men who will also be qualified to teach others.[23]
Discipleship does not become a movement within a church or community until it is several spiritual generations deep!

Disciple making in a rural setting also requires a strong constitution. The more rural the ministry context, the more

---

23 *The Holy Bible: New International Version.* 1984 (2 Timothy 2:2). Grand Rapids, MI: Zondervan.

likely you will disciple plainspoken, salt-of-the-earth people. Because discipleship is life-on-life, some of these discipling relationships will be challenging and messy. You may be invited into family conflict situations that have lasted a long time, even generations. You'll be brought into conversations and experiences in your relationship with these folks that may surprise you – especially if you were not raised in a rural community yourself. These folks have a better grasp on chemistry from fertilizer, herbicides and insecticides than many college chemistry majors. These are folks who can castrate a goat and deliver piglets without having to call a veterinarian. Rural life is different, but amazing. Having your identity firmly rooted in Christ, resting your ministry in the Word of God, preparing with ongoing prayer and acting in genuine love are vital.

Finally, I (John) have found that rural disciple making requires a great sense of humor. I have heard way too many stories about pastors who could not bring themselves to laugh at life or themselves. These pastors don't last long in rural churches, and if they do they tend to suck the joy right out of them. Genuine love and laughter open many doors for discipleship. People will show their true colors if they trust you and enjoy being around you. I had a few pranksters in my church – and their humor usually struck between 11:00 am and noon on Sunday (I could tell you stories!). One of the things that catapulted my relationship forward with key people in that church was accidentally blowing my nose into my lavaliere microphone, having forgotten to turn it off – it echoed through the whole church during worship! Laughing with people on genuinely humorous occasions breaks down huge relational walls. Don't be a stuffed shirt.

Rethinking the Discipleship Emphasis

Because discipleship in North America has now become largely academic, and most churches place the majority of their planning, resources and energies into the Sunday morning experience, discipleship is now often fit into that framework. It's a part of the Sunday routine rather than being the primary ministry all week long. The problem is that very little actual discipleship can take place as part of a typical Sunday School or worship experience. There is precious little time for real interaction. There is little if any ministry modeling or accountability happening. Too many relationships remain comfortably superficial. And there is simply no expectation that people will literally put into practice what they are being taught (obedience) and accept loving assessment of it. Teaching and worship can be excellently done in a congregational gathering; discipleship cannot. Disciple making is most fruitful one-on-one and in smaller clusters of people in relationship with each other.

So how do we move the disciple-making emphasis from the large gathering back down to the few where it was always intended to be? Here are some principles to help you answer that question for your setting:

1. Communication

Good, thorough communication is a must. The disciple-making process is sometimes so foreign to church people that they respond with great opposition saying things like, "That's not the way WE do church!" Grace and planning are important. If you have a generation of folks in a congregation that have lived the better part of their lives in their rural, family church with no expectation of making disciples for Christ, a new discipleship emphasis will cause two things to happen: first, they will be fearful because they have no frame of reference for what you're expecting, and second, they will worry that their whole Christian experience has been inadequate. These are real concerns and you have to be ready for them.

Before the first steps toward a new disciple-making emphasis are made, it is imperative to explain as much as possible beforehand. Begin with clear and biblical teaching – from the pulpit, in small groups, in the newsletter and in conversations – on the *what, why* and *how* of disciple making. Let them know this is not a program (short-term), but a lifestyle change (ongoing). Work with your leaders to determine ways to measure how well the congregation is receiving and understanding the message. This kind of communication will continue through implementation of the new emphasis and with each new person or family that joins the church.

2. Prayer & Intercession

The foundational nature of prayer cannot be overstated. Pray for your leaders that they would personally engage the new emphasis and begin making disciples. Pray for your congregation that each member would accept Jesus' Commission and would begin asking the Lord to guide them to at least one person to disciple. Ask the Lord into whom you should invest your life for His kingdom and take steps to build a discipling relationship with them that is loving and trustworthy. And in all this, be ever watchful to see who God may be raising up for a greater role and mentor them in it.

I am concerned about the general lack of prayer and intercession in the American Church today. Even among congregations of solid biblical background, prayer is often cursory at best. And it's not much better among pastors. There are a few who are faithful in practicing both the discipline of prayer and of maintaining an ongoing conversation with God throughout the day, but many others will tell you that their prayer life is inconsistent and, in some cases, missing altogether. A church will never surpass the level of her pastor in any area: if the pastor is not praying, this will ultimately be true for the congregation as well. And when it comes to revitalization – especially in rural congregations – consistent intercessory prayer is mandatory.

3. Identification

The next step in shifting the disciple-making emphasis away from the larger group gathering is to prayerfully identify those who are willing (and especially the eager) to be discipled and to disciple others. Pastors often become discouraged when the whole congregation doesn't begin to show movement, but this is typical. Focus on the "low-hanging fruit." As individuals begin to catch the vision for the new disciple-making emphasis, it will be important to match up disciples with disciple-makers. Ideally every Christian should be both a disciple and discipling others. It does not matter how old or spiritually mature one becomes, the discipleship process does not end until we stand before the Savior in glory, seeing him as He is because only then will we be fully like Him (1 John 3:2)!

4. Avoid Unnecessary Offenses

As with the implementation of any significant change in local church ministry, it is important to follow the established protocols as much as possible. It is never good to cause an offense unnecessarily and doing an end-run around policies, the church constitution or people will always break trust and cause strife. The notion that "sometimes it's better to ask forgiveness than to get permission" is a lie. It's never good for a believer in Jesus to purposely do something for which they will need to ask for forgiveness. That's unholy arrogance. Resist the pull of impatience and give the Holy Spirit time to do His work in the church. If policies or guiding documents need amendment, then follow the rules and bring the leadership together on that point. If a particular person consistently influences the congregation away from obedience to Jesus' Commission, then converse with them, pray with and for them, and then lovingly hold them accountable if their heart doesn't change. I (John) have worked with many churches and leadership teams to clean up messes that did similar damage and were completely avoidable. Few things are as important in the life of every church than the making of disciples. Don't risk souring people on that effort by acting outside of the appropriate structures and systems of the church.

5. Think "Generationally"

A very common mistake in disciple making is to unwittingly make the outcome too narrow. Again, the goal is not simply to make disciples, but to make disciples that make disciples. The difference is critical. When developing a discipling pathway for your church, it should always end in multiplication. Part of the process of *being* discipled is guidance and a living example of *making* disciples.

Paul's instructions to his son-in-the-faith, Timothy, are very helpful here (see 2 Timothy 2:2 above). Inherent in his own demonstration is a discipling influence to four generations: Paul himself is the first, Timothy his protégé is the second, "faithful men" is a plural third, and "others also" is a plural fourth. We know that Paul discipled multiple people, and here he is instructing Timothy to do the same. The expectation is that each of Timothy's disciples will also pour into multiple people. The multiplication impact is important. If we just use a factor of three as an example, by the fourth generation ("others also") we are already at 27 disciples. As those disciples enter into the work, the next level is 81!

Developing a Life-on-Life Approach

When it comes to discipleship and mentoring, I am indebted to my own mentor, Tom Johnston. Tom has done extensive work on this topic – especially as it relates to the rabbinical, life-on-life approach Jesus took. While there are many books on discipleship available, few really delve into a critical understanding of how disciples were made in the early church. Tom is truly an expert in this area and practices what he teaches. There are four important considerations I would make here from what I have learned from him.

1. Relationship is Key

Our Great Commission is to make disciples of all nations (*ethne* here in Greek might be best translated as "people groups"). But this last instruction of Jesus cannot be accomplished without relationship. You can teach people without a relationship (think of all the teachers you've had in school with whom your relationship ended the last day of that class); however, you cannot disciple someone outside of a real, personal relationship. This differentiates much of what is called discipleship today from the actual practice of making disciples. Taking an academic approach is easier because it can be standardized. The problem is that people are not standardized. Discipleship must be personal. The goal is not passing on information but life transformation. What is taught is not just known but lived.[24] Relationship is the key.

The kind of relationship that fosters life transformation takes time and effort. Therefore, it is important to note that the level of discipleship of which we speak can only be done with a few people, in close proximity, at any given time. Jesus

---

24 Thomas Brian Johnston, The Way of the Master: The Rabbinical Process of Jesus as an Adult Integrated Learning Methodology, Master's Thesis, ACTS Schools, Bangalore, India, 2012, p. 11.

was the Second Person of the Godhead, and he only chose to disciple 12 men. This should be instructive to us. Our American bent to "mass disciple" has hurt us in this regard. We've unwittingly reduced the impact of our work by systematizing it. We've created a Christian culture that knows a lot about the Bible but isn't very good at actually living it out. This is just as true in a rural setting as it is in the cities.

Close relationship allows for a life-on-life impact. There certainly is instruction, but there are also example, mentoring and accountability. There are expectations that what is taught will actually be lived out, and life itself provides both the curriculum and the laboratory. It is a form of spiritual apprenticeship that blesses both parties.

2. The Disciple's Needs Set the Agenda

Because discipleship is personal, the needs of the student dictate the discipleship agenda.[25] More will be said about assessment below, but suffice it to say here that it is important to determine where a disciple needs to grow in areas like character, spiritual maturity, calling, specific competencies and especially in rooting his or her identity firmly in Jesus Christ as God's precious son or daughter.

Again, life is both the curriculum and the laboratory. As the disciple receives instruction in any area of life, that instruction should then be tried and tested. For example, if the disciple has conflicted relationships, then he must be taught how the gospel applies to personal reconciliation and must take that understanding into the broken relationships to pursue any possible healing. There is a biblical process for reconciliation. Discipleship teaches one how to live life in a way that honors God and serves his fellow man.

---

25 Tom Johnston, "Session Six: The Rabbinic Mentoring Cohort: Creating the Environment," Trivium Institute, February 4, 2014.

As the disciple grows, the expectations of the discipling relationship can grow as well. As his or her needs change, the discipleship agenda changes with them. The goal of this ever-adapting process is to produce a follower of Christ who is mature, faithful and reproducing.

3. Assessment and Planning

This is an area that is truly lacking in most American discipling relationships. Because we have opted for a standardized curriculum approach, the need for assessment is all but overlooked. It is critical to begin with a good evaluation of the disciple's life and ministry. There are various tools available – some are good and some are simply not helpful.[26] As you search for a good tool to use, consider the following as important components:

Identity – the disciple's identity should be buried in Christ. Most Americans find their identity first and foremost in their dominant role (career, family, sports, etc.). This is why the first question we usually ask when meeting someone is, "What do you do?" Our culture teaches us to identify (pigeonhole) people by their role or job, and this has crept into the church as well. Even pastors often find their identity primarily in their pastorate – which is very unhealthy! We need to assess the disciple's identity so that correction and support can be provided where necessary.

Spiritual Maturity – the disciple should be growing in Christ. Few American Christians today pay intentional attention to their own spiritual disciplines (i.e., prayer,

---

26 I (John) recommend using the VISTA Assessment Tool produced by The Praxis Center for Church Development, www.praxiscenter.org.

study, Sabbath rest, generosity, etc.). Yet, these disciplines are the very things that deepen our vital connection with God. We need to assess the disciple's spiritual maturity so that direction can be given for living out these spiritual habits.

Character – the disciple should be displaying the character of Christ. The character of Jesus is best seen in what we typically refer to as The Fruit of the Spirit. When reviewing the entire New Testament, it is clear that Paul's list in Galatians 5 is not exhaustive. But these 9 character traits are a great start! We need to measure the disciple against such a list to determine any areas of character growth on which the discipling relationship should focus.

Calling – the disciple should have an awareness of his or her personal calling in Christ. Every believer has a calling – and that calling will always revolve around Christ's Great Commission (Matthew 28:18-20). But exactly *what* that calling is will be unique to every believer and will be consistent with his or her own divine design. We need to assess their spiritual gifts, ministry passions, life experience and skills to better understand how to guide them toward that unique destiny.

Competencies – the disciple should be growing in the skillsets needed to live and minister for Christ.[27] These include personal skillsets (e.g., prayer, worship, submission, repentance, etc.), relational skillsets (e.g., reconciliation, love, etc.) and ministerial skillsets (those specific to the disciple's ministry and calling). We must assess their skillsets so that discipleship can include investment and training into any areas of lack.

---

27 Tom Johnston and Mike Chong Perkinson, *The Organic Reformation: A New Hope for the Church in the West*, Manchester, NH: Praxis Media, 2009, pp. 98-102.

Actual Fruitfulness – the disciple's life should be bearing noticeable kingdom fruit for Christ. Great questions to ask are: How is God actually using this disciple for His kingdom purposes? How are people's lives being affected by this disciple for the glory of God? We must assess the actual fruitfulness of the disciple to ensure that their impact for Christ is on target and growing.

Once a thorough assessment has been completed, then a unique discipleship plan can be created for that disciple. It will focus on both increasing general understanding of Christ and His kingdom, and specific points of interest from the assessment that will help the disciple grow in those areas where he needs it most. This greatly increases both the intentionality of the discipling relationship and its expected fruit. It also provides a great set of potential milestones by which the disciple can mark personal growth in Christ.

The one blessing of discipleship in a rural setting is an increased ease of fostering life-on-life relationships. Work in rural communities is more often "shoulder to shoulder" than those in urban and suburban office cubicles. People tend to know each other (for better or worse) in rural communities. And most rural congregations in America still have a culture of "community" that many urban churches would envy. But discipleship in rural churches must still be intentional. These kinds of relationships might be easier, but they are not automatic. It still takes time and effort.

Results

The results of shifting the disciple-making emphasis from the larger gatherings to a one-on-one or cluster approach can be significant. Momentum will take time, but as more and more people catch the vision for both discipling others and being discipled themselves, it will increase. This kind of discipleship changes the priorities of a church. Disciple making (really, the Great Commission) becomes primary and it impacts everything else. Relationships change, but so do programs. Children's ministry and youth ministry focus on growing authentic, reproducing disciples and soon even the young will be impacting their peers for the kingdom. Evangelism shifts from a programmatic approach (following a predetermined outline) to a lifestyle that affects every relationship. Ultimately, a whole new way of life emerges in the church.

Rural congregations can be a bit more skeptical than their more urban counterparts, and this will mean communication and modeling is non-negotiable. But once people begin to see the fruit of this new emphasis, they will put their energy behind it. Even the smallest of congregations can experience health and make a wonderful impact on their communities for Christ.

Chapter 5
Resuscitating the Rural American Church (TC)

You're my place of quiet retreat; I wait for your Word to renew me.[28]

In order to resuscitate the rural church in north America, there must be an all-out blitz on attracting new members to one's church. There are a large number of rural congregations which are struggling to retain current members and attract new ones. The rural church must begin reexamining everything in an effort to more fully engage present members and appeal to potential new participants. Rural church revitalizers need to focus more on engaging the gifts and passions of their followers in the ministries and outreach of the rural church. It has to be in large part one of the big things rural church focuses upon. There has never been and will never be a time where the rural church can stop doing the work of equipping the rural church member for the work of ministry into the rural landscape. The rural church revitalizer affects how ministry gets done by the process we utilize in recruiting and releasing volunteers into the rural church ministry. We must be supportive, encouraging of their efforts, and celebrating of the effort even while it is still in the incubator stage. The one question we need to remain focused upon as the leader of a rural church is "how can I rally me parishioners to come along side and grow the church?" Remaining focused as the rural church revitalizer on this single question is often the thing which will allow others to embrace the vision for the church to flourish once more.

Paul in his initial advice to young Timothy in the second Epistle of Timothy provides great advice to all of us as church revitalizers. He admonishes: *"For God has not given us a*

---

[28] Eugene H. Peterson, *The Message: The Bible in Contemporary Language* (Colorado Springs, CO: NavPress, 2005), Ps 119:114.

spirit of fearfulness, but one of power, love, and sound judgment.'[29]
When resuscitating the rural American church, it is often easier to approach the declining rural church like a new church plant. By that I mean there is a high degree of operating as a catalyst for the rural church leader. Church planters are catalytic and have the ability to start something from dirt. They can land in a place and in six months they have a core group developed and moving towards launch. In rural church revitalization, the ability to be catalytic is a strong asset to gathering those who are disenfranchised or unreached. For the catalyst, he must think like an evangelist over a maintainer of the status quo. Breaking a rural church out of its comfort zone might be the hardest thing you will have ever done. Changing the structures and patterns of operation is difficult. Spending time with the key influencers is a must if they are going to embrace your new vision and direction. As the key influencers go so will the rest of the rural congregation. Here are some things which will help you as you begin to resuscitate the rural American church.

Challenge Obsolete Rural Church Rational

I.M.P.A.C.T. is a foreign word for many a rural church. The idea of reaching into one's community will often be met by "We tried it before but nothing happened." Survival is the name of the game for many and you must work to turn that around. Vision for many is to just keep the doors open. Remind the rural membership that they have something new to offer. Create a discussion group that meets regularly and discuss how they could reach further into the community. Talking about future possibilities helps your members enlarge their vision. Potential is a key ingredient you must works toward in the discussion groups sessions. Develop a brief mission statement that they can all remember. Church Revitalizer's are the key spark plug to get the church moving

---

29 C.f. 2 Timothy 1:7.

again. If the Church Revitalizer is a "can do" type of leader they can make an immediate impact. It might take a while for others to embrace the new future but the revitalizer can begin the journey with a tremendous spirit of optimism. Beginning by coaching and equipping a small few will lead to greater impact later. Far too many rural church leaders wait too long to do anything. The first year is a good time to begin the journey and the free pass you are often given in that time must not be wasted. Passivity is not something you can afford. Continue to be diplomatic but keep the end view in focus.

Focus on Evangelism Efforts Initially

Church Revitalizers working in the rural landscape must keep outreach a primary focus. In a day where it is vital to equip the laity for the work of the ministry (including evangelism) the one who leads the church must become the model for the rural church membership in the area of soul winning and outreach. Personal evangelism must be a key skill set in the rural churches pastoral leadership. Far too many churches today have pastors who are not modeling this key ingredient and it shows in their baptisms and lack of new people entering the church through an effective personal witness. Teach your people how to reach their friends and bring them to church.

Keep Missions Out Front Despite Those Wanting to Abandon It

Nothing gets a rural church more energized than when members return from a mission trip sharing how they were used by the Lord to make an impact on the mission field. In a day where there are those who go and those who stay and pray, getting more of your membership actively involved in mission works is a huge win for the rural church. Begin with local missions in your area which can be done on weekends and then advance to going across the nation. Stretch your people to consider going abroad in an effort to do mission work. Begin a special offering during Sunday School for the purpose of raising the support for those who go. Understand who really is your audience. Probably people similar to who you have right now. Do not try being everything and start focusing on who you really are. Do what you can do. Reach others through your sweet spot not your weak spot. Remember it takes all types of churches to reach all types of people. Keep your mission dollars local at first. Remember the local association of churches, is your first and foremost group that can provide help so stay faithful. Doing missions as a rural church is important to begin ones focus locally trying to be the lighthouse to your region first. Much work can be done in this area which will influence families for the cause of Christ with a focus on your immediate area. Concentrating on home missions in your local area will bring about greater dividends to your church than sending them all across the world.

Give the Church New Vision

Begin by listening to your rural church influencers first. Hear their hearts and ideas. Understand what gets them excited and would get them involved in ways they have not been before. Discover the past history of the church and why it is wired the way that it is.

Ask some of these questions:

What kind of church would you like to see us become? What suggestions to you have to make us better and stronger?

What could we do this year that has never happened before?

If we could do anything as a church body, what would it be?

Vision is led by the rural church revitalizer but it is also fueled by the group dynamics of the entire congregation. Ask for their opinions and thoughts first before you begin to launch a twenty-step plan that they were not part of crafting. If you start out becoming the church dictator, you will be counterproductive to the end goal of creating a viable new vision to grow the church.

In the area I serve locally, I met with a young pastor who just came to revitalize a rural church. He was a recent seminary grad and this was his first church to lead. During lunch one day he told me he would have the church "whipped into shape" (his words) within the next twelve months. I tried to get him to slow down and listen to the wonderful people which make up his congregation. He then opened a folder and gave me an assignment he had completed during his final year as a seminary student in Memphis. In that document, he shared twenty-seven things he was going to do in order to revitalize the rural church. I suggested that he do very little the first year that was not something the members thought would be a good initial step. I suggested what he did in seminary was a good thing to think about but in a vacuum, it does not always work the way it does in an academic institution. Then he rose his voice and told me that because he made a 98 on that paper in seminary, it was the Lords sign that he was to push hard to accomplish all of this in record time. I told him that if he persisted with such haste, he would be fired somewhere around the eighteen-month period of his tenure. You know what happened, almost to the day, a year and a half later, he was released. Vision is developed in unison in almost all rural churches and never forced upon a congregation.

Phase Out Antiquated Activities

In any declining church, there are things which have become antiquated and should be discontinued. The outdated stuff does not work for you and it is best if you remove these activities slowly and replace them one at a time with activities which work. Ask yourself if the ide or activity would still continue to bring wither good will or future prospect in one's church. Having an annual dinner on the grounds to celebrate formers members while being defeating in its concept, if refurbished a little it could become something which showcases the new things you are doing to regrow the rural church. Many rural churches have big days designed to promote the past but stall in moving it towards the preferred future. While you must honor the past, it is never wise to live in it.

Look towards the future not the past. Did you know that younger families feel out of place when they attend events that are primarily focused on what a church did fifty years ago? Younger and newer leadership within your church will not dwell on the past. They want a new day designed for their time, seeking to reconnect with a rural church that is advancing is their goal. Recreating yesterday only leaves you in yesterday looking back but rarely advancing and looking forward into the future. Evaluate all that you do in the church and in your ministry. What is not evaluated is not important.

Encourage Hospitality

Within the rural church there are many who enjoy hosting events such as fellowship dinners or lady's connection times. A wise rural church revitalizer will discover those people who love to host events in your church. That is a special gift. I was in one rural church in Franklin, North Carolina which really had it going on and they were drawing interested younger families from two other counties into their church. Utilize these gifts sets towards some sort of assimilation process in your church. In any rural church, there are those who have been there for a long time and have their own groups of friends well established in the fellowship. Meet with them and ask if they would consider some sort of hospitality event where the long tie members could meet and connect with the new potential members who are attending the church. Carl George taught us more than thirty years ago of the importance of introducing the new berries to the former berries. Putting some fun back in church is a great way to start. Begin building friendship towards you and your church by having fun doing life together. This will create new entry points into your church for those not presently part of the rural church family. Do not forget to do a few events designed for men that men are comfortable doing. Have events for men like basketball or softball. Have a fishing outing or big game dinner. Encouraging hospitality with new groups of individuals is a great way to begin the revitalization process of a declining rural church. Remember to include the nurals.

Rally the Congregation Through "BIG" Rural Events

In a rural landscape developing big events for the local church takes quite a bit of doing. Part of the reason is that often the sheer numbers required to pull off such an undergoing takes more volunteers than you might have within the church. Yet, even in small rural areas an event can be designed to draw the community. Events build up the morale, give a winning team sensation, makes an impact into community, says something is happening, pulls in a pack, expands a churches faith, provides a chance to invite friends, achieves something for the church, unites members and develops future volunteers. When a rural pastor considers doing big events you might want to consider my formula I used when revitalizing a rural church in West Virginia. To make a big impact in a rural community:

B – Build on What You and Your Church Members Can Accomplish

I – Invest in Your Rural Area for Greater Impact

G – Gather Others with Similar Interests

Remember, holding a successful church event takes your planning to the next level. Whether you are hosting a community wide picnic, worship event, youth day-camp, seasonal festival, Christmas extravaganza, or any other special event, you need to think through many things. Keeping the acronym in mind will help. Developing a plan with a long enough timeline is crucial. Gathering others who have similar interests in rural community that will handle the various manageable parts is necessary. Begin early developing streams of marketing that will not cost you anything or very little. Get the word out early and often. Six months before an event is not too early to begin thinking and doing low key marketing events. In my Church Marketing book, *Total Church Communication Plan Book*[30], I suggest seven ways to market an event that will cost you absolutely nothing. A good promotion plan will help lay the groundwork and set the course for every big event your church considers. Promote your church to your rural region. Most churches make no noise and no one knows where they are or who they are. In a rural setting get your region talking about you early and often. Newcomers respond to the noise. Write a community blog and have a regional Facebook page. Become a voice for positive change in your rural area. Create a Church Website, it is the fellowship hall for the new millennium. Get on your local radio station somehow. Creating a big event for a rural

---

30 If you are interested in a free download of this resource go to: RenovateConference.org/resources and look for the title *Total Church Communication Plan Book* by Tom Cheyney.

community must be an event that the entire community will support and participate in. Creating fun is often a great way to connect with a community to emphasize that we are all working together for the betterment of our area. If your church membership lacks enthusiasm for creating big events, while such events could help your church revitalize, unless you develop other forms of assistance it is not advised you utilize such a strategy.

Thom Rainer in his weekly blog says there are three reasons big events are ineffective.[31] He says that most of them will fail to reach their intended purpose. His reason is that most are supposed to be outreach events designed to reach people and share Christ. But for the rural landscape, it is wise to make connections through acts of kindness or having fun. While Rainer says that "church leaders often point to the large attendance of the event, to the hundreds of guest cards completed, or to the decisions noted by these guests. But when the same leaders try to assess how many people have actually become integrated into the life of the church, the reality is usually disturbing."[32] I would suggest this is the wrong idea for doing events. In rural areas being a major player is far more important than being able to say you had three hundred join one's church as a result. Thom, Rainer does make a good point what he says that most churches doing events are not outwardly strategic in preparation, follow-up, and possess a DNA of outward focused for the event.[33] Stop thinking about cost and start thinking connection in your rural events.

---

31 C.f. NOVEMBER 23, 2015
http://thomrainer.com/2015/11/three-reasons-most-churches/

32 Ibid.

33 Ibid.

Put the Fun Back in the Church and Others Will Begin to Have Fun as Well.

One of my best all time themes as a rural pastor was when for two years our major church emphasis was: Putting the Fun Back in the Son! Here is what I began teaching that declining church during the time we made this theme our guiding vision. Fun is something that is often overlooked in declining churches, both rural and urban. Fun is a contagious ingredient for the initial effort of revitalization. Declining churches which bring back the joy will be remembered. Enthusiasm is infectious. When a declining church developed a new environment of joy and celebration it has a better chance to achieve revitalization. If you are not having fun in your work of the ministry, no one else will. Some rural churches have forgotten what fun is all about. The point is that the more you laugh, the more others will begin to sense something is changing within your church. Frowning ministers often are such a turnoff to potential members that it is impossible to make a connection. A reconnection will not be possible if you are always acting like our Christian journey is nothing but solemn and depressing. Rural church revitalizers who are adept at humor and telling interesting stories are an asset to such churches.

Ask the Opinion of the Gatekeepers and Caretakers

Your matriarchs and patriarchs have much invested in their church and while they want you to be instrumental in saving their church, they want you to hear what are their opinions. Wise rural church revitalizers focus on the opinion makers in one's church. They are the influencers which can help you. Taking the time and making the time to work towards gaining their backing is a critical investment. Such gatekeepers and caretakers can make you or break you. Listening earns you the right to be heard. Solicit their consent to make changes and include them in the process. Their feedback is a friend and not your enemy.

Teach the Notion of Change

In my book, *The Church Revitalizer as Change Agent*[34], I suggested that if you are going to be an effective revitalizer of plateaued or declining churches, you must be a deliverer of change. It is a simple point; revitalized churches do not stay the same. There is movement and not lethargy. Long-lasting improvement is the goal not just changing because you want too. The Bible speaks of change. Church Revitalizers need to show how the Holy Spirit is our greatest means towards change. So, allow one's body of believers to present new ideas over you presenting them. Members like other member's ideas.

Update the Music in the Worship Services

It is interesting that in most rural churches the style of music has been around for a long time. In fact, most are utilizing a worship music selection that has been around for more than one hundred years. Then we wonder why we are not able to keep younger family members and their children. Grandmother and mother have come to realize that quilting your children into worship does not go as far as it has in the past. I was in a church in the pan handle of Florida not long ago doing a revitalization consult when a gentleman raised his voice and said, "You can do anything you want to revitalize this church, except for changing the music!" While he was good intentioned, it spoke of why the church was unable to keep their younger members and not able to draw new ones.

---

34 You can search via Amazon, Tom Cheyney in books for this resource or go to RenovateConference.org/bookstore for the latest church revitalization and renewal resources.

Do whatever you can to recuperate your music. Ask yourself the question, "would my kids and grandchildren want to worship here? Stop using guilt to get you kids to attend. They deserve a vibrant worship experience and you should not keep them from such intimate connection with their Lord. If you are not using sound and video get your sanctuary up to speed. Say we are just a small church and it is not necessary is just living in denial. Reformat your song selection and stop providing a litany of dirges and discouraging songs. Rural church music does not need to be perfect just participatory. One pastor I follow says rural churches might want to contemplate a "New Country" type of feel for the worship music. Remember and emphasize that Kids begat kids and kids begat parents into your church. Kids should matter to a rural church. Show it in your budget. Develop activities for them because there is so little for them to do in rural areas, make your church a place for kids. Parents want their kids in a church which loves them. Is yours that church? Celebrate new things and positive things. Clapping is not the unpardonable sin! Make worship fun. Clap more often. A new volunteer is worthy of clapping. Someone getting saved is worthy of clapping. A new youth coming to youth group is worthy of clapping. Model and teach your participants how to clap over remaining silent. Church Revitalizer, start clapping and laughing more often. It will not keep you out of heaven.

Put Your Cheerleaders at Your Entrances and Exits

If you want to resuscitate a rural church put your cheerleaders at the entrances and exits. Stop placing those introverts at the doors which say nothing to individuals entering your campus. Talking about games and gossip is not the type of individuals which will help a first-time guest feel welcomed. Your church cheerleaders are the best individuals to man the doors. Cheerful people help guests feel welcomed. In fact, take the time to consider what a new prospect needs as they enter worship and begin developing leaders who could meet those necessities. Utilize positive ushers and friendly people to take offerings and make announcements. Ushers must "Ush." They are there to assist those who enter the worship center and not to catch up on the latest gossip. Name tags for these leaders help visitors know they have the information they need to get to where they need to go. Always escort guests to the furthest front areas as possible. Work at becoming visitor friendly. Teach your people how to make friends of visitors. People are looking for a place to make friends not a friendly church today. Help visitors to find a place and not feel out of place.

Protect Your Congregation and Defend It

Remember as the rural revitalizer that the rural church must be protected. That is the job of the church revitalizer. Make it a safe place for the wounded. Church disciplined must be practiced. When disgruntled members leave remove them from leadership positions right away. Committed church members must protect their pastor while he is protecting you. Make being a church member mean something special. It was John Maxwell who taught me that membership is a privilege and not a right. It should mean something. Get rid of inactive membership rolls. Take care of the pastor's family and he will take care of you. Stop over working him so you can do nothing.

Work Towards Creating Multi-Cells

Work towards creating multi-cells and move past the single cell concept of a rural church. Move from being one cell for everyone to as many multi-cells as possible. A single cell is what keeps most rural churches small and ineffective. The *"We are one big happy family"* idea must be replaced with *"we are many and there is the right group for you here."* There will be a road block if the rural church does not create and develop small groups and a multi-cell mentality.

Become More Male Friendly

Far too many churches are designed for women worshippers. Then we wonder why men refuse to go to such churches. Men are spiritual but many are not excited about the style of worship in many rural churches. Men like to worship where the songs do not cause them to go in for surgery the following day! Move towards a male friendly church over a women centric service. Men like male things not female things in worship. Stop dominating the service by women participation and get some men up before the church. Have men take up the offering and pray. Have men make the announcements. Develop a men's gathering led by a man the others respect. Begin working on your rural Male leadership at church.

Move Back to a Church Bulletin

Granted most contemporary churches do not use a worship service program but in rural areas it is still a good mechanism. Make the bulletin a big deal and improve its appearance. The chief reason for this is because the weekly church bulletin is often the rural churches only promotion tool for advertising so make it count. As I worked to revitalize a rural church in one of my former pastorates I always included a pastor's column in it each week with a challenging idea and thought provoking content. It was also where I developed vison and goal statements that would compel participants towards a desired outcome. Utilize the piece as a positive informative piece and less about who was there and how much was given. Negative numbers are not impressive so delete them and allow for other ideas to present a more positive picture of your church body. A jam-packed bulletin gives the impression that a lot is going on here.

Revamp, Refurbish, & Repair

It is amazing how those who go to the same church each week become blind to the disarray and disorder of the campus. Having a slow plan to renovate the church is a must. A little paint now and then when you can afford it goes a long way. Begin revamping the facilities utilizing your membership and you as the leader. It takes time but slow going is a win here. New paint and the updating of bathrooms goes a long way. The often-overlooked area in declining rural churches is the nursery so begin cleaning it up and making it an area that invites young families with infants. Refurbishing has a way of boosting morale. Get your men to build a new sign with the men of your church. Design and display directional signs around your area on Sunday. Signage can be done inexpensively with a color copier and a laminator. Make it easy for people to find their way around your church. Develop a few inexpensive brochures. Excellence is doing the best with the resources you have! Consider Yard Signs which can be put up and taken down each week.

Count the Cost for Saving One's Church

The rural church revitalizer must be willing to count the cost for new growth. He must have an unwavering resolve for including new participants in the work of the church. He needs to be tough skinned because as a rural church grows, some people will leave. As you grow your time will be spread to a greater number of people and families. Remember that always growth cost more in supplies and materials. But grow anyway.

Wrapping it Up!

The diminishing spiritual condition of rural regions, coupled with the challenges of small-town communities, calls for a renewed focus on church revitalization and renewal in rural America. One out of seven individuals live in rural America. That is a little over 50,000,000 Americans live in the rural American landscape. A significant proportion of unchurched individuals reside in rural communities of America. Not only is there a significant population in these communities, but the needs are just as significant or greater than their urban/suburban counterpart. Drug and alcohol abuse, breakdown of the family, physical abuse and child neglect, poverty and unemployment describe several of the challenges facing these communities. For much of the twentieth century, most rural communities experienced population loss as millions of rural residents left for the opportunities in booming cities. More people consistently left rural areas than came to them. This trend ended in the 1970's when rural population gains exceeded those in urban areas. Gains in rural areas waned in the 1980's, rebounded in the early 1990's and slowed again in the later 1990's. Rural growth picked up again after 2001, although recent gains remain smaller than in the early 1990's. Currently, seventeen percent of the population (50 million people) and seventy five percent of the land area of the United States is nonmetropolitan.[35] From the 1920's to the 1960's, people left rural America in substantial numbers, but rural counties still grew slowly due to natural increase. In the 1970's a dramatic and surprising shift occurred when more people moved to rural areas than left.[36] Tragically, a dramatic demise in the presence and influence of the church is accelerating the destructive impact of these problems. Many churches are quietly dying off without so much as a fight, unless it is

---

35 C.f. Demographic Trends in Rural and Small Town America by Kenneth Johnson.
http://scholars.unh.edu/carsey/?utm_source=scholars.unh.edu%2Fcarse y%2F5&utm_medium=PDF&utm_campaign=PDF REPORTS ON RURAL AMERICA Volume 1, Number 1.

36 Ibid.

among themselves! Rural America is being shunned by some of the larger denominations which were once known for aggressive church planting. This forgotten landscape will survive and be rejuvenated through medium size churches heading the call to partner with near rural locales. The eternal fortunes of those living in rural America are just as important as those who have migrated to urban centers. Invest in a small town that needs your help. We need lay individuals who have the ability to minister in a rural landscape to become equipped and deployed as a bi-vocational pastor. We must reverse the downward spiral through revitalization and renewal. Get to know the "Nurals" that inhabit your rural landscape. Revitalizing of the rural church matters to the Lord.

CHAPTER 6
The Peacemaking Imperative in Rural Revitalization

Oh! May the God of great hope fill you up with joy, fill you up with peace, so that your believing lives, filled with the life-giving energy of the Holy Spirit, will brim over with hope![37]

There are few things as disconcerting and damaging to local church ministry as is unresolved conflict. And in the rural setting, where relationships often go back generations and most folks know each other well, conflict can have a particularly devastating impact. This impact is multiplied when the congregation has slowly drifted into a self-focused agenda over time. The truth is, as the Immanuel agenda (the Great Commission) wanes in a church, multiple human agendas always arise to fill the void. When this happens, the good and expected conflict that comes with the transformation of souls gives way to the aggressive and damaging conflict of competing personalities. Revitalization is impossible until such conflict is addressed and resolved. Many a church that could otherwise experience revitalization has succumb under the influence of unforgiveness.

Conflict, simply defined, is a difference in opinion or purpose that frustrates someone's goals or desires.38 People

---

[37] Eugene H. Peterson, *The Message: The Bible in Contemporary Language* (Colorado Springs, CO: NavPress, 2005), Ro 15:13.

38 This practical definition is from Peacemaker Ministries. I (John) have been personally blessed by their excellent training and materials. Before pursuing certification with them, I was ill equipped to deal with conflict and would usually avoid it until someone exploded. I highly recommend that pastors and church leaders seek out the training to gain both skills and perspective, learning to bring even long-standing conflicts to a resolution. I also recommend they read two books: *The Peacemaker: A Biblical Guide to Resolving Personal Conflict* by Ken Sande (Grand Rapids, MI: Baker Books, 2004) and *The Peacemaking Pastor: A Biblical Guide to Resolving*

typically fall into one of two camps – they avoid conflict like the plague, or they try to control conflict – both of which only make things worse. Bringing conflicted parties together is challenging and can even be unnerving. And when that conflict is in a rural congregation, its tentacles can indeed be long and can impact not only the church but also the entire community.

I (John) know of one town where a local grain storage operator (and a church elder) cheated several farmers. Most of these parties were in the same congregation. You can imagine the impact such a conflict had on that little church. Everyone in town knew what had happened and the battle (though only verbal) had deeply damaged not only the reputation of those directly involved, but of the church as well. To allow such a conflict to remain unaddressed can annihilate a church's witness to its own town.

The Uniqueness of Conflict in a Rural Community

While there are peacemaking principles that work in virtually every environment, there are also nuances in each situation that require these principles to be contextualized. Nowhere is this truer than in a rural church setting. There are really five key aspects of conflict in rural communities that make it unique:

1. A Different Quality of Relationship

In urban and suburban congregations – especially larger ones – it is possible to maintain a very superficial relationship with fellow church attenders. People attend church for months without really ever meeting someone. And even when there are relationships, they may be jovial on Sunday

---

Church Conflict by Alfred Poirier (Grand Rapids, MI: Baker Books, 2006). These will become oft-referenced guides in your pastoral library!

and then not even interact the rest of the week. Unfortunately, some folks prefer it that way – and will find another church to attend if people start getting to close. This scenario is near impossible in most rural congregations. Rural churches tend to be smaller and far more familial (i.e., attended by extended family in multiple generations). People in rural settings tend to know each other more fully. In many cases, these generations have grown up together. Folks in rural churches likely see each other more often. These are all good things, but they make any conflict within the church far more personal and potentially damaging – especially if it's between members of the same extended family.

2. A Different Response to Conflict

Because of the more-personal nature of rural relationships, the pain produced by conflict is often experienced as betrayal. This makes conflict more challenging to address. Betrayal destroys trust at a deeper level. And betrayal between brothers or cousins impacts a whole family. The response to conflict is not just between the conflicted parties, but encompasses more people and more volatile emotions.

3. A Different Network of Communication

Every church has to endure some level of gossip. But gossip in rural communities is particularly heinous. Again, because of the kind of relationships, both good and bad forms of communication are more far-reaching and more devastating. News of a conflict in a rural congregation often quickly spreads to the whole community. What happened in a Sunday School classroom can literally change relationships at the grocery or barbershop.

4. A Different Intensity of "Memory"

Conflict "memory" can be a huge problem in rural churches. In one church with which I (John) worked, there was an unresolved conflict between two families that I would later learn stemmed back to something that happened between their grandfathers! What I call conflict memory is really an issue of unforgiveness. And, as we'll see below, Christians are not allowed to harbor any kind of unforgiveness. Conflict resolution is not really complete until all parties and their extended families have released the offense in Christ-like forgiveness.

5. A Different Level of Damage

Finally, conflict in rural churches can potentially cause greater harm than that in their city counterparts. Because of the closer, more personal nature of the relationships, and the familial ties within rural congregations, the chances of hurting someone (and causing collateral damage in the larger family) are much higher. Fear of being "blackballed" is very real in some rural communities, where conflict in the local church can translate into loss of business or opportunities. Again, this is primarily a forgiveness issue, but it's still a driving consideration in rural church conflict.

A Biblical Theology of Conflict Resolution

It is surprising how many pastors and churches lack a biblical understanding of conflict resolution. Few churches have adopted formal conflict plans that are rooted in the gospel. Even fewer churches have church discipline policies based upon such plans that lead toward reconciliation, forgiveness and restoration. And those policies that mention church discipline at all often articulate punitive statements relating to the removal of membership privileges. While Scripture does express the need to protect the flock by separating out certain kinds of people, it is to be the exception not the rule. And even when such a separation occurs, the biblical authors are clear that it is with the purpose and hope of repentance and eventual restoration. Bringing biblical clarity is important here. And there is no better place to start than with the instruction of James, the half-brother of Jesus, on the topic.

> [1] What causes fights and quarrels among you? Don't they come from your desires that battle within you? [2] You want something but don't get it. You kill and covet, but you cannot have what you want. You quarrel and fight. You do not have, because you do not ask God. [3] When you ask, you do not receive, because you ask with wrong motives, that you may spend what you get on your pleasures.
> [4] **You adulterous people**, don't you know that friendship with the world is hatred toward God? Anyone who chooses to be a friend of the world becomes an enemy of God. [5] Or do you think Scripture says without reason that the spirit he caused to live in us envies intensely? [6]

But he gives us more grace. That is why Scripture says:

> "God opposes the proud but gives grace to the humble."(James 4:1-6)[39]

This letter is written to believers, yet James calls them "adulterous." That's strong language. Why would he say such a thing? To better understand the answer, we need to look at a few more passages. Paul instructs us how to relate to one another in his letter to the Church at Ephesus:

> [29] Do not let any unwholesome talk come out of your mouths, but only what is helpful for building others

---

[39] *The Holy Bible: New International Version.* 1984 (Jas 4:1–6). Grand Rapids, MI: Zondervan, **emphasis mine**.

up according to their needs, that it may benefit those who listen. [30] And do not grieve the Holy Spirit of God, with whom you were sealed for the day of redemption. [31] Get rid of all bitterness, rage and anger, brawling and slander, along with every form of malice. [32] Be kind and compassionate to one another, forgiving each other, just as in Christ God forgave you. (Ephesians 4:29-32)[40]

Note that he tells us that we must forgive each other, just as God has forgiven us. He says the same thing to the Church at Colosse in Colossians 3:12-13. But perhaps the strongest instruction on this comes from Christ himself. As he relates the Parable of the Unmerciful Servant, he contrasts the forgiveness of the king with the lack of forgiveness of his servant. When the king finds out that his servant has acted wickedly toward another servant who owed him far less that he had owed the king, the king sentences him to ongoing punishment. The story itself is a great reminder of how we should forgive people in light of our own forgiveness from God, but Jesus makes it even stronger by ending the story with this warning:

> "This is how my heavenly Father will treat each of you unless you forgive your brother from your heart." (Matthew 18:35)[41]

Forgiveness is the reason Jesus, the Second Person of the triune Godhead, left the glory and majesty of his throne and took on human flesh. Forgiveness is the reason Jesus paid the incredible price at Calvary – giving his own life for us.

---

[40] *The Holy Bible: New International Version.* 1984 (Ephesians 4:29–32). Grand Rapids, MI: Zondervan.

[41] *The Holy Bible: New International Version.* 1984 (Matthew 18:35). Grand Rapids, MI: Zondervan.

Forgiveness is the heart of the Gospel, and thereby the very heart of the whole Christian faith! Forgiveness is non-negotiable for the follower of Jesus Christ.

Now back to James. An adulterer is someone who has cheated. It's someone who has committed infidelity. It is someone who is in a covenant relationship and then violates that covenant. This is precisely why James chose such a strong word. In the upper room, as Jesus shared his last Passover meal with the disciples, he told them of the New Covenant in his blood for the forgiveness of sins.42

Here's the point: When someone turns their life over to Christ, they enter into a covenant relationship with him. They enter the New Covenant community, the communion of the saints. The basis and the heart of this relationship with Christ and other believers is *forgiveness*! For Jesus' own people to allow (let alone to harbor) unforgiveness – to actually remain in broken, unreconciled relationships with each other – is nothing short of infidelity to Christ our Lord!

As followers of Jesus Christ, we cannot *not* forgive! It's not allowed. We have been made citizens and ambassadors of another kingdom in the Great Commission (Matthew 28:18-20) by virtue of our faith in Christ, and along with that citizenship and ambassadorship is a message and ministry of forgiveness. Paul writes to the Christians in Corinth:

> [11] Since, then, we know what it is to fear the Lord, we try to persuade men. What we are is plain to God, and I hope it is also plain to your conscience. [12] We are not trying to commend ourselves to you again, but are giving you an opportunity to take pride in us, so that

---

42 C.f. Matthew 26:27-28; Luke 22:20; 1 Corinthians 11:25; & Hebrews 9:15.

you can answer those who take pride in what is seen rather than in what is in the heart. [13] If we are out of our mind, it is for the sake of God; if we are in our right mind, it is for you. [14] For Christ's love compels us, because we are convinced that one died for all, and therefore all died. [15] And he died for all, that those who live should no longer live for themselves but for him who died for them and was raised again. [16] So from now on we regard no one from a worldly point of view. Though we once regarded Christ in this way, we do so no longer. [17] Therefore, if anyone is in Christ, he is a new creation; the old has gone, the new has come! [18]

All this is from God, *who reconciled us to himself through Christ* and *gave us the ministry of reconciliation:* [19] that God was reconciling the world to himself in Christ, not counting men's sins against them. And *he has committed to us the message of reconciliation.* [20] We are therefore Christ's ambassadors, as though God were making his appeal through us. We implore you on Christ's behalf: Be reconciled to God. [21] God made him who had no sin to be sin for us, so that in him we might become the righteousness of God.[43] We are called to be reconcilers! He's given us our marching orders – our Commission – the ministry of reconciliation (v. 18). He's given us the primary tool we need for this ministry – the message of reconciliation (v. 19 – that's the gospel). We are God's instruments in Christ to bring gospel reconciliation to the world!

Please understand, friends, it is inconceivable to God in light of the cost of our own forgiveness that we would *ever* withhold forgiveness toward someone else. It is forsaking our first love! To do so calls into question our own salvation – and at the very least our understanding of Christ's gospel.

---

[43] *The Holy Bible: New International Version.* 1984 (2 Co 5:11–21). Grand Rapids, MI: Zondervan.

Christians are not allowed to leave broken relationships unaddressed.

The Critical Need for Conflict Coaching

We've discussed the uniqueness of conflict in the rural setting and the clear mandate to pursue forgiveness in every relationship. We've noted that church revitalization is impossible when conflicts in the church family remain unaddressed. So just how does one practically foster the kind of biblical peacemaking and reconciliation that promotes revitalization? The rest of this chapter provides some guidance, and chief among the suggestions is that the church establish a cadre of mature believers with a gentle spirit, a reputation of genuine love and some critical training in biblical peacemaking to be conflict coaches.[44] This ministry team will be ready to serve the church family and community when such help is needed.

The Coach

A conflict coach, of course, cannot be a party in the conflict. This is someone who is called to help fulfill the ministry of reconciliation with both brothers and sisters in Christ, and also folks in the community, by coming alongside them in this time of need. In fact, once news about conflict coaching moves beyond church walls, it's not unusual for this to become a primary way to serve the community and demonstrate the power of the gospel to those who desperately need it.

Another essential factor when prayerfully recruiting conflict coaches is to only consider those with a track record

---

44 As noted above, Peacemaker Ministries provides training on various levels for this exact purpose. They also have several DVD studies local churches can use to get the ball rolling. www.peacemaker.net

of trustworthiness. Reconciliation ministry cannot happen without trust – period. For this reason, it is a mistake to ask for volunteers. Too often, volunteers will not have the right gifts and temperament. Instead, after much prayer, candidates should be selected for such a ministry. People will only respond to a coach they trust, so having a team of several available people is always helpful.

Finally, a conflict coach must be patient and gentle, and have his or her identity firmly rooted in Christ so that truth can be spoken in genuine love. This is non-negotiable. As noted above, conflict (especially in rural settings) comes with high emotion. The coach must be someone who can receive that emotion without taking it personally, and then help the parties (individually and then together) to process their perspectives in a healthy way. Wounded people may need to be protected in reconciliation and mediation. Angry and belligerent people may need to be held accountable. A patient and gentle spirit can impact both of these needs with the peace of Christ's gospel.

The Process

The process of conflict coaching is straightforward. It begins with a bit of triage individually with each party to get a general understanding of the conflict. This first meeting is mainly relational to ensure that there is trust. Additional meetings are then schedule with each individual to do fact-finding and "emotional mining." Fact-finding is just that, personalized research to learn all the pertinent facts regarding the situation. This includes taking notes about conversations, getting copies of any needed documents and learning the complete story of each party.45 Emotional mining is also an

---

45 Peacemaker Ministries' training is outstanding on this process, providing both essential resources and role-playing practice to hone one's skills.

important aspect of this process. This is where the coach gains a thorough understanding of each party's perspective and their emotional responses to the situation. Sometimes perspectives are skewed and emotions are misplaced, but even this is critical knowledge for the coach so he can help the party navigate back to a healthy place and ensure forgiveness. This part of the coaching process takes time – do not cut it short. The reconciliation process will only be as solid as are the facts used to foster a true understanding and forgiveness. If several meetings are needed with each party, it's worth it.

Once the coach understands the situation well, he or she can then begin helping the two parties to understand each other. The coach can clear up misunderstandings and offer guidance on ways the parties might move toward common outcomes and reconciliation. As the process continues, it is always important to coach both sides on biblical confession and forgiveness. It is amazing in the American church today that so many people really have no concept of what biblical confession and forgiveness look like. We have made assumptions for at least a generation that people just know how to do these critical Christian practices. This is simply not the case! Churches teach people that they *must* confess their sin but never really teach them how to do it. Likewise, churches teach people that they *must* forgive others but never really teach people how to forgive like God forgives in Christ. The conflict coach has a primary role in this so that real reconciliation can happen – for without confession of wrongdoing and real forgiveness, reconciliation is unlikely and restoration is probably impossible.

The Seven A's of Confession46

The Seven A's of Confession tool is available in many different publications from Peacemaker Ministries. It provides one of the most useful, concise outlines to guide people in forming a solid, biblical confession in reconciliation.

1. Address everyone involved (All those whom you affected)
2. Avoid if, but and maybe (Do not try to excuse your wrongs)
3. Admit specifically (Both attitudes and actions)
4. Acknowledge the hurt (Express sorrow for hurting someone)
5. Accept the consequences (Such as making restitution)
6. Alter your behavior (Change your attitudes and actions)47
7. Ask for forgiveness

A good conflict coach will work through each of these points in detail with the parties, helping them to write a heart-felt confession to be used in the reconciliation meeting. Such a confession is often very powerful and sets the stage for genuine forgiveness to be offered. It is likely that both parties will have things to confess to each other as a result of the conflict.

---

46 Ken Sande, "The Seven A's of Confession," *Peacemaker Ministries Website (www.peacemaker.net)*, 22 September 2014, Web, 01 July 2015.

47 I (John) have found it particularly helpful here to lay out your plans to make sure you never make that infraction again. It shows that you are serious about reconciliation.

Before outlining the Four Promises of Forgiveness, it's important to explain what forgiveness is not. Because the Church's teaching on forgiveness has not been thorough, church folks have often had to figure out this essential skill on their own and have come up short. The conflict coach will have to clarify these things with the parties to make sure that their understanding of forgiveness is Jesus' understanding of forgiveness.

Forgiveness is not a feeling – many people will tell you plainly that they do not feel like forgiving the one who hurt or wronged them. This is actually natural, but we must explain that forgiveness is supernatural and not contingent on our feelings. It is only as they take steps (sometimes out of sacrificial obedience to Christ) toward forgiveness that the Holy Spirit will give them the capacity for genuine forgiveness.

Forgiveness is not forgetting – our flesh has a long memory and loves to mull over past hurts. In addition, our enemy, the Devil, has a vested interest in keeping the reconciliation power of the gospel through forgiveness at bay. We will be reminded of some wrongs from time to time. Eventually there will be no more death or mourning or crying or pain (Revelation 21:4), but for now only God has the ability to truly forget wrongs against him (Isaiah 38:17; 43:25; Jeremiah 31:34; Ezekiel 18:22; Hebrews 8:12). Just because a hurt or wrong is remembered does not mean it remains unforgiven.

---

48 Ken Sande, "The Four Promises of Forgiveness," *Peacemaker Ministries Website (www.peacemaker.net),* 22 September 2014, Web, 01 July 2015.

Forgiveness is not excusing behavior – our forgiveness is modeled after God's forgiveness of us. God in no way excused our sin. Christ paid the full penalty for it on our behalf. Think of it this way: God's forgiveness is an act of both grace and mercy – grace in that he extended to us something we didn't deserve, and mercy in that he did not extend to us what we really did deserve! When we forgive someone, we are leaving the payment of that sin up to Christ. We are not excusing it, but are appropriating our faith in Christ and offering both grace and mercy to our offender.

Forgiveness is not saying "I'm Sorry" – the words "I'm Sorry" only mean that you feel sorrow for what you have done. They are not an expression of forgiveness. For that matter, they are not an expression of confession either. Unless one is expressing "godly sorrow that leads to repentance" (2 Corinthians 7:10) as a first step toward real repentance and confession, "I'm sorry" is completely insufficient for our purposes.

Forgiveness and Trust are not the same thing – and this is a critical point! When trust has been violated and a relationship has been broken, trust must be re-earned! It is completely biblical to grant full forgiveness toward someone and then not trust him or her. As noted above, forgiveness is non-negotiable for the Christian. But we are commanded in Scripture only to trust God (Christ).

Extending trust to anyone else is in response to his or her level of trustworthiness. When it comes to trust, forgiveness simply means that we are offering the offender the opportunity to earn our trust back. But the work is on his or her shoulders.

Now that we understand what forgiveness is not, lets clearly define what we mean when we say the words, "I forgive you." Forgiveness offers four promises. The first three of them are a matter of the heart and apply to all situations. The fourth is transactional (meaning that both the wounded party and the offender are working toward reconciliation and forgiveness has been requested).49 As such, the fourth may not be possible in some circumstances. Ken Sande outlines the promises as:

1. "I will not dwell on this incident."
2. "I will not bring up this incident again and use it against you."
3. "I will not talk to others about this incident"
4. "I will not let this incident stand between us or hinder our personal relationship."

Sande further explains,

> By making and keeping these promises, you can tear down the walls that stand between you and your offender. You promise not to dwell on or brood over the problem or to punish by holding the person at a distance. You clear the way for your relationship to develop unhindered by memories of past wrongs. This is exactly what God does for us, and it is what he calls us to do for others.50

---

49 *Resolving Everyday Conflict: Biblical Answers for a Common Problem,* Billings MT: Peacemaker Ministries, 2010, p. 35.

50 Sande, "Four Promises."

The need for conflict coaching is huge today, and it can be highly successful in rural churches as both a service to the church body and the community at large.

Getting Started in Your Congregation

Bringing biblical peacemaking to a congregation where it has not been practiced is no easy thing. It is critical to bring the church family back to the Scripture to see that what you are doing is not "new," and that a vital part of the Christian life together has been missing. It will usually require a firm gentleness at the beginning, in a spirit of genuine love. Great intentions are ruined when pastors or church leaders come across to their memberships as dictators or control freaks. There is no place for that in the pastoral ministry, and certainly not in helping a congregation rediscover the mandate for peacemaking!

It is best to work hard from the beginning to fully embed biblical peacemaking into the church's overall discipleship process. Jesus said, "Blessed are the peacemakers, for they will be called the sons of God." (Matthew 5:9) To become more like Christ – *the* Son of God – is to become a peacemaker. Arguably, there are few times we are more like Christ than when we're about the process of bring reconciliation to those around us. Therefore the overall discipleship strategy of the church should include peacemaking for every age group – children's ministry, student ministry, sr. adult ministry, etc.

Biblical peacemaking must be modeled; therefore, it is essential that the pastor and the church leadership fully practice biblical peacemaking in their own families, around the leadership table and in their other relationships. One cannot export what he does not own. Only after the congregation sees peacemaking bearing its fruit among the pastor and leaders should they be called to join in as well.

Finally, biblical peacemaking in any congregation must be consistently applied to every conflict situation. This is critical – because God exempts no believer from living out the gospel. There can be no personality in the local church who is "above" reconciliation and forgiveness. Period. In one of my former churches, I (John) was once approached after Sunday worship by one of the most kind, gentle souls you'd ever want to meet. But she made the mistake of starting the conversation, "Several people are saying…" The subject of her statement is not important here. What *is* important is that she unloaded on me some information that was a complete misunderstanding, and this misunderstanding had now been spread by gossip to a large audience (even outside of the church). I asked her who the "several people" were and she refused to tell me. This was not a lady I wanted to confront, but I knew that no one is exempt from peacemaking. She had burdened me with the knowledge that I was misunderstood and that the audience was growing but gave me no way to respond. I persisted. After a very long conversation with a lot of "hemming and hawing," she finally told me from whom she had heard it. That lady happened to be standing just across the sanctuary from us. I took the divulger by the hand and we went to meet the other lady. Both were shocked that I would lovingly hold them accountable – no one had ever done that before! By the time the conversation was done, we had exposed the problem, reconciled our relationships and had produced a quick plan to set the record straight backwards up the local grapevine. And there was another benefit: I was never approached with the words "Everyone is saying…" in that church ever again!

A Final Word

Please be patient as you rebuild this foundational aspect of Christian life in your church. If you're like most churches in rural America, it took your congregation a long time (likely generations) to lay the framework for the conflict and power brokering you now face. It takes a long time to reverse that trend. Remember, revitalization in any local church is impossible in the midst of unaddressed conflict. Again, be patient. God is more interested in establishing a culture of peace in your church than you are! Get the needed training and resources, patiently invest yourself, and watch what God does as the powerful gospel of peace bears its fruit.

Chapter 7
Preparing for the Spiritual Battle of Rural Renewal

True to your word, you let me catch my breath and send me in the right direction. Even when the way goes through Death Valley, I'm not afraid when you walk at my side. Your trusty shepherd's crook makes me feel secure.[51]

Let me say at the outset, rural America is worth fighting for. The rural church is in a battle. We curse the days of war until we are enslaved in a prison camp. Then we pray that God will rescue us, which, if He often does. He usually uses days of war to accomplish it. Rural communities are facing challenging times. Rural churches are going to have to fight to preserve their existence. There is a reprehensible abandonment of rural America. About 60 million people, or one in five Americans, live in rural America.52 In general, rural areas are sparsely populated, have low housing density, and are far from urban centers. Urban areas make up only 3 percent of the entire land area of the country but are home to more than 80 percent of the population. Conversely, 97 percent of the country's land mass is rural but only 19.3 percent of the population lives there.53 To understand the battle in which the rural church faces, we need to begin with recognizing that we are in a war. Battles make up smaller sections of the bigger picture. By definition, battles involve combat between two persons, between factions, between armies and they consist of any type of "extended contest,

---

[51] Eugene H. Peterson, *The Message: The Bible in Contemporary Language* (Colorado Springs, CO: NavPress, 2005), Ps 23:3–4.

52 "One in Five Americans Live in Rural Areas" America Counts Staff, August 2017 https://www.census.gov/library/stories/2017/08/rural-america.html

53 Ibid.

struggle, or controversy."54 Rural churches and their leaders, are in a spiritual battle of some sort often daily. In warfare, battles are fought on different fronts, for different reasons, and with fluctuating levels of concentration. The same is true in spiritual warfare. Our spiritual battles and warfare are real, even though we cannot physically see the attacker. But, we can educate ourselves on how the battles are fought and how they impact our lives daily.

The rural church revitalizer must stand for his community and be a vocal expression for the cause of rural town and country communities. One day he might be fighting against the rising drug epidemic facing their community and on another he might be rallying the community to keep from losing its supermarket or gas station. Next month the rural pastor might need to be a local voice against the consolidation of schools. One month he will stand against the governments regulation of fertilizers and pesticides which have made it almost impossible to successfully grow strawberries. This is a market which once was the bread and butter for the rural aquiculture farmer, but now it has moved to China. What rural America once owned as a key crop for over twenty-five years is now sliding to another country.55 Time and time again if you are ministering in the rural community we hear about the struggle of individuals and families to make ends meet. You will hear about the lack of response from anyone with the authority to make life better for rural America. These things are disappearing all across the rural landscape. Most people who live in urban centers view rural as someplace where there are farmhouses and large pastures. The U.S. Census Bureau defines rural as what is not urban—that is, after defining individual urban areas, rural is what is left. Other federal agencies and researchers may use a

---

54 C.f. Webster-Merriam.

55 http://www.debate.org/opinions/is-rural-america-dying.

different definition of rural. For example, the U.S. Department of Agriculture's Economic Research Service illustrates that there are several different ways to measure rural communities.56 Our urban centers are growing as they push out into suburbia. The suburbs that once were looked at as urban fringe, are now often considered part of the urban landscape. Urban land areas are growing. What once was a smaller city has now become a larger urban center. While all of this has happened, the rural population and land mass has declined. Over the past century, the United States has experienced substantial urban growth. The suburbs around large cities have expanded, and in many areas account for a large proportion of an urban area's population and land area. Midsize cities and small towns have now grown into larger urban agglomerations. As urban areas and their populations have increased, the rural population has declined as a percentage of the total population, from 54.4 percent in 1910 to 19.3 percent in 2010. Changes to settlement patterns have necessitated periodic recalibrations in methods and definitions of what constitutes urban and rural.57 Nobody desires to farm anymore. The prices of most commodities have fallen. Most of our countries grocery stories are filled by huge farms originating in south America.

---

56 See Defining the "Rural" in Rural America available at <www.ers.usda.gov/amber-waves/2008/june/defining-the-rural-in-rural -america/> and "Rural Classifications" available at <www.ers.usda.gov /topics/rural-economy-population/rural-classifications/>.

57 U.S. Census Bureau, 1910 to 1990 Censuses, <www.census.gov /population/censusdata/urpop0090.txt>; 2000 decennial census, Table P002; 2010 decennial census, Table P2.

The Coming Warfare

There will be spiritual warfare so get ready for it. Martin Manser says that "spiritual warfare has its beginning in a uprising of many angels against God. Satan is seen as the prince of this world, leading an array of forces opposed to God. Although disarmed by Jesus Christ on the cross, they remain a powerful threat to the church and to individual believers."[58] The phrase 'spiritual warfare' never appears in the Bible. It is a pastoral, theological term for describing the moral conflict of the Christian life. It is a metaphor for our lifelong struggle with our lies and other liars, our lusts and other tempters, our sins and other evildoers, the present darkness that continually unsettles us. Our sufferings, whatever their form or cause, provide occasions either to stumble or to stand. Our warfare is over which it will be."59 In Ephesians 6 we are given our tools to overcome spiritual when we read:

> *So, take everything the Master has set out for you, well-made weapons of the best materials. And put them to use so you will be able to stand up to everything the Devil throws your way. This is no afternoon athletic contest that we'll walk away from and forget about in a couple of hours. This is for keeps, a life-or-death fight to the finish against the Devil and all his angels. Be prepared. You're up against far more than you can handle on your own. Take all the help you can get, every weapon God has issued, so that when it's all over but the shouting you'll still be on your feet. Truth, righteousness, peace, faith, and salvation are more than words. Learn how to apply them. You'll need them throughout your life. God's Word is an*

---

[58] Martin H. Manser, *Dictionary of Bible Themes: The Accessible and Comprehensive Tool for Topical Studies* (London: Martin Manser, 2009).

59 David Powlison, in Beilby and Eddy, *Understanding Spiritual Warfare*, 2012, p. 92.

*indispensable weapon. In the same way, prayer is essential in
this ongoing warfare. Pray hard and long. Pray for your
brothers and sisters. Keep your eyes open. Keep each other's
spirits up so that no one falls behind or drops out.*60

Scripture traces the roots of spiritual warfare in the revolt of
Satan and his angels against God and asserts the confidence
of God's final victory over such forces through the Lord
Jesus Christ's death and resurrection. The primary name
given to our enemy is Satan. This name is used 53 times in
the Bible. It means adversary. The primary thing Satan wants
to do is destroy. He wants to destroy God and he wants to
destroy us because we are the acme of his earthly creation.
We are created in God's image. He is our adversary. Satan is
also called the devil. While Satan is his name, the devil is his
game. Devil means tempter. This is what our adversary does.
He specializes in tempting us to sin. Chuck Lawless states
that much of the teaching about spiritual warfare lacks a
biblical base, and we should be careful to filter everything
through the scriptures.61 He suggests three basic issues we
face in the midst of spiritual warfare. They are:

1. *We are Trying to Reach Lost People Who are Blinded.*

2. *Un-discipled Believers are Targets for the Enemy.*

3. *We Cannot Overcome the Enemy Apart from God's Word.*62

---

60 Eugene H. Peterson, *The Message: The Bible in Contemporary
Language* (Colorado Springs, CO: NavPress, 2005), Eph. 6:11–18.

61 Church Lawless, *Spiritual Warfare and Church Growth*,
http://chucklawless.com/category/spiritual-warfare/.

62 Ibid.

I hope you know that we are in the fight of our lives. Far too many churches in the rural landscape are made up of individuals that are fighting one another for positional authority. There is fighting within the membership. There are factions and estrangement, and there are all sorts of exhibitions of one's old nature, the flesh, which Paul says is seen and manifested when we bite and devour one another. Instead of walking in faith we walk in the flesh. Paul declares:

> *The world is unprincipled. It's dog-eat-dog out there! The world doesn't fight fair. But we don't live or fight our battles that way—never have and never will. The tools of our trade aren't for marketing or manipulation, but they are for demolishing that entire massively corrupt culture. We use our powerful God-tools for smashing warped philosophies, tearing down barriers erected against the truth of God, fitting every loose thought and emotion and impulse into the structure of life shaped by Christ. Our tools are ready at hand for clearing the ground of every obstruction and building lives of obedience into maturity.*[63]

Satan the enemy hates you. He detests every about you. He wants to destroy you. He wants to do a number on you completely. Corrie Ten Boom who endured the Nazi concentration camps, said, "The first step to victory is to recognize that we are in a war." We have an enemy, an enemy who is intent on our destruction. If he could take you to hell, he would take you to hell. That's what he wants, for every human being made in the image of God, and you need to be aware of this. Do not give the devil any glory. But we need to realize there are demons, spirits, that form a hierarchy in the kingdom of darkness and they're out for our destruction. Peter says: "He goes around like a roaring lion, seeking whom he may devour. Him resist, steadfast in the faith."

---

[63] Eugene H. Peterson, *The Message: The Bible in Contemporary Language* (Colorado Springs, CO: NavPress, 2005), 2 Corinthians 10:3–6.

If you are sincere in your faith, and if you are desirous to go on with God, I'm telling you: you will face a Satanic onslaught, you will face a barrage of darkness and evil, and you need to know how to stand, how to cope. You ought to be in a war. If you don't know that there is a war on, something is wrong. Either you're not saved, or you're not in a correct relationship with God, or you're just rolling over and giving in - you've complied with the enemy, compromised. Eugene Peterson says: *Keep a cool head. Stay alert. The Devil is poised to pounce and would like nothing better than to catch you napping. Keep your guard up. You're not the only ones plunged into these hard times. It's the same with Christians all over the world. So keep a firm grip on the faith.*[64] We will never earnestly put on the whole armor of God if we do not trust that this spiritual battle is real. The Christian's warfare is not physical but spiritual. This is very clear from the whole of the subsequent teaching of the New Testament, especially from Paul's statement that *"The weapons of our warfare are not of the flesh, but mighty before God"* (2 Corinthians 10:4). We never see the apostles to which these words were spoken carrying swords as they pursued their ministry. The Bible is clear that unseen dark powers that the Bible calls Satan and his demons exist, and they are fighting against us physically and mentally. Just like the Ephesian Christians who found themselves in battle with powerful demonic forces in the city on a daily basis, the rural church revitalizer will sense the same forces.

Satan's Strategy in Spiritual Warfare

What is Satan's strategy in spiritual warfare? Paul outlined his strategy speaking to a carnal church, when the apostle wrote, *"I am afraid, least as the serpent deceived Eve by his*

---

[64] Eugene H. Peterson, *The Message: The Bible in Contemporary Language* (Colorado Springs, CO: NavPress, 2005), 1 Peter 5:8–9.

craftiness, your minds should be led astray from the simplicity and purity of devotion to Christ" (2 Cor 11:3). Satan's strategy is simple, he is out to deceive us, to trick us into buying his lies and temptations. He has been at his plan for numerous years, and he is good at it. Paul even said that Satan can disguise himself as an *"angel of light"* (2 Cor. 11:14). You and I are at war! In fact, we are engaged right now in the mother of all battles. No war in history can compare with the battle you and I fighting. It can be either the cause of your greatest joy as a Christian, or of your deepest pain. The war I am talking about is the spiritual warfare that you became a part of the day you trusted the Lord Jesus Christ as your personal Savior.

The Church Revitalizer's Battle

It is easy as we pastor a church that has a pace which is a little more laid back to remember that we are in a battle. We must prepare for it with purpose. We are the Lord's soldiers so it is wise to understand the battle. Often in such communities we credit our troubles to other causes. We must not become preoccupied with secondary causes, people and circumstances, when the real issue is that portion of spiritual evil which is the real enemy. There is a warfare in heaven and from this, circumstances can be created and people affected. When, in New Testament language, we speak of heaven, do not let us think of that which is remote and far away, somewhere in or beyond the clouds. Heavenly warfare is in the atmosphere all around us. The Devil is called "the prince of the power of the air" (Ephesians 2:2). Now the air is not all above the clouds, but it is where we are as we breathe it now. The heavenlies are wrapping us round all the time and the spiritual conflict is in this very atmosphere. There is an illustration of this in the Old Testament story, when Elisha prayed: "Lord, I pray thee open his eyes that he may see" (2 Kings 6:17), and the young man had his eyes opened to see how near as well as how real were the unseen armies of God. Because we have a spirit, which is the medium of connection with that which is spiritual, this evil atmosphere is not always outside of us but sometimes seems to make the conflict inward. In one way or another, the spiritual conflict is very real and for it we need the Spirit's sword.

The Church Revitalizer's Battleground

The occasion of this conflict is the destiny of the Church. All departments and realms of really spiritual work seem to provoke the opposition of spiritual forces, but the nearer we get to the great, eternal conception of God's destiny for the Church of Christ, the Church which is His Body, the more pronounced the enemy's hostility becomes. We meet spiritual opposition in seeking to win souls for Christ, because it is only in this way that the Church is born. When, however, the full thought of God is brought into view, then the greatest challenge of the forces of evil is registered. This is because it is in the Church and in relation to the Church's destiny that the whole kingdom of Satan is to be met and overthrown. Even by small and seemingly insignificant means, moodiness or trifling disagreements, Satan breaks up the flow of fellowship among the saints. It seems strange that the vital power of the Church should be weakened by the moods and temperaments of God's people but so it can be. Spiritual fellowship becomes a real battleground. We praise God for all the joys of fellowship, but the matter is more serious than that, and is so important that it can become a matter of real battle. Fellowship is not just something that happens. We must fight for it. It is a great factor in the spiritual battle.

The Rural Revitalizer's Prayers for the Community

The rural pastor is not only the shepherd of a local church but also of a community. They operate as a watcher for the spiritual needs of a community. The rural pastor develops the activity of united prayer not only for the local church but also for everything that is needed in the community. Prayer for the rural community is one of the things such a watcher does to embrace his community. We need to be reminded that our seasons of coming together for prayer are more than occasions for bringing to the Lord a list of items. It is far more than praying over gallbladder x-rays. The real goal of our praying, however, must be not merely personal blessings but the triumph of the will of God. In the Old Testament the prophet Daniel provides us with a wonderful example of such prayer. He not only prayed, but he prayed a lot. Daniel was stretched out for three entire weeks, fasting and praying, as he gave himself to prayer for the fulfilment of the great purposes of God. His prayer was based on what he "*understood by the books*" (Daniel 9:2). He knew what other servants of God had written about the divine purposes and he had those purposes within his own heart. Because those purposes were in apparent suspension, because there was a contradiction of them since the Lord's enemies had been given an advantage through the unfaithfulness of the people of God - this was why Daniel was so drawn out in his praying. We are told that the result was great warfare in heaven. During the twenty-one days of this particular season of prayer, a terrific conflict had been taking place without his being aware of it. The very principalities and powers had been so stirred and roused by this kind of praying that they had withstood the messengers of God. A fight had been going on, and one great angel needed to come to the support of another, as if one angelic being was not enough and needed help to get through. The value of prayer is not decided by asking for things but the nature of the things asked for.

The rural church revitalizer faces darkness daily and must pray with intention. What God needs are rural churches who have seen His intentions and purpose, seen the destiny of His Son and of the Church which is His Body, and devote themselves to the fulfilment of His will. When we are that intentional we cannot help but be drawn into spiritual warfare. A lot of Christians do not even know they're at war. But others can see the results of the battle in their lives because they have become casualties of spiritual warfare. They are disheartened, dejected, demoralized, and overwhelmed.

Where the Church Revitalizer Gets His Protection

Paul admonishes in Ephesians where we are to get our protection. He charges us to *"take up the whole armor of God"* (Ephesians 6:11). It is not that we enter a prayer session by some mental process of thinking of the armor. The power of which Paul speaks comes from being equipped by God for the battle. The spiritual body armor will equip the soldier so that he can stand firm in the fight. It is no use when you sense that the battle is on that you should try to concentrate your thoughts on the various items of the armor. To do that would be to find yourself too late. You can only begin to stand if you are already girded beforehand. This is not an emergency outfit for special occasions but a manner of life for the Christian warrior. There will be times in our lives of severe demonic attack where demons are working hard to tempt us to sin by placing thoughts in our minds, or difficult conditions in our lives. Paul called those times, *"in the evil day."* In Jesus' life in Luke 4 and Matthew 4, we find intense demonic attack took place at the beginning of his ministry. After 40 days without food, he was physically exhausted and stressed, and Satan set out to attack him with powerful temptations. Christ's victory over sin is our victory over sin. Christ's victory over death is our victory over death. Christ's strength over demonic attack is our strength. The key to winning any demonic attack is to rely more deeply upon Christ, his love for us and who we are in Jesus. When we face strong times of temptation, read the Bible. The Holy Spirit will take his word and apply it to our lives and bring home to us what we need to hear. We need to pray. As we pray, we rely on Jesus' strength rather than our own strength. Satan and his demons wait for the opportune times in or lives to tempt us. It is when we are tired. It is when we are stressed. It is when we are away from home. It is when we are away from church and Christian accountability. It is when we are away from reading our Bibles and prayer. Those are opportune times for the devil. Expect that.

May I share the passage in Ephesians once more. I would like you to notice some six specific things:

> *Put on the full armor of God so that you can stand against the tactics of the Devil. For our battle is not against flesh and blood, but against the rulers, against the authorities, against the world powers of this darkness, against the spiritual forces of evil in the heavens. This is why you must take up the full armor of God, so that you may be able to resist in the evil day, and having prepared everything, to take your stand. Stand, therefore, with truth like a belt around your waist, righteousness like armor on your chest, and your feet sandaled with readiness for the gospel of peace. In every situation take the shield of faith, and with it you will be able to extinguish all the flaming arrows of the evil one. Take the helmet of salvation, and the sword of the Spirit, which is God's word. Pray at all times in the Spirit with every prayer and request and stay alert in this with all perseverance and intercession for all the saints.[65]*

Notice the Importance of Truth

Truth is so critical in a world that knows not truth. We are to be girded with truth. This means that things must be real in our lives. If there is anything false about our position, anything artificial or unreal about our profession, then we will be ineffective in the spiritual battle. We must be free from

---

[65] *The Holy Bible: Holman Christian Standard Version.* (Nashville: Holman Bible Publishers, 2009), Ephesians 6:11–18.

errors in doctrine, that is very important. More than that, though, we must be living in the good of what we believe, not just holding some mental ideas without real heart knowledge of the truth. The spiritual warrior needs to be girded with the truth if he is to triumph. As Paul wrote this letter from Rome, he was most likely chained to a Roman soldier. As he looked at the soldier, he described some of his pieces of his armor and analogized it to important parts of the Christian life to win when attacked by Satan.! The first piece is the belt of truth. After instructions to put on the full armor of God and the promise of the power of God in victory over the devil, Paul specifically describes the various pieces of armor. *The belt of truth* pictures the large leather belt the Roman soldier wore. It held other weapons and kept his outer garments in place. To put on the belt of truth can be understood as accepting the truth of the Bible and choosing to follow it with integrity.[66] A Roman soldier wore a long shirt. It looked like a bed sheet with a head hole in the middle. It draped down the front and the back and needed to be gathered. The belt is what gathered it so it didn't flap around. If your shirt was flapping around in a fight, all the enemy had to do was grab your shirt and throw you to the ground. The belt is what holds everything together. It is called the belt of truth. I believe Paul meant that having the truth and living the truth protects us from demonic attack. As Christians, we have the truth about what the real problem is in the world, sin. We have the truth about what is the real solution, Jesus. When Satan is trying to discourage us, we know the truth. God loves us and will not let us go. Everyone else is living a lie because that is what Satan spins. Having the truth about life protects us. In the same way, living truthfully protects us. Truthfulness is protection against demonic attack. When we

---

[66] Max Anders, *Galatians-Colossians,* vol. 8, Holman New Testament Commentary (Nashville, TN: Broadman & Holman Publishers, 1999), 190–191.

lie, we give Satan and his demons an opportunity to attack us. Tell the truth. It is spiritual protection from demonic attack.

Notice the Importance of Righteous Living

The Roman soldier wore a breast plate that covered his front and his back. The goal was to protect his vital organs so when he was in hand-to-hand combat, if somebody shanked him with a knife, he would survive. In the same way, when we are attacked by Satan, Christ's righteousness is what protects us. When Satan helps you remember you never do anything right, what protects us is that our relationship with God is not based on what we do right, it is based upon what Christ has done right for us. God looks at us and sees the perfection of his son. Just as Christ's righteousness protect us, our righteousness also protects us from demonic attack. What matters is what is satisfying to God, for that is His righteousness. The whole question of righteousness is that of God's rights, what He has a right to; and what God has a right to must accord with His own nature. God is always right, He is just and true. He therefore must have that which satisfies Him and He has found this in His Son whose righteousness is imputed to us. The wiles of the Devil are always directed against that, trying to get us off the ground where we stand in the absolute satisfaction of God by faith. The enemy keeps saying, "God is dissatisfied with you, He has this and that against you" so to counter his accusations we must hold fast to the fact that full righteousness is supplied to us through faith in Jesus Christ. It is His righteousness which alone can protect that most vital part. No doubt this also makes a reference to the need for that righteousness to work out in our lives in a practical way, for anything unrighteous in our dealings or behavior will mean that we cannot stand against Satan. Paul is saying that the church's basic equipment in the spiritual battle is integrity and righteous living, and they are effective because these qualities

bear the stamp of Jesus and the new creation he brings [67]
Doing what is right is always right. Doing what is right, even
though it is hard, protects us from being attacked and
tempted by Satan.

Notice the Importantance of the Good News of Peace

A Roman soldier wore a heavy duty, open-toed sandal.
What made it unique is that while your toes were exposed,
the Romans fitted nails into the tread of the shoe. Think of
cleated football shoes. The goal was that they didn't slip in
battle. Paul's point seems rather to be that the footwear
provides preparation or readiness for battle. What soldiers
need in a holding battle is the good grip provided by nails
driven through the sole, so that the front lines are not sent
reeling and slithering by an enemy charge.[68] The Apostle was
saying that when we are tempted by Satan, we don't get
pushed over or tripped up by him when we are relying on the
gospel. The gospel means good news and it is good news of
peace. As a Christian, all of our sins are paid for. God is not
angry at us. We have complete and total peace with God. He
loves us. He will never let us go. When Satan tells you that
you have messed up and God is done with you, you go back
to your firm footing. I have complete and total peace with
God. We must go to the world with the good news that God
offers perfect peace to the troubled heart and mind. Satan
never minds us going to people with bad news, or with a face
that suggests gloom, but he hates to have Christians
spreading the glad news of peace. Paul and Silas went to
Philippi with good news, the gospel of peace, and the enemy

---

[67] Max Turner, "Ephesians," in *New Bible Commentary: 21st
Century Edition*, ed. D. A. Carson et al., 4th ed. (Leicester, England;
Downers Grove, IL: Inter-Varsity Press, 1994), 1243.

[68] Max Turner, "Ephesians," in *New Bible Commentary: 21st
Century Edition*, ed. D. A. Carson et al., 4th ed. (Leicester, England;
Downers Grove, IL: Inter-Varsity Press, 1994), 1244.

did his best to take that off their faces and out of their voices (Acts 16:11-34). He did not succeed. They triumphed over him because the very spirit of the good news was in their hearts. It is a tremendous strength against the Devil to be standing in the good of the glad tidings of peace. God is for you. He has shown that in Christ. Stand and walk in the power of His peace.

Notice the Importance of Real Faith

The Roman shield Paul was talking about was not the small Roman hand shield used in battle, it was the big Roman shield used as a column of Roman soldiers advanced. It was approximately 4 feet tall by 2 and a half feet wide. It looked like a door. It had metal edging and was covered in cloth and animal skins. The covering was soaked in water. As a Roman column advanced the enemy would shoot arrows at them. They usually dipped the arrows in pitch so they were flaming arrows. If a flaming arrow hit somebody it created quite a bit of damage. First, the arrow could kill them. If the arrow didn't hit a vital organ and they could continue, the flaming pitch went into the wound and all around the wound. When you have burning tar all over the side of your arm it really freaked you out and ruined your day. The idea with these shields was to hide behind them and the wet covering kept them from burning with the flaming arrows. Paul said that Satan will launch arrows at us. Arrows of anger, envy, pride, doubt, fear, despair and every temptation he can think of. What we hide behind is the shield of faith. That means I know that I can trust God. Faith takes hold of God's resources in the midst of the onslaughts of evil and produces the firm resolve which douses anything the enemy throws at the believer.[69] No matter what is going on, I have faith that he loves me. I know the plans he has for me. They may not be

---

[69] Andrew T. Lincoln, "Ephesians," vol. 42, Word Biblical Commentary (Dallas: Word, Incorporated, 1990), 449.

easy but God is good. He will use me for his kingdom. When life is falling apart, we protect ourselves with our faith and trust in God. He is reliable. We can trust him. Faith is all-embracing and relates to every possible aspect of the conflict. There can be no triumph in the spiritual life without the full exercise of vital faith. The evil one wants to destroy our hope and diminish our convictions, but the shield of faith will quench all his fiery darts. But we must lift it up. We must believe what God reveals and do what the Lord requires. This is biblical, shield-like faith.

Notice the Importance Fully Embracing One's Salvation

The last piece or armor we will look at is the helmet of salvation. The Roman soldier wore a helmet of either metal or thick leather that extended down the back of his neck and the sides of his head. Some helmets also had something to protect the face and the nose. According to Ephesians, he gives his helmet to believers for their protection. This helmet is salvation itself, and believers are urged to lay hold of it as they engage in the spiritual warfare. Earlier in the letter, salvation language was used to summarize what God has already accomplished for believers: his making them alive with Christ, raising them up, and seating them with him in the heavenly places[70] are comprehensively described as his having saved them by grace. The present aspect of salvation is emphatically stressed. God has rescued them from death, wrath, and bondage, and transferred them into a new dominion where Christ rules. The position of power and authority with Christ to which they have been raised is greater than that possessed by their mighty supernatural enemies. As they appropriate this salvation more fully and live in the light

---

70 C.f. Ephesians 2:5-6.

of their status in Christ, they have every reason to be confident of the outcome of the battle.[71]

The reason they protected the head is because everyone knows if you are going to take somebody out, the quickest way to do it is a head shot. In ancient warfare, horsemen had a special long-handled ax they would ride with just lopping off heads like a weed whacker cutting the grass as they rode through the enemy. The Roman soldier's helmet protected him and kept his head on his shoulders. In the same way, God's salvation is what saves us. God has promised to rescue us from Satan, sin and death through Jesus. No matter what happens to us, Satan cannot take off our head. He cannot deliver a lethal blow to Christians. Clear assurance about salvation needs to cover the head as a helmet. How many arguments, debates, fears and uncertainties are ready to impinge upon our minds and paralyze our value to the Lord. The salvation of the Lord is mighty, and we must use it to protect our minds from succumbing to satanic assaults. His strong salvation is the only cover which can do this. Satan would tempt us to minimize the importance of salvation. He would like for us to think of it as a past experience only. Paul encourages us, however, to recall and consider the meaning of salvation today. We are saved by the grace of God through faith, and therein we stay. We have had our access by faith into the grace in which we abide, and *we must remain in it* (Rom. 5:1-2). If, at any time, we rely on our own merit, we are severed from Christ and fallen from grace (Gal. 5:4; cf. 1 Jn. 1:7-9). If we fail to spiritually develop, Peter says that it is because we have forgotten the cleansing of our old sins (2 Pet. 1:9; Acts 2:38). Salvation! Receive it and be moved by the great love

---

[71] Peter Thomas O'Brien, *The Letter to the Ephesians,* The Pillar New Testament Commentary (Grand Rapids, MI: W.B. Eerdmans Publishing Co., 1999), 481.

wherewith he loved us, and salvation constantly appreciated will be your helmet.

Notice the Importance of Holding Fast to Scripture

We know how the Lord Jesus met the enemy in the wilderness with apt quotations from God's Word. He had so soaked Himself in the Old Testament that the right emphasis came to Him at the right moment. The final piece of equipment in the believers' armor which Paul urges them to grasp is 'the sword of the Spirit'. They must not only withstand the devil's fiery missiles; they must also take the offensive against the powers of darkness. As the sword was the soldier's only weapon, so God's Word is the only needed weapon, infinitely more powerful than any of Satan's. [72] Warren Wiersbe states: "A material sword pierces the body, but the Word of God pierces the heart. The more you use a physical sword, the duller it becomes; but using God's Word only makes it sharper in our lives. A physical sword requires the hand of a soldier, but the sword of the Spirit has its own power, for it is "living and powerful" (Heb. 4:12). The Spirit wrote the Word, and the Spirit wields the Word as we take it by faith and use it. A physical sword wounds to hurt and kill, while the sword of the Spirit wounds to heal and give life. But when we use the sword against Satan, we are out to deal him a blow that will cripple him and keep him from hindering God's work."[73] We, too, are told to let the word of Christ dwell in us richly (Colossians 3:16). Do not let any of us think that we are going to triumph in the spiritual warfare if we neglect our Bibles, any more than we can do so if we neglect prayer. Try to do without prayer and the Word and you will be worsted in the fight. You will be a soldier without a sword!

---

[72] John MacArthur Jr., ed., *The MacArthur Study Bible*, electronic ed. (Nashville, TN: Word Pub., 1997), 1815.

[73] Warren W. Wiersbe, *The Bible Exposition Commentary*, vol. 2 (Wheaton, IL: Victor Books, 1996), 59.

The believer whose mind is fixed on Christ's imminent coming will not fall into Satan's traps.

Wrapping it Up!

As Christians, the devil and his demons will tempt us and put us through trials. We do not have to be defeated. Jesus defeated the devil on the cross, and as Christians, our victory doesn't come from our strength but through him. By relying on Jesus, we find victory over Satan's attacks. We have the truth while Satan spins lies. We have Christ's righteousness. When God looks at us he doesn't see our sin, he sees the purity of his son. We have peace with God. We can have faith in God. We can trust him. We have the helmet of salvation to protect us against a lethal blow.

Paul said we don't wrestle against flesh and blood. It is interesting that Paul used the term wrestling to describe our battle with Satan and his demons. This is hand to hand combat. It is close quarters. It is not like firing a gun at somebody or launching a missile. If you have ever wrestled you know it is a sport of raw will, intensity and emotion. It is very hard with absolutely no break in the action. It is mano-a-mano. We are a wrestling family, and I can tell you wrestling is a hard sport. It is a lot of sweat and hard work. Why did Paul use this analogy? Ephesus had a colosseum. As a city, the people were into sports. What was one of their favorite sports in the colosseum? Wrestling! A church revitalizer will wrestle against the challenges that come his way. The battles of spiritual warfare are intense when a person decides to accept Jesus as their Savior. The enemy will attack from all angles, hoping to dissuade the person from fully giving their heart to Jesus. He will use circumstances, events, people, things and even doubt in their minds to steal their heart back to his ways.

CHAPTER 8
Developing New Leaders in Rural Churches

I want you to get out there and walk—better yet, run!—on the road God called you to travel. I don't want any of you sitting around on your hands. I don't want anyone strolling off, down some path that goes nowhere.[74]

There are many factors that lead a local church toward decline. The problem is often theological in nature as the congregation slowly becomes more self-centered and less Jesus-centered over time. The problem can be cultural in that priorities from ethnicity, heritage or even the community are allowed to rise above the gospel priorities to which the church is called. The problem can be related to poor discipleship as people are taught Bible stories and doctrine but not shown how to consistently live an obedient, Christ-honoring life and how to pass that lifestyle on to the next generation. The problem can be evangelistic if the church ceases to intentionally build redemptive relationships with pre-Christian people in their own community to influence them toward the Savior. The problem can be social, where the focus on fellowship and camaraderie becomes the primary driver of church life. The problem can be structural in that the traditions and systems of doing "church" become unchanging and no longer bear kingdom fruit. All of these and more can play into the slow demise of a congregation. There is one factor, however, that has a direct impact on all of the above either for good or ill: Leadership.

The single biggest factor in the health of a local church is the spiritual health, maturity, strength and character of her leaders. Unfortunately, not all church leaders are prepared to lead God's people. Truly biblical leaders will guide the

---

[74] Eugene H. Peterson, *The Message: The Bible in Contemporary Language* (Colorado Springs, CO: NavPress, 2005), Ephesians 4:1.

church toward ongoing health, fruit and revitalization. More business-oriented leaders, on the other hand, may help a local church to function well organizationally, but are unlikely to provide the spiritual guidance needed for her to flourish in kingdom priorities. And then there is a third kind of leader – those that mean well but have not been discipled or trained in any biblical leadership process. Without the proper guidance, these leaders give the church their best, but such leadership is often inadequate to shepherd God's people toward fulfillment of their divine design. It's amazing how many churches place unspiritual or unprepared people in positions of spiritual leadership and then wonder why their congregation is fraught with problems and division.

In my work with churches across the country, I (John) have learned not to fault local congregations for poor or unhealthy leadership choices. In many cases, such churches have been left to figure out spiritual leadership on their own. Often, they have had to navigate this journey while also trying to hold outspoken people and power brokers at bay, realizing that such personalities are the first to rush in and fill any leadership vacuum. Local churches look to their associations and denominations for help, guidance and resources only to learn that such assistance is frequently hard to find. They may also look to outside "experts" for help, nearly always eliciting advice from local business and civic leaders with good reputations who have seen success in their own work.

While these issues plague churches everywhere, they can be particularly problematic in small towns and rural communities. It is not unusual for a rural church to be "ruled" by a particular family – and while many may deny it, such families have a huge influence on who is elected to church leadership. Strong personalities are often masterful at gaining positions of authority or making sure decision makers are sympathetic to their wishes. And even unhealthy pastors (i.e., those that are angry, hurt, controlling, narcissistic) seem to migrate toward rural congregations. A church's leaders can make or break her life and ministry.

To address this huge need – especially for rural congregations – we're going to begin by developing a clear biblical theology of leadership. From that we'll discuss the true purpose of church leaders, how to develop leaders to that purpose and briefly outline some key criteria for finding the kind of pastors that will flourish in the rural setting. Finally, we'll discuss how to implement this leadership approach in a local congregation where it has been waning or missing altogether.

A Biblical Theology of Leadership

One of the biggest problems in the American church today is the treatment of theology. Theology and doctrine are read and studied, but few people practically live their theology out anymore. The disconnect is enormous and has had a devastating effect on most local congregations which are now filled with people who have bible or doctrinal knowledge but do not bear consistent fruit from living it out. Writing about stumbling blocks when it comes to food sacrificed to idols, Paul warns, "We know that we all possess knowledge. Knowledge puffs up, but love builds up. The man who thinks he knows something does not yet know as he ought to know. But the man who loves God is known by God." (1 Corinthians 8:1-3)[75] The warning for us is to avoid stopping at "information" when it comes to doctrine and vigorously pursue "transformation."

Transformation is primarily seen in how we love. For this to happen in your church, it is important to develop this theology *with* your church family (in meetings, media,

---

[75] *The Holy Bible: New International Version.* 1984 (1 Co 8:1–3). Grand Rapids, MI: Zondervan.

sermons and bible studies) taking enough time to ensure they not only understand it but also are beginning to live it out. In particular, it will change their entire view of church leadership.

Compassionate Laborers for the Harvest

Much has been written about the task of church leadership in recent years. But less attention has been given to the qualities of leaders and how they are developed and recruited. In the Gospel of Matthew, Jesus teaches about the need and source of kingdom workers.

[35] Jesus went through all the towns and villages, teaching in their synagogues, preaching the good news of the kingdom and healing every disease and sickness. [36] When he saw the crowds, he had compassion on them, because they were harassed and helpless, like sheep without a shepherd. [37] Then he said to his disciples, "The harvest is plentiful but the workers are few. [38] Ask the Lord of the harvest, therefore, to send out workers into his harvest field." (Matthew 9:35-38)[76]

There are three important things we can learn from this passage. First, note the tone of Jesus' response to the crowds of people who had yet to encounter the kingdom of God (and by kingdom we mean primarily his dominion; his rule and reign). Jesus' heart is broken. His immediate and guiding response is that of compassion for them because they were harassed, helpless and like sheep without a shepherd. These were people who were living completely lost, as ready prey for the devil and without guidance, nurture or protection. People in our towns and villages today who are without Christ are in the very same condition. All Christians, let alone those who lead Christ's church, must have the same response

---

[76] *The Holy Bible: New International Version.* 1984 (Mt 9:35–38). Grand Rapids, MI: Zondervan.

as Jesus. If a person's heart is not truly broken for those who have yet to meet Jesus, he is probably not ready to be considered for a leadership role in the church.

The second thing we learn from this passage is that Christ's instruction for increasing the church's labor force is to pray. This is so important because it is all but overlooked in most congregations today. When leaders and laborers are needed for the local church, the first and strongest commitment should be to "ask the Lord of the harvest to send out workers into his harvest field." And yet, if any prayer is offered in most churches today, it's a cursory prayer at the beginning of a nominating committee meeting. If a congregation will not take the time to thoroughly bathe her need for leaders and laborers in prayer before any steps are taken toward their selection, she is likely to succumb to wrong criteria, wrong candidates and the pressure of powerful people.

The third thing we learn from this passage is about God's response when the church beseeches him for laborers: it's powerful! The Greek term Jesus uses in this passage, translated in the New International Version as "to send out," is better translated "thrust out" or "drive out (i.e., *into* his harvest field)." It's the very same term used in Matthew 21:12ff to describe Jesus' response to the moneychangers in the temple – where he forcibly drove them out of the temple courts! It's the same term used in Mark 7:26 to describe the way in which Jesus cast out a demon! It's a term of power and authority, of controlled ferocity. In other words, *if* God's people in a local church will pray as they should, he will respond by thrusting laborers forward into his harvest field! When a church cries and complains that it cannot find laborers and leaders, it is a definitive indication that they are not taking the call to prayer seriously.

Critical Leadership Emphases

Our next leadership lesson comes from Paul's letter to
the church at Ephesus. Paul is writing about true Christian
unity – the real fruit of hearts entwined together across racial,
economic, cultural and even denominational lines beating in
unison with the Father's heart in worship and service. After
calling the believers to unity, he explains how church
leadership "builds up" the body both to this unity and the
maturity it eventually fosters.

*It was he who gave some to be apostles, some to be prophets, some
to be evangelists, and some to be pastors and teachers,* [12] *to prepare God's
people for works of service, so that the body of Christ may be built up* [13]
*until we all reach unity in the faith and in the knowledge of the Son of
God and become mature, attaining to the whole measure of the fullness of
Christ.* [14] *Then we will no longer be infants, tossed back and forth by the
waves, and blown here and there by every wind of teaching and by the
cunning and craftiness of men in their deceitful scheming.* [15] *Instead,
speaking the truth in love, we will in all things grow up into him who is
the Head, that is, Christ.* [16] *From him the whole body, joined and held
together by every supporting ligament, grows and builds itself up in love,
as each part does its work.* [77]

There are at least three things we can learn from this
passage. First, the phrase "It was he who gave..." shows us
the critical importance of what follows. Clearly the context
tells us that the "he" here is Jesus. In fact, the *'he'* in Greek is
emphatic. The nuance here is that Christ himself appointed
or entrusted the listed leadership gifts/offices to the church
for a purpose. These are precious to our Lord and his
mission and must be taken as such.

---

[77] *The Holy Bible: New International Version.* 1984 (Ephesians 4:11–16).
Grand Rapids, MI: Zondervan.

The second thing we learn from this passage is the multifaceted purpose for which Jesus gave these particular giftings. They are to prepare God's people for works of service *so that* the body of Christ may be built up until we all reach three things:

1. Unity in the faith,
2. Unity in the knowledge of the Son of God, and
3. Maturity, which Paul defines as "attaining to the whole measure of the fullness of Christ" himself.

These points cannot be overemphasized! When talking about the revitalization of Christ's church, all three of these are absolutely essential. Jesus had a transformational plan embedded in the combined ministry of these leader roles. But, when one assesses the overall condition of American Christianity today, all three of these intended outcomes are seriously lacking. Conflict and disunity in local congregations is at an all-time high. Because we have not been discipling people as we should, biblical illiteracy is a major problem and too many Christians' relationship with the Savior is more academic than personal. For many, it gets harder every year to find mature believers who are ready and willing to actively serve Christ's kingdom purposes in their own churches and communities. Something's gone wrong.

The third thing we can take away from Paul's instructions to the Ephesian Christians is that there are five critical emphases in the realm of church leadership that are necessary for the three outcomes above to become a reality within any given congregation. And these emphases, which are hard-wired into the design and function of Christ's church, are discovered in the five leadership roles Christ gave his church:

Sending/Innovating – local churches continuously strive to find new ways to reach people with the love, service and gospel of Christ. As their community changes, so must their gospel tactics and processes. They raise up and send out pastors to continue leading established churches in new directions. They raise up and send out church planters to start new Christ-centered congregations. They raise up and send out missionaries to take the gospel in new and innovative ways to the ends of the earth. This is the timeless emphasis of the *apostolic* role. By this understanding, every person who is "sent out" is doing an apostolic kind of work (the Greek word *apostolos* literally means "one who is sent"). When I have worked with small and rural congregations on this topic, I often hear someone say something like, "Raising up and sending out missionaries and church planters is something bigger churches do – we're too small..." That is a lie—don't buy into it. This is something *obedient* churches do! And the reality is that most pastors, church planters and missionaries have been raised up in congregations of 100 people or less. I would argue that the reason it's not happening today like it should is that we have ignored the apostolic sending/innovating emphasis among our local leaders. Churches have largely stopped intentionally seeking such people to serve on their leadership teams. When a church has someone who will pick up that sending/innovating clarion call, the church will soon start experiencing its fruit.

Standard Bearing – local churches live out counter-cultural truths and ideals in their respective communities. They are instruments for Christ's kingdom (again, read "rule and reign"), advancing through unconditional love, service and disciple making. But they can't do that well if their own people are living just like the world around them. This is where the timeless *prophetic* emphasis comes in. The prophet's ministry was always mainly to God's people, calling them back to the standards and decrees of the Lord. Without sounding too legalistic, it is certainly true that many local congregations have become frighteningly carnal today. And this dilemma is just as common in rural churches as it is in the city – sometimes more so. When a church intentionally places some prophetic voices on their leadership teams, God's standards are lovingly held ever before the congregation.

Evangelizing – local churches regularly lead people to Christ. They build relationships with pre-Christian individuals, groups and families in their respective communities to draw them toward the Savior. There are many evangelism programs available today, but they tend to be canned, mechanical and often show little fruit. Congregants feel awkward in their witness and evangelism, and there is usually no one in the church leading, coaching and resourcing them for that work. The need for the timeless *evangelistic* emphasis is clear. And in a rural setting with a deeper sense of relational community and familial relationships that may go back generations, resistance to evangelizing one's neighbor tends to be higher. Churches that intentionally place such leaders on their leadership teams see the work of evangelism remain a priority, and resources and energy are allocated for its ongoing success.

Caring/Nurturing/Protecting – local churches do care ministry. They care for their own, and they use loving care as a means to connect with their communities. They also nurture people spiritually through worship and discipleship so folks grow in Christian maturity. They also remain aware of threats (particularly spiritual and doctrinal ones) in an effort to warn and protect people from being led astray. All of these are included in the timeless *pastoral* emphasis. When these things are not being done well, it's usually a sign that a congregation expects their pastor to do all of this by himself. But a quick perusal of the New Testament (particularly the pastoral epistles) shows us that it was always meant to be done by a plurality of leaders. Rural congregations tend to have higher expectations of their pastors, requiring him to be a "jack of all trades but a master of none." A church that builds pastoral people into her leadership team will foster an environment where such ministry is done better, more consistently and will even multiply as the congregation grows.

Teaching/Training/Discipling – local churches make disciples. They don't just teach people the truth (although they certainly start there); they train them for faithful obedience. Disciple making is primarily a transformational work, not an academic one. As noted earlier, when a local church overemphasizes information over transformation they produce people who are in love with the idea of Christ and Christianity, but do not effectively live out Christ's priorities and lifestyle. This is where the timeless emphasis of the *teacher/discipler* is so critical. In many rural congregations today, there is a misconception that teaching and discipling are primarily the work of the pastor. While pastors certainly lead in this area, disciple making is the commission of *every* believer. When a church intentionally puts such people on the leadership team, biblical disciple making remains a priority and participation in this vital ministry increases over the whole church family.

Jesus knew what he was doing when he gave these emphases to his church. When all five are active within a local church's leadership, it can have an enormous impact for that congregation's revitalization and for Jesus' kingdom.

Criteria for Leaders

Now we turn to Paul's leadership lessons to his son-in-the-Faith, Timothy. He writes,

¹ Here is a trustworthy saying: If anyone sets his heart on being an overseer, he desires a noble task. ² Now the overseer must be above reproach, the husband of but one wife, temperate, self-controlled, respectable, hospitable, able to teach, ³ not given to drunkenness, not violent but gentle, not quarrelsome, not a lover of money. ⁴ He must manage his own family well and see that his children obey him with proper respect. ⁵ (If anyone does not know how to manage his own family, how can he take care of God's church?) ⁶ He must not be a recent convert, or he may become conceited and fall under the same judgment as the devil. ⁷ He must also have a good reputation with outsiders, so that he will not fall into disgrace and into the devil's trap.[78]

Paul here is giving guidance to Timothy about the criteria he should be looking for in those who would be elders. He provides a similar list to Titus (see Titus 1:5-9). Many churches review these criteria when nominating folks to leadership, but most seem to miss the main idea. The traits listed by Paul fall mainly into two categories: traits of spiritual maturity and traits of Christ-like character. These are not competencies, but qualities. Arguably, the only item on the list that could be a competency is "able to teach." In addition to all that we've noted thus far, two non-negotiable qualities a local church must seek when appointing leaders are spiritual maturity and Christ-like character. It is far better for a church to temporarily choose fewer leaders than their constitution may require than to fill the leadership quota by adding people who are immature in their faith or who are dealing with character issues (or both). Doing the latter will always cause problems. This becomes particularly important for smaller congregations like those in many rural areas where the number of potential leaders is fewer and strong personalities are vying for control. Do not give in on this point. Those

---

[78] *The Holy Bible: New International Version.* 1984 (1 Ti 3:1–7). Grand Rapids, MI: Zondervan.

who lead must be spiritual mature and must have evidence of Christ-like character the whole congregation can readily affirm.

Competencies can be taught, but spiritual maturity and character can only be grown over time. This means that the church must be very purposeful in growing such leaders on an ongoing basis. Leader development is not something that just happens, it is something that is planned and executed. The passage above gives us several goals at which to aim. And while only Jesus can perfectly fulfill the list, an intentional process will repeatedly prepare leaders who are clearly growing in all these areas. One on one mentoring by current leaders with future leaders is key. Practicing the spiritual disciplines together will set the stage for growth in the area of spiritual maturity. And holding each other accountable on the Fruit of the Spirit will go a long way to growing leader candidates with respect to their character. Paul says that those who aspire to be leaders in Christ's church "desire a noble task." It is important the church not cheapen that task by giving it to unprepared leaders.

Generational Leadership

Finally, Paul gives Timothy another critical leadership principle later in his ministry: "And the things you have heard me say in the presence of many witnesses entrust to reliable men who will also be qualified to teach others."[79] Herein is the mark of success in leader development for a local church – the leader development becomes "generational." There are four spiritual generations in Paul's lesson:

1. Paul himself
2. Timothy, who was mentored/trained by Paul

---

79 *The Holy Bible: New International Version.* 1984 (2 Ti 2:2). Grand Rapids, MI: Zondervan.

3. "Faithful Men," who would be mentored/trained by Timothy
4. "Others Also," who would be mentored/trained by the Faithful Men

This is so important! Each leadership generation is making a very real investment in the leadership generation that follows. Every leader is pouring into at least one leader candidate so that leader development multiplies in that congregation. This actually happens quite naturally in the rural setting if people let it. While our world is changing, many rural communities still live along strong generational lines. Families are farming land their grandfather or great grandfather farmed. They learned farming from their own father and practiced it as they grew up. This generational idea of leader development is, perhaps, less foreign in rural America than anywhere else in our nation. We just need to do it.

The Purpose of Church Leadership

As one reviews what Jesus and the New Testament writers say about leadership in Christ's church, it quickly becomes apparent that Christ-oriented leaders live out a dual role with a singular focus. They are both overseers and servants. As overseers, they shepherd and guide, enabling the congregation to flourish. As servants, they actually enter into the vital work of the church according to their own gifts. Church leaders must be both at the same time – servant-leaders – in order to correctly lead Christ's people. And this dual role always has a singular focus: Christ's harvest.

The Church's commission is to make disciples from every people group. All disciples come from Christ's harvest field – whether they are pre-Christian people sitting in our pews or unreached people groups in remote places across the oceans. Everything church leaders do is ultimately to foster the worship of God and to effectively reach the harvest for Christ. So important is this understanding that my friend and mentor, Tom Johnston, has said, "The needs of the harvest drives the need for leaders. If you aren't going to engage the harvest, there is no need to develop leaders."[80] When church leaders become so encumbered with the needs and problems of the local congregation they serve that they take their eyes off of the harvest, the stage is immediately set for the church to decline.

Church leadership is charged with protecting the flock (Acts 20: 27-31; Titus 1:6-9). But that protection is not just for the sake of the flock (inward) but also for the purity of their gospel (outward) so that they may be instruments of transformation to the world! Leaders are to nurture and disciple the flock. But that discipling is not so the flock will know more; rather it is so that they can demonstrate what Jesus has done as they live it out before those around them. Leaders are to serve. But that service is not exclusive to the congregation. Rather they lead the congregation outward by being first in line to serve and bless their communities. Church leaders lead by example in all things. If the leadership does not labor to reach the harvest themselves, the congregation will not follow suit.

Developing Leaders to that Purpose

So church leaders must be spiritually mature and must be growing in and demonstrating the character of Christ. Church leaders must lead the congregation into the harvest so they can fulfill the Great Commission together. You now see that unprepared leaders and those who are over-focused on church organization are usually ill equipped to help the

---

80 Tom Johnston and Mike Perkinson, Journey: *The Descent to Servant Leadership*, Manchester, NH: Praxis Center for Church Development, 2009, p. 3.

congregation actually obey the Savior's instruction to be laborers for the harvest. Every local church needs fruit-bearing leaders who lead by example. The kind of leaders we're describing do not just happen, the church develops them. And this development is more an extension of discipleship than it is anything else.

We develop leaders as we teach them to love and obey God with every fiber of their being (Matthew 22:37-38). We develop leaders as we teach them to love people with true humility and service (Matthew 22:39-40). We develop leaders as we teach them to make disciples themselves for Jesus (Matthew 28:18-20). We help such leaders to engage an ever-deepening walk with Christ. We hold high expectations of such leaders relationally, that they can develop both peer and mentoring relationships for the sake of the kingdom and they also know how to reconcile broken relationships so that peace may reign in their lives. This kind of leadership development does not happen quickly – the investment takes time. It requires commitment on both the part of the church and of the leader candidate. And those would be leaders who reject these essential components of their development necessarily disqualify themselves from leading Christ's church.

The Need for a Settled Pastor

Church leaders are only part of the equation for revitalizing a rural congregation. They are critical, but so is having the right kind of pastor at the helm. Because of their relative size and smaller budgets, rural churches tend to be a landing spot for all kinds of pastors. Some rural congregations sense a calling to be a "starter" church for young pastors right out of seminary. This is a great mission, but it's not for everyone. In reality, many rural churches suffer because they've endured a series of pastoral mismatches and high pastoral turnover. It hurts the church's mission and often leads a congregation to conclude there is something wrong with them. It is rare to find a pastor who actually feels a deep sense of call to rural ministry – and the rural church that finds him is truly blessed.

In my work with congregations around the country, I (John) have come to the conclusion that the majority of pastoral candidates that end up in rural and small town churches come to their new charge with unhealthy expectations. Some of these pastors see themselves as "cutting their teeth" on their little country church. And while the scenario may indeed be true, what's communicated to the congregation is that the pastor's time with them is temporary. Once his theological teething is complete, he'll move on. Many pastors see small, rural congregations as mere stepping-stones to "bigger and better" things. Tragically, I've heard pastors even say this about their ministries! Still other pastors come into their farming community or village with grandiose ideas about how their church is going to become the next Willow Creek or Saddleback Church while totally missing the incredible ministry opportunities that already exist. Attitudes like these do not serve the church well, nor do they lay the foundation needed for long-term relationships through which spiritual growth can be fostered.

To experience revitalization, rural congregations need a pastor who actually feels called to their church for the long haul – especially in smaller congregations. While God does move pastors onto other ministries, the pastor should otherwise love serving in that setting and intend to remain there. He should love the people enough to say that he's staying to retirement and mean it. He should love the community enough to fully embed there – even buying a home or raising his children there. And he should be patient enough to wait for the congregation to realize that he is truly not going to abandon them – especially if that congregation has experienced high pastoral turnover. By the way, that realization will usually take one year longer than the tenure of the longest pastorate in that turnover cycle.

If you are a pastor of a rural congregation, prayerfully consider what we're saying here. In some cases, the biggest obstacle to revitalization is a pastor whose heart is not engaged. That is a hard truth to hear if you're already feeling mismatched to your church. On the other hand, you may be reading this with excitement as you confirm the call God placed on your heart for your particular church. In any case, start with the truth and work from there. Allow the Holy Spirit to prepare your heart and then plan some one-on-one time with each of your key leaders to talk about the role they must play. Revitalization is led first and foremost by demonstration, so alignment and fruit must always start with pastor and leadership.

Final Thoughts

If you're serious about developing leaders in your church, you will likely experience some opposition if you do it right. When a pastor starts spending more time with a few leaders in order to invest in them, two things happen: his own priorities will begin to change, and people who are not getting as much time with their pastor will get jealous. You will have to take the congregation back to the New Testament example – and more than once. We'll close with some thoughts on minimizing resistance.

Begin with Intercession

We'll spend more time on this vital component of revitalization in a few chapters, but for now just know that everything related to the revitalization of a church is rooted in intercessory prayer. The pastor must be daily interceding. The leaders of the church must be daily interceding. The congregation must be regularly interceding. Remember, all intercession is prayer but not all prayer is necessarily intercession. It's important to understand what intercessory prayer is and apply it to the transformation of the church's life and ministry.

Refer them to Jesus' Example

The church belongs to Jesus. He is her Savior and her Lord. It behooves us to study his example with our congregations so they begin to get a New Testament vision for their own church. Jesus ministered to the masses, but he *invested* in only a few. This is a good pattern for us to follow as well – and if we do it right, the multiplication effect can put Amway to shame!

Jesus taught the multitudes (academic)
Jesus trained the 70 (tactical)
Jesus lived with the 12 disciples (daily life-on-life example)
Jesus poured himself into Peter, James and John (life investment into a few)

The pastor and leaders cannot (and should not) have the same level of investment into everyone in the congregation. Again, if we expect the pastor to do everything and take care of everyone, nothing is done well and no one is fully discipled. It's simply not possible to invest in the "many" for real life transformation. But when the pastor teaches the congregation (classes, studies and sermons), trains key people in specific areas of ministry (visitation, youth ministry, etc.) and then spends much more time with his leadership group, he has the personal bandwidth to really disciple a few. As the few begin to disciple their few, the multiplication begins. Most rural congregations are fully engulfed in this discipling process (and it's already spilling over into the community) by the fourth level. More people will have a deep investment, and more laborers are truly prepared for their Great Commission work.81

Lead by Consistent Example

It is critical that the pastor and leadership lead by a consistent example. Anything that is expected of the believers in the church must be first lovingly demonstrated by the leadership. Leader development processes must be put in place with clearly defined, biblical outcomes. And the pastor and leaders need to be in ongoing discipleship relationships – both receiving the investment of their own mentors, and pouring into their own disciples. As more leaders take on disciples of their own both inside and outside the church, people will finally experience the value of revitalization on a personal level and the resistance will diminish.

---

81 C.f. Matthew 28:18-20; John 13:15-17; 20:21; & 2 Timothy 2:2.

Chapter 9
Why Indigenous Leadership in Critical in Rural Renewal

What a God! His road stretches straight and smooth. Every God-direction is road-tested. Everyone who runs toward him Makes it.[82]

I have served as a Bi-vocational church planter and pastor at a few particular points early in my ministry. Each of these were a choice I willingly made in order to birth a new church in one instance and save another through revitalization and renewal in another. The number of bi-vocational ministers is increasing rapidly. Many pastors who work full-time jobs and serve in congregations part-time receive little or no pay for their church service. This trend has been described as "the future of the church" and extolled because the model is a return to "the original church" that will "enliven congregations." There is a growing need for what has been known as Bivocational Pastors which is being re-coined by some who prefer a statelier name as Marketplace Leaders. While I suppose the later sounds like it has more clout either expression is still worthy of our investment. Indigenous leadership is critical in rural renewal. Many churches would love to have five full-time ministers, but their budgets rarely allow for more than one. We can – and should – lament the trend towards bi-vocational ministry as the norm, but there's no escaping it. All we can do is accept the situation as it is, while looking for ways to make some really good spiritual lemonade out of these lemons. We can improve lay leadership, strengthen communal bonds, and think of new ways to conduct worship that are less dependent on professional clergy. Bi-vocational pastors deserve our support for the incredible work they do in service to God, neighbor, and church. At no time in recent North American history has there been both a greater opportunity for the

---

[82] Eugene H. Peterson, *The Message: The Bible in Contemporary Language* (Colorado Springs, CO: NavPress, 2005), 2 Sa 22:31.

expansion of the kingdom of God coupled with a seemingly inability of the contemporary church to meet that challenge.

A clear example of an indigenous Church is easily found in the New Testament, namely the Church in Jerusalem. In fact, this Church was so strongly Jewish, that the members resented the conversion of Gentiles unless they joined the ritual adherence to, and performance of, the law, required by Judaism. Yet, Paul taught in his Gospel – from revelation - that Gentile converts need not be circumcised as the law of Moses required for Jewish people. Further, the Christians need not meet in the Synagogue but could form their own associations and use their own buildings. Paul emphasized that the moral content of the law was what was important – not the actual framework of the accompanying ceremony. This was significant, because the apostles had previously grappled with the issue of making Gentile converts conform to the standards required for Jewish people. Hence, the indigenous Church continued with an important message, but saw its expression in ways relevant to its membership. In 1 Corinthians 3:5-8 we read:

"Who then is Paul, and who is Apollos, but ministers through whom you believed, as the Lord gave to each one? I planted, Apollos watered, but God gave the increase. So then neither he who plants is anything, nor he who waters, but God who gives the increase. Now he who plants and he who waters are one, and each one will receive his own reward according to his own labor."

The New Testament, thus, repudiates the views of the Judaizers, and proceeds to set up the Church as a group of believers within its own society.

Today the term "indigenous church" is commonly thought to be one that meets the "three selfs." It is a church which is:

Self-Supporting (able to finance its vision)
Self-Sustaining (able to provide the necessary leadership required)
Self-Propagating (able to govern and grow)

Melvin Hodges (1909-1988), an Assemblies of God missionary to Nicaragua, again popularized the idea in the 1950s with his book, *On the Mission Field: The Indigenous Church.*[83] He defined the indigenous church as *"a native church . . . which shares the life of the country in which it is planted and finds itself ready to govern itself, support itself, and reproduce itself."* Hodges believed that foreign money creates dependence and establishes paternalistic patterns within mission movements, leading to an unhealthy, anemic church. His experience as a missionary no doubt influenced his presentation of the three-self principle. He emphasized the need for flexibility and tailoring the principles to fit the need of the local believers.

Charles Brock added further three more when he stated that indigenous specifies that something or someone is native rather than coming or being brought in from elsewhere. In the church renewal context, indigenous would refer to the church becoming:

Self-governing - The new church can make its own decisions under Lordship of Jesus Christ.
Self-supporting - The new church can provide for its material needs through the tithes and offerings of the members.
Self-expressing - The new church can express itself according to local culture. This has to do with times of worship and ways of expression in worship. All should be within Biblical guidelines and teachings.

---

83 Melvin Hodges, *On the Mission Field: The Indigenous Church.* pg. 58.

Self-teaching - Each member influences and teaches the other members.
Self-propagating - The new church will be involved in starting other new churches.[84]

Warrick Farah in his online book "The Seven Selfs of Contextualized Churches offers a few more. He ads his take by sharing two additional selfs in the "Seven Selfs" of indigenous or contextualized churches:

1. Self-governing
2. Self-supporting
3. Self-propagating
4. **Self-identifying**
5. Self-teaching
6. Self-expressing
7. **Self-theologizing**

Doctor J. D. Payne[85] does a great job of explaining these in his new book *Discovering Church Planting*.[86] The indigenous church is never mentioned in the New Testament. It is, however, obvious in the sense that the church took root and grew naturally. In the New Testament we see no outside participation and assistance. Paul and others were planting

---

84 Charles Brock, *Indigenous Church Planting in Review*, 11.

85 J. D. Payne serves as the pastor of church multiplication with The Church at Brook Hills in Birmingham, Alabama. Prior to moving to Birmingham, J. D. was a National Missionary with the North American Mission Board of the Southern Baptist Convention and an Associate Professor of Church Planting and Evangelism in the Billy Graham School of Missions and Evangelism at The Southern Baptist Theological Seminary in Louisville, Kentucky, where he also directed the Center for North American Missions and Church Planting.

86 J.D. Payne, *Discovering Church Planting*, Paternoster: August 4, 2009. pgs. 18-24.

churches but they did not stay long enough for the people to become reliant on their ministry. The one time that Paul does stay too long he apologizes because he has caused them to become a mediocre church. In staying he had worked another job, making tents, without having them pay his salary. They had a church that cost them nothing. That meant Paul wasn't burdensome and this caused them to become stuck in an expectation that someone else would take care of them. Indigenous pastors have always been a key part of rural revitalization. That coupled with bi-vocationalism or marketplace leaders is the growing norm for rural. If these churches are to survive then it will require ministers who make such sacrifices in order to have a continued gospel witness in the rural landscape.

Thom Rainer and Jonathan Howe share in their podcast an interesting new series of thought relating to indigenous pastors. They call the episode "The New Marketplace Pastor."[87] In their discussion on a new trend regarding pastors they share that many pastors are choosing to continue to serve in secular vocations even when a church can afford to pay them for full-time work. These marketplace pastors are a growing trend worth a further look. They concluded that:

Marketplace pastors serve for part-time pay because they chose to, not because the church can't afford full-time compensation.

Marketplace pastors often have more opportunities for gospel conversations than those who are full-time pastors.

Pastors sometimes don't say or do things that need to be done because their salary is tied to keeping peace in the church.

---

87 Thom Rainer and Jonathan Howe, *Rainer on Leadership: The New Marketplace Pastor* #193, January 26, 2016

I (Rainer) would say about 60% of active church members believe they are "the pastor's boss."

Pastors who are not completely dependent on a church financially tend to deal with critics differently.

Online training is the way to go for marketplace pastors.[88]

They provide eight insightful characteristics of new marketplace pastors. They say:

1. The marketplace pastor serves in churches that could offer full-time compensation to the pastor, but they choose not to do so.
2. Marketplace pastors get their name by their desire to stay in the marketplace with one of their vocations.
3. Marketplace pastors tend to have extraordinary leadership skills.
4. These pastors have a high work capacity.
5. These pastors will have long tenures.
6. Marketplace pastors will be able to deal with critics more freely.
7. Marketplace pastors will be serving in a wide range of churches of varying sizes.
8. Marketplace pastors will get their ministry and theological training online.[89]

One of the most vital yet understudied streams of church ministers is the bivocational pastor. This is that pastor who, either out of necessity or intentionality, works as both the pastor of a local church and in the secular marketplace. Already, more than one-third of all American pastors are

---

88 Ibid.

89 Ibid.

bivocational, and this number will probably keep growing. Ed Stetzer says, "bivocational pastors are uniquely positioned to live out their pastoral calling as the lead missionary to their local community. As a well-equipped and gifted emissary of the gospel, these ministers can lead their congregations by demonstrating the power of evangelism to build the local church. In a mission field that is moving in an increasingly secular direction, bivocational pastors are on the frontlines of gospel witness."[90]

Indigeneity in Rural Renewal is Critical

Indigeneity in rural renewal is critical. God is calling many individuals who formerly resided in the city or suburbia back to rural heartland. Having planted a church in New England, my wife and I had an understanding of the people and place. Much like a foreign missionary will study a new language and a new culture in order to be more effective in reaching that culture, we feel like we had a head start when it came to doing ministry in Massachusetts. Because of this, it only made sense that we considered a life of mission in a context where we could "hit the ground running." God did just that when He called us back to the rural heartland for seven years to revitalize a rural church in West Virginia. If you are pastoring in a rural area remember that much of rural America is still a critical mission field. As stated previously 46.2 million people reside in the rural heartland. That would be roughly 15 percent.[91] Sharing the gospel message is critical to these communities. Many people believe that rural

---

90 Ed Stetzer, The Exchange: *Bivocational Ministry as an Evangelism Opportunity*, October 15, 2017.
https://www.christianitytoday.com/edstetzer/2017/september/bivocational-ministry-as-evangelism-opportunity.html.

91 https://www.pbs.org/newshour/nation/rural-america-thing-past.

America resides in the southeast and southwest. It might surprise you to know that a large portion of rural resides in the northeast. Within the northeast are the ten least evangelical states in our land.[92] When I pastored in New England some thirty-two years ago it had the lowest number of evangelical church attenders and still does today. It hovers around 3.7 percent. Think about that for a minute. An area with almost fourteen million people that have no relationship with the Lord Jesus and have never made a profession of their faith and followed Him as savior and Lord. It should break your heart when you think about the historical activity of the great awakenings.

Geography Does Not Define Us

As church revitalizers who are interested in multiplication, we know that Jesus' mission is to "…make disciples of all nations…"[93] including our own! However, when it comes to doing gospel-centered ministry in more rural areas, I have seen a tendency to want to frame these contexts as lessor ministries that are not as important. But if we are to remain faithful to this Great Commission, we have no choice but to be concerned for all people, in all places. Geography does not define this mission, people do. That said, as rural America becomes more secular and established churches continue to close their doors, we will see an increased need for renewed churches, new church plants that reach new generations, new residents, and new people groups.

---

92 Go to:
http://www.thearda.com/ql2010/QL_S_2010_1_27p.asp.

93 C.f. Matthew 28:19-20.

We Still Need these Mission Outposts

Rural churches are often mission outposts in a penurious environment. Each one has great potential. They proclaim Gospel in an indigenous setting. They are relational and diverse. These churches are a channel of contagious joy and continual blessings. They connect people to God and each other in very personalized ways. If they can celebrate the spirit of their heritage and yet distinguish between the power and purposes of God and the vehicles of a previous day then they have a glorious future. Anthony Pappas has written in *Entering the World of the Small Church,* that there are six challenges that small churches must address if they are to become healthy. They are:

> traditionalism,
> congeniality,
> club mentality,
> conflict management,
> negative self-perception, and
> finances.[94]

Rural churches battle with traditionalism, congeniality, club mentality, unhealthy conflict management, negative self-image, and property (and personnel) expense. Pappas makes a good case in suggesting that small churches function like a tribe. Every tribe has stories that are woven into the very fabric of tribal life and he believes that stories are at the heart of small rural church life.[95] When an outsider attempts to lead the charge for change it is usually ineffective. However, rural church pastors can still be facilitators for change. But, transformation will never occur unless the call comes from

---

94 Pappas, Anthony G. *Entering the World of the Small Church.* Herndon, VA: The Alban Institute, 2002. Pg. 7-9.

95 Ibid., Pg. 127-129.

indigenous leadership. The key to rural renewal is the understanding that in the heart of a few people in every local expression of the true church beats God-given passion. Discovering and utilizing those people and the passions they have can set a rural congregation on fire from the inside out. That is rural revitalization in its best example. According to Dean McIntyre there are eight obstacles for the small church: psychology, facilities, leadership development, finances, use of technology, travel gap, burnout, limited talents and gifts.[96] Ed Stetzer declares, "ultimately, a church is only indigenous when it is similar enough to its surroundings that it can reach the community around it, while not being so similar it is unfaithful. It must be contextualized but not compromised."[97]

We Must Renew and Re-establish the Indigenous Rural Church

The goal of rural Church Revitalization and Renewal should be the re-establishment of indigenous churches. Indigenous methods are not "new" methods. They are patterned after the Apostle Paul. Paul was an itinerant church planter, not a permanent pastor. He never stayed in one place for more than 2-3 years. Paul appointed leaders to provide watch care and instruction to the new believers who had gathered together as a new church plant. Paul never appealed to the home church of Antioch or Jerusalem to request funds for church building construction or to support new pastors. Paul did not export leaders from home churches to pastor the new churches. Leaders emerged out of the new congregations. Although Paul wrote periodic letters or visited

---

96 Dean McIntyre. *The Small Church Primer: Strengths, Weaknesses, Worship, and Music In The Small-Membership Church*, www.gbod.org (2002), July, 2006.

97 Ed Stetzer. Church Planting Village, North American Mission Board, SBC: *Indigenous Church Planting*. www.churchplantingvillage.net.

these new churches, they were not dependent upon Paul or the "mother churches" to provide leadership, finances, decision-making, or evangelism initiatives. It was Anthony Pappas who said, "Certain small churches have a future. Others do not. Those that can rediscover joy, those that reconnect people to their God-given purpose, those that can love others, those that can preserve the spirit of their heritage will have a glorious future. But those that fail to do so will wither away."[98] In other words, if a congregation is willing to turn its gaze from pictures of the past to a vital future hope, then the future is bright. Unless a rural renewal church can be taught the necessity of shouldering its own burden and facing its own problems it will not see the outpouring of the Lord once again upon His church. The true measure of success as a rural church revitalizer, is not that which the revitalizer accomplishes while he walks among his community and people but the health and vitality of the work that stands after he has gone.

Wrapping it Up!

Depending on your source, the median American church size is 75 to 90 people. Many of these congregations are vibrant, healthy, effective, and gospel-centered—yet they remain small. Their budgets are often tight, and they provide the level of support they can. Such churches and their pastors should be commended for serving God to the best of their ability. A congregation makes a meaningful and tangible impact when they sacrifice so that their pastor can minister on their behalf and labor to expand the kingdom of God. All across the rural heartland there is a rise in indigenous bivocational ministers. They are a great asset to the Lords work and we should honor them for all that they do to keep a gospel witness viable in a rural community. These pastors

---

98 Pappas, Anthony G. *Entering the World of the Small Church*. Herndon, VA: The Alban Institute, 2002. Pgs. 37-140.

apostolic hearts are blessing and transforming the lives of so many. When you meet a rural church revitalizer, encourage them for the great sacrifice they are making so that there will be a strong voice for the Lord in that area.

Chapter 10
Christ Centered Clarity & the Rural Church
Chris Irving

A cheerful disposition is good for your health; gloom and doom leave you bone-tired.[99]

In my time as a pastor, I have served only in rural churches. From my first church in a community where the cows literally outnumbered the people, to my current location, which is an agricultural community, each stop along the way has displayed different qualities, characteristics, strengths, and weaknesses as well as some commonalities among these churches found in rural settings.

I began my tenure at my first church with 40 worshipers whose history of fighting and dismissing pastors was well known in the area. They had not seen any kind of baptism in several years. Upon our arrival, my wife had to climb into the church attic to bring down the crib for the nursery because they had not had a baby in the nursery for 5 years. In this rural setting, I was the only full-time employee in town on a regular basis as the US Postal Service reassigned our local post-master to just a half day. I was the pastor, volunteer fire department chaplain, grass fire-truck driver, and I once drove the ambulance into the small community for one of my oldest church members who was suffering with a stroke. Most of the fires for which I drove the truck were actually started by one of my deacons who loved to burn brush on his ranch. So yes, I was a rural pastor who literally was putting out church fires. The rural church can be a beautiful place to serve.

Glenn Daman, author of *The Forgotten Church*, writes that many people see rural America as an escape from the wild

---

[99] Eugene H. Peterson, *The Message: The Bible in Contemporary Language* (Colorado Springs, CO: NavPress, 2005), Pr 17:22.

and wooly life of the city and still others see it as a desolate dying waste land where people cling to their guns, bibles, and religion. I might add that they very well could be married to their cousins and not know it because family ties run deep. These people are often said to reject change, hold on to the past and refuse to move into the 21ˢᵗ Century. They are believed to be closed-minded, bigoted, and Republican. God, family, and country in that order are the core convictions they strongly hold. But Daman also says, "Christ sees people who are without a shepherd. To Him, these communities represent individuals who have been devastated by the ravaging effects of sin and are in desperate need of the gospel."[100] I could not agree more with a hearty "amen!" Those who speak ill of the rural church are speaking ill of the bride of Christ. When large institutions turn a blind eye to the thousands of rural churches in America today, they turn a blind eye to the bride of Christ.

The reality a young pastor in the rural church setting might find is that this ministry boils down to the *constraints* and the *ain'ts*.

Constraint #1. Rural church resources are usually quite limited, which often lead congregations to feel isolated and abused.

Constraint #2. One of the resources needed in the rural setting are pastors who will stay long enough to bring the church back to health.

Constraint #3. Small budgets and the lack of potential growth in the budget leave rural churches feeling desperate and hopeless.

---

100 Daman, Glenn. *The Forgotten Church: Why Rural Ministry Matters for Every Church in America.* (Chicago, IL: Moody Publishers, 2018) Kindle Edition. 15.

There are other constraints of course, such as staffing, adequate training of laity, effective ministry systems, clear lines of communication, and the list goes on. But in the rural setting you may find the "ain'ts" more detrimental because the "ain'ts" are imposed by the people themselves. Our church "ain't" going to be this or that. Our pastor "ain't" going to stay long because we are a stepping stone to bigger churches and more prestigious positions for ministers. The "ain't" mindset is a large hurdle to overcome but it *is* possible because all things are possible with God.

The rural church and community need revitalization as much as any urban or suburban church. Though rural churches might be harder to turn around, it is not impossible. That little rural church where I started experienced a turnaround in just 3 years. Three years was a fast start for this little congregation, considering the general rule of a thousand-day investment before a pastor really begins to see change take place. These people were aware of the rapid change taking place around them, but they were not in any hurry to join in. The change that happened was truly a movement of God and the response of faith of His people to His movement. Take heart pastor, there is always hope. As the title of this chapter says, every ministry must be centered around Christ Jesus and His mission for the local church.

The rural church will not be able to offer every ministry and program that their larger counter-parts provide, but her mission remains the same. Acts 1:8, "you will receive power when the Holy Spirit has come on you, and you will be my witnesses in Jerusalem, in all Judea and Samaria, and to the end of the earth," does not just apply to the mega-church because they have more money and more people.[101] Their

---

[101] *Christian Standard Bible* (Nashville, TN: Holman Bible Publishers, 2017), Ac 1:8.

abundance of money and people often brings an abundance of problems, so let us not put all the responsibility on the mega church. Acts 1:8 and the disciple-making Great Commission of Matthew 28:18-20 are issued to every church, regardless of size. When you pastor a rural church, there are days when it feels like you are pastoring in the most remote parts of the earth, but the mission of the church remains the same.

Watch Out for the Dangers in the Countryside

Revitalization has no one-size-fits-all approach, but many of the stumbling blocks look the same in the different contexts of local churches. In the book of Revelation, the seven churches of the apocalypse receive this letter from Jesus through John and five of the seven receive dire warnings of their need for revitalization. Though not all are located in rural settings, the troubles they had are very similar to any setting today and most certainly in the rural church.

Losing Your First Love – A Lack of Visional & Missional Clarity

Ephesus is the first church mentioned in the letter. Jesus mentions their works, labor, endurance, and lack of tolerance for evil people. They have endured great hardships and persevered for the sake of the name of Jesus and they have not grown weary in doing so. But the one thing they lacked was the most important thing. They abandoned their first love. It was not as if it happened by accident, but they intentionally *left* their first love. Their love for God first above all else and their love for each other, abandoned. Because of this lack of love for God they ceased to be a loving church. If the church cannot love one another, how are they supposed to love the lost and tend to the harvest?

Their visional clarity was skewed, as if looking into a cracked mirror. The reflection is unclear and distorted. God's purpose is to shape us into the image of Jesus. My, how we have messed up the image. Without the visional clarity of loving God first, the missional clarity of loving each other and loving the lost with the intention of sharing the Gospel, is lost. The Ephesus church was doing good work, but they lacked what mattered most. How many rural churches have ministry in place but are in decline because they lack the one thing that matters most? A love for God above their own family, preferences, modern forms of idolatry and programs? If this might describe your setting in rural America, Jesus is calling you to repent just as He did the church of Ephesus. Repentance is always a vital step in the process of revitalization and it must begin with the leadership in the church. A church that will repent of her sin is a church that is one step closer to health.

False Teaching and Tolerance – A Lack of Gospel Clarity

We will look at the church in Smyrna as we examine the church in Philadelphia. But first, the congregations in Pergamum and Thyatira had a few good things going for them. They were holding on to the name of Jesus and had not denied their faith in Jesus. In the past, Antipas was faithful even unto death. But the past does not last and in the present a serious problem was diminishing the light of this once great beacon of light. They are guilty of mixing a false teaching with the truth of the Gospel. It is no secret that a rural church can lack high-quality, developed leadership. What I witness pastoring rural churches is what I call "Warm-Body-Syndrome." Churches have a list of positions that need to be filled. "Warm-Body-Syndrome" is nothing but placing a warm body in a position so the list is complete and everyone is happy while not considering the warm-body's beliefs, commitment or spiritual gifts. I have pastored churches where committees were willing to insert a teacher who was not even a member of the church just because that warm-body was willing to fill a position. The problems with this are many, but among them are the creation of confusion in doctrine and teaching leading to confusion in the teaching of the Gospel. This is no small matter.

In Pergamum, they had several who held to a different type of Gospel. Jesus calls it the teaching of "Balaam" and the teaching of the "Nicolaitans." There is not sufficient time and space to cover the different takes on this except to say they were teaching extreme liberty, leading to a cheapening of the grace of God. The Gospel is clear that Jesus died to save sinners and was raised to raise us to walk in a new life, a life that is defined by following Him in faith. A lack of gospel clarity can lead people to never experience the true life transformation that occurs with the Gospel. That lack of true transformation is a detriment to leadership development in the rural church. Again, the same first step is issued to Pergamum and Thyatira…repent!

Dead or Alive – A Lack of Convictional Clarity

Sardis and Laodicea are an altogether different case. They have a reputation of good works, but in reality they are dead, or at least they are in the process of dying. The Laodicean church is luke-warm, virtually useless to the Kingdom, and is about to be vomited out. The Gospel ought to create a conviction to take the good news to the ends of the earth, to reach out into the fields for the harvest. Yet, if your church is like Sardis, it is nothing more than a reputation and that will not get you very far. A reputation reaps no reward but death. Programs, people and old, sacred church idols from the past need to die so that the church can truly live!

In any church there is always a faithful remnant and, Pastor, you need to discover who they are. Jesus gives five imperatives for the Sardis church that each church in need of revitalization today can follow to rebound to health. The lack of convictional clarity can be fixed by an awakening of sorts and a strengthening of what remains. Perhaps this happens through an old fashioned revival! The church must find the conviction to honestly assess each ministry and to seek to adjust ministries to a new methodology with the goal of more effectiveness in outreach and disciple making. Now this takes time because rural churches are generally weary of outside programs and people, but given enough time the pastor can earn the trust of the people and lead them to make the necessary adjustments.

Faithfully Holding On – A Proper Way Forward

Looking at the church of Smyrna and Philadelphia, we find two churches small in stature yet faithful to Jesus. Both churches face pressure from outside forces and yet they remain faithful to the Gospel and service to Jesus. Both are suffering, yet faithful. Philadelphia is of "little power" yet they have not denied the name of Jesus. He places before them a door that He opens and closes, and no one else can control that door. Many scholars believe this open door is a reference to evangelism and missions. The proper way forward for any church is a healthy evangelism and missions strategy. This takes endurance though, which both Smyrna and Philadelphia both possess. However, the question remains if the rural church will find the conviction to hold on to what they have, keep it and endure. So many critics write off the rural church because she is not able to hold large conferences, she does not have a book-writing pastor, or a pastor who is well known with high levels of education. But what the seven churches show us is that size does not matter when it comes to effectiveness for the gospel.

When I attended the *Renovate National Church Revitalization Conference* in 2017, Karl Vaters told us a story of the importance of the small, rural church. He illustrated the point by telling us about the landing craft used in the attacks of D-Day. The allied forces had their large ships stationed off the coast, but those ships could not reach the beach head to deliver the invasion force. The only way the forces could be delivered were by smaller boats and landing craft. In the same way, 90% of the churches in the United States are small and many of these are in rural settings. Your rural church has value in the Kingdom of God and your church's health is important. So remain faithful and hold on to the true Gospel. If needed, repent and turn back to the Lord!

Establish a Christ-Centered Rural Church Ministry

The need exists for rural churches to develop leadership on multiple levels. Not everyone can lead, but everyone can serve, which is the essence of New Testament leadership. In John 13, Jesus makes this clear and in Mark 10 as the Sons of Zebedee ask Jesus for positions of power, He makes it clear that kingdom leadership is first and foremost from a place of humility and service.

The rural church needs to develop leadership through authentic discipleship. This can be daunting but in thinking about one of the greatest characteristics of the rural church, relationships, the natural bridge is already in place between discipleship and leadership because the people have deep relationships already established. The pastor should spend his first years developing his own personal relationships and learn the intricacies of the people in order to establish the best path forward for disciple-making and leadership development.

Develop the Heart of Your Church

One thing you are called to do as a pastor is to disciple your people and equip them for the ministry.[102] First and foremost they must love Jesus and follow Him. It is certainly a real possibility that those who sit in the pews do not have authentic relationships with Jesus. They might have a relationship with the church without having ever come to the life-changing decision to follow Jesus by faith, never having experienced His amazing grace. This could certainly be why their works are useless and dead! The heart of the church is that she has a heart that follows and loves Jesus. Everything is centered on this one relationship for no other relationship will suffice as a substitute. The church belongs to Jesus. He is the one who purchased her, therefore the heart of the church must love Him and seek to serve like Him. You will develop the heart for the church through text-driven preaching, authentic worship, prayer and personal discipleship. The more your people encounter God, the more they will love Him and desire to serve Him.

Develop the Understanding of the Church

The church must understand her purpose, mission and vision. There are chapters in this work that will help you develop these for your rural context. Your purpose is simply the reason you exist. You must teach your church the theology of the local church as found in Scripture. The church must understand her mission is the Great Commission and the Great Commandment and not to serve as a personal-preference-pleasing community organization. People's eternal destiny is at stake and the church must be about the Father's business! Beyond the Great Commission, the church needs a healthy theology of corporate worship and

---

102 Ephesians 4:11-13.

179

corporate prayer. John 4 serves as a great reminder of the nature, time, and location of worship in the New Testament. Worship wars have not waned going into the 21st Century and many rural churches are still worshiping with hymn books and have no projection system. Fortunately, a rich theology of worship is not determined by smoke, lights, lasers, and styles, but rather hearts that seek to glorify Jesus.

Discover the Motivation of the Church

What is it that motivates the church in a rural setting? Is your church open to new people, outsiders? Here in my current rural setting, we are experiencing suburbanites and urbanites moving into the country in their retirement years. These are people who do not have deep connections to this community. In fact, if your family was not a part of the original settlement from the 1820's, then you are not really considered "from" the town I now pastor. But the church is very much open to newcomers and new faces. Ultimately, our motivation must be the glory of God. The glory of God compels us to love Him and love others which means we exist to serve others. If the church is motivated by anything else above the glory of God, that motivation will eventually give way and your church will just be a reputation with nothing to show for it. Motivate your people by keeping them before the Cross of Christ and reminding them just how great the love of God truly is, that we (the church) should be called the children of God.

Determine to be Biblical

That term, "biblical," can mean many things in our post-modern era. I define "biblical" with a simple understanding of the Bible as the inerrant and infallible Word of God. 2 Timothy 3:16-17 says, "All Scripture is inspired by God and is profitable for teaching, for rebuking, for correcting, for training in righteousness, so that the man of God may be complete, equipped for every good work."[103] All of your ministries, all of your sermons must be text-driven. Feel-good sermons with warm-fuzzy platitudes won't cut it in the work of revitalization. Ezra stood before the people of God upon their return from exile and proclaimed the very Word of God to them and led them to repent of their sin. Notice the Bible is God's word and is useful for all that we need: teaching, rebuking, correcting and training in righteousness so that the church is complete and equipped for ministry. You must be a biblical church!

Develop Leadership in their Giftedness

The Holy Spirit provides the church with spiritual gifts. The gift of leadership is listed in Romans 12 and the gift of administration is listed in 1 Corinthians. Perform a spiritual gifts inventory and find out who your spiritual leaders are. Those who are given the gift of leadership by the Holy Spirit are the ones who should be in place as leaders in your church. Certainly anyone can be developed into a leader, but I believe Scripture clearly teaches that there is a gift of leadership from the Holy Spirit. Now Jesus set the tone for leadership in the Gospel in John 13, and Mark 10 where He clearly demonstrates that leadership is first and foremost servanthood. Jesus said, "I didn't come to be served, I came to serve and give my life as a ransom." Leadership is giving oneself up, even to the point of exhaustion.

Develop the Evangelism Ministry

Churches in decline are mostly lethargic when it comes to evangelism. A lack of love for Jesus leads to a lack of love for the lost. Jesus came to seek and to save that which was

---

[103] *Christian Standard Bible* (Nashville, TN: Holman Bible Publishers, 2017), 2 Ti 3:16–17.

lost, and the church has that same purpose and calling. You must be intentional about evangelism. My experience informs me that churches do not just naturally practice evangelism unless the pastor demonstrates and leads them to be a soul-winning church. In a rural setting, a robust evangelism ministry might upset the apple cart because "new people" will suddenly arrive at the church. Rural churches are not always friendly to new faces and they are usually skeptical of the town drunk and other sinners who are suddenly in church on Sunday morning. Because of this, a healthy evangelism strategy must be buffeted by a strong discipleship strategy. As your church members learn to follow Jesus through discipleship, they'll be more open to the inevitable change that evangelism brings.

God has called you, Pastor, to serve in your rural setting for a time such as this. The temptation is great to bring in outsiders, purchase the next great program from a Christian book store, jump on the next big wave of ministry ideas or even to use your rural church as a stepping stone to something bigger. But God has called you to pastor right where you are for a very specific reason. Paul's words to the church in Philippi apply to us as rural pastors too, "Just one thing: As citizens of heaven, live your life worthy of the gospel of Christ."[104]

A prayer I pray often is one that I was blessed to have been shown long ago by a dear friend of mine in the ministry. This prayer of David Brainerd's says simply, "Lord, let me make a difference for You that is utterly disproportionate to who I am."[105] My prayer for the rural church is similar. "Lord,

---

104 *Christian Standard Bible* (Nashville, TN: Holman Bible Publishers, 2017), Philippians 1:27.

105 Brainerd, David. http://www.azquotes.com/author/1806-David_Brainerd. Accessed June 21, 2018.

let us make a difference for you that is utterly disproportionate to their size and setting." Believe He will do it!

Chapter 11
Nineteen New Realities for the
21st Century Rural Church

God doesn't want us to be shy with his gifts, but bold and loving and sensible.[106]

The world is changing and for the local church that is a challenge. It is even a greater challenge for the church of the rural heartland. While far too many rural church books write about the negative of pastoring rural church we have sought to be positive and provide illustrations and examples of rural churches doing great things. Growing a rural church through revitalization and renewal is a choice and many ministers in the heartland are making it each and every day. They are courageous crusaders which love those who live in the less populated areas of our lad and know they need a shepherd with a clear voice that speaks for the Lord our God. I wanted to examine twenty-one newer realities for the rural church ministering in the twenty-first century.

Most Rural Communities are Plateaued or in Decline

There are few rural communities where you discover that they are remaining vibrant growing environments and possess a strong population. While the population has declined there is still a need for a new testament church to be the lighthouse and spiritual voice to those who remain. Not everybody is moving away from the rural landscape so ministries must decide that a continual effort is still important. Within my own denomination, where once we were all about helping the rural landscape through the planting of churches, we have now withdrawn from such efforts choosing to focus on a small number of urban centers instead. What we are left with

---

[106] Eugene H. Peterson, *The Message: The Bible in Contemporary Language* (Colorado Springs, CO: NavPress, 2005), 2 Ti 1:7.

is a denomination that has at its conception a rural and urban fringe focus, now has withdrawn from the rural landscape and seems impotent to keep our denomination from declining meteorically. I had a group of rural pastors I was working with recently ask me if our national agencies were giving up on the heartland and fringe areas of our country. That is a valid question of which I no longer have to answer for, yet it is tragic to see such withdrawal and how it is affecting the rural community. If you live in a rural community you have just as much right to a local church expression as does the big cities across our land. The formula will look quite different, but there is still a great opportunity for growing churches in the rural areas.

That Does Not Mean Your Church Must Be Also

While most rural communities are plateaued or in decline that does not imply that your church needs to just throw up its hands and do nothing to impact your community for Jesus Christ. There is still a voice that needs to make a clarion call for the Lord in such areas. Jesus walked all over rural areas presenting the gospel and so should we. Granted some rural churches will not be able to survive because they want a model that no longer appeals to those who live in the area. I am asked all the time by rural churches what will happen if they do not make changes to reach those who still live there. I try to respectfully declare that if they isolate themselves from those which still reside in that town, some new church plant and church planter will come in and gather all of the younger occupants in town together leaving the former churches as landmarks and no longer as lighthouses. There is an old song that says, "it only takes a spark to get a fire going and soon all those around will warm up to its glowing. That's how it is with Gods love once you experience." The rural church which brings a new spark has a greater chance to impact the area than one which wants to stay stuck in outdated formats failing to reach those who make up the community. During my sabbatical of 2017 the number of new churches surprised me and to the letter, each pastor spoke of the existing churches unwillingness to try new things to gather the community to the Lord. Does your area have a new church plant in it? Often that is in direct response of a rural community saying and acting like they must be plateaued or in decline like their community.

Agriculture, the Once Lifeline of Rural Communities Has Moved Off to Larger Enterprises

In the past, the rural heartland had many farmers who worked the soil and farmed the land. If you were willing to work hard you could have a nice livelihood and great life being a farmer. Providing for the food needs across the land was a tremendous blessing to both the urban and rural population. But the day of the small farmer growing and providing for the population had declined. Now there are large enterprises which do the farming and hire fewer and fewer farmers to work the land. The rural community no longer can sustain itself through the agricultural enterprises of the past. Big companies have moved in with all of their technology and have made the farmland more sufficient while lessening the need to have individual farms and farmers developing crops. The once strong financial base of farming has lessened due to corporate agriculture companies buying out the land or leasing the land for pennies while squeezing out the rural agriculturalists. Something else must take the place which was held by farming enterprises.

A New Rural Set of Enterprises, Featuring Mom and Pop Businesses are Surfacing

In the rural communities that are prospering what has taken the place of the agriculture lifeline has been a new set of rural small enterprise featuring Mom and Pop businesses. With the ability to have high speed internet at your fingertips in even rural areas you can run a small online business. I met some who worked for companies providing customer service assistance. Others created start-up business such as food catering, children's novelty items, furniture creation, and one of my favorites was a lady who developed a thriving granola business with well over fifteen different morning granola flavors. One family developed a pop tart type of dough where they utilized the fruits from their farm to make these delicious treats. All of these had one thing in common, a willingness to think outside of the box and be creative.

There are Still People Who Need the Lord Around the Church

Regardless of your community's population, there are people who live there that need the Lord. When God first formed Adam from the dust, he was the only human on the planet. Can you imagine how lonely he must have felt? But it didn't last long. God said it wasn't good for man to be alone (Genesis 2:18) and decided to give Adam some company, so He created Eve. There you have it the creation of the first rural community in scripture! If you live within an urban city demographic it really does not feel all that lonely. Regardless of one's community it is easy to get so wrapped up in our own lives that we don't take the time to really get to know others. Everywhere you look there are people, lot of them.

But that is not true in town and country areas or rural America. It is easy to live in isolation if you reside in a rural landscape. The Lord never intended for that to be the case. In the rural churches which are successful they understand the need for connection and work hard at providing interesting and enlightening opportunities for the community to connect with the church and the church to connect with the community. We are designed to thrive and blossom in relationships with others. We're our best selves when we're experiencing life's highs and lows with other believers. That means everyone, whether you're single or married, needs community. The Bible has much to say about this idea of relationships and connection! Here are four motivations the Bible says living in community is so important.

1. Living in Community is Encouraging.

Being in community gives you the chance to be around people at different stages of their faith journey—and to bear their burdens alongside of them (Galatians 6:2). That's awesome, because everyone has something to teach and to learn. In fact, it creates the ideal environment to be a Barnabas, pursue a Paul, or train a Timothy. What it comes down to is lifting each other up, learning from one another, and being the friend each of us needs.

2. Living in Community is Fun.

Community should never feel boring or forced. In fact, it should be the exact opposite. Psalm 133:1 (NIV) tells us, *"How good and pleasant it is when God's people live together in unity!"* *Living* in community has a higher purpose. But it should also be enjoyable!

3. Living in Community Attracts the Holy Spirit.

The Bible says the Holy Spirit is present whenever believers gather together.[107] A great example of this was the early church of Acts, which made a habit of meeting together, eating together, and worshiping together. As a result, *"the Lord added to their number daily those who were being saved."*

---

107 C.f. Matthew 18:20.

4. Living in Community Nurtures Friendship.

When you live in community it has the ability to nurture friendships and that is very important for the rural church. Having those relationships that foster deep relationships and love are a great way to advance the rural church. Paul held love above all else in his letter to the Corinthians and he did the same with his letter to the Colossians: *"Bear with each other and forgive one another if any of you has a grievance against someone. Forgive as the Lord forgave you. And over all these virtues put on love, which binds them all together in perfect unity."*[108]

The life giving nature of living in community is essential to following Christ. Scripture says that's because we're better together than we are alone.[109]

It can be awkward for some of us to commit to community, especially if we are cautious or favor privacy. But community is God's desire for us and a sign of a mature faith. Because at the end of the day, when we grow in our relationships with others, we're growing in relationship with Him!

Compassion Ministries Will Become an Ongoing Connection Point

There is much work to be done within the rural landscape in the area of compassion ministries. The rural American community has been hit hard with the exodus of businesses which formerly supported the town and country community. Families are suffering and need the church to be the church it was intended to be. One rural pastor I met wrote a series of letters to fellow pastors within one hundred

---

108 C.f. Colossians 3:13–14 NIV.

109 C.f. Romans 12:4–5.

miles of his rural community asking if they would assist him in providing clothing for those in need in his area by asking for their church members to contribute unwanted clothing and in particular heavy jackets for children, youth, and adults. Five churches led by loving and compassionate pastors responded to his simple and humble request. The result was that not only did they meet this rural pastor needs for his community he cared so much about, but also provided a touch ministry for the urban churches to participate in acts of kindness. Eventually because the members in the urban churches got so excited about what they were doing twice a year they provided bags of groceries for the rural church to distribute. The most interesting one was the food drive right as the rural public schools were closing for the summer. These five churches understood that many children would go hungry because they no longer had the food program going on at school. These churches did an old fashion pounding and provided meals for the pastor to give away in his community. The other one was at the beginning of the winter break where students were away from school for about two weeks and would go hungry. What a wonderful blessing these five churches are and were to this rural pastor as he sought to embrace his small town. The end result was that the community came to understand that that church cred for them and that they were the real church in the rural landscape. The result was that the church grew. It still had little money, but loving churches helped this pastor touch his community for Christ Jesus. All because he sent out twenty-five letters to these pastors asking humbly for any kind of assistance they could provide.

The Age of Bi-Vocationalism Will Be the Rural Norm Not the Exception

Bivocational ministry is the new normal. Bivocational ministry may be God's tool for such a time as this. It continues to grow and can make a big difference in strengthening existing churches and helping to launch new ones. Ed Stetzer professor at Wheaton University has observed, "If you are a bivocational pastor, you are a gift to the kingdom. That is unquestioned." The "norm" is changing in some parts of the United State from a majority of full-time pastoral positions to a majority of part-time pastoral positions. The Southern Baptist Convention is currently the leader in promoting and supporting bi-vocational pastors. It is reported that 75% of their churches run under 100 people, many of which are bi-vocational. About 10,000 bivocational ministers were working in the Southern Baptist churches in 1998. By 2004, that number had doubled, to 20,000. In 2014, Frank Page, the president of the Executive Committee of the Southern Baptist Convention, said, "I'm convinced that in the 21st century, the best stewardship is bivocational. Some would say 35,000 of our 46,000 churches — maybe more than that — are in the two categories of small church or bivocational." Some observers have indicated that as many as 80 percent of all ministers are bivocational, while others fix the number at 40-60 percent. The Church of the Nazarene denomination reports that about 40% of their ministers are bi-vocational. The Pentecostal Holiness churches also report a number of their pastors working outside of the ministry due to declining attendance. While George Barna of Barna Research reports that 87% of Protestant churches have full-time ministers, there are concerns that only 7% of our pastors are between the ages of 28-45. The rest is made up of Baby-boomers or older, which may have different financial make-up. Being a bi-vocational pastor brings challenges and opportunities for the pastor as well as the church. Paul never apologized for being bi-vocational so why should you? Both bi-vocational and full-time pastors are very important in the Kingdom of God. Each have a call, purpose, and similarity.

The pastor of a large church is the one who usually gets all of the accolades. But bivocational pastor; such as real estate brokers, information technology professionals, house painters, teachers, and lawyers, who work both in the church and in the secular world outnumber those big names. Their numbers are likely to grow in the future. Fewer than two-thirds (62.2 percent) of churches in the United States have a full-time pastor, according to the 2015 Faith Communities Today survey. That's down from 71.4 percent in 2010. Median Sunday attendance dropped from 105 people to 80 during the same time, and the median annual budget fell from $150,000 to $125,000. Ray Gilder who leads the Bivocational and Small Church Leadership Network says, "A lot of churches can't afford to take care of their pastor." The reality in the rural context is that most pastors are bivocational ministers. Finding the right 'second' job is critical and challenging as a rural pastor. The rural pastor which has a second vocation must keep in mind that serving in a rural context is all about the mission you are on and finding a way to do it. It can never be solely about the financial remuneration. A proper fit that will allow you time to do the necessary things required in ministry is vital. Also finding a second job that will not suck all of the energy and time out of the rural pastor is important. I worked as a contract worker for a construction company in an early bivocational ministry and it allowed me to meet our needs and yet remain open to a flexible schedule. Often church planting teams will plant a new church utilizing the bivocational model so as not to drain any early resources from the new church. You must be willing to share the responsibility of leading a church if you are bivocational. Having a bivocational pastor means the rural congregation members need to take leadership roles.

Doctor Randy Singer, a lawyer by trade, has been a bivocational pastor at Trinity Church in Virginia Beach the past nine years. He also runs a law firm and writes novels on the side. The church could afford to pay him full time, but Singer isn't interested. He believes bivocational ministry helps bridge the gap between professional staff and people in the pews. "Being bivocational sends the message that we need all hands-on deck," he says. Having a secular job also keeps him from being trapped in a church bubble, where his primary social contacts are with fellow Christians. Being in the courtroom and working at his law firm keeps him in touch with the rest of the world. "I am no less a minister of the gospel when I'm at my law firm than when I'm at the church," he says. "I'm on mission just as much at one place as I am at the other." Singer believes bivocational pastors need to share leadership in order to be successful. At times, he says, pastors are afraid to give lay leaders control over essential parts of the ministry. His advice for bivocational pastors: Delegate as much as you can. Find and develop leaders who can run ministries at the church and let them do their jobs.

Thriving Rural Churches Will Have Additional Funding Streams Above the Weekly Tithes and Offerings

During my study sabbatical of 2017 while researching the rural church landscape what quickly became apparent was that all of the churches which had been revitalized had discovered ways to acquire alternative funding streams. Some rented out their facilities such as a gym to the county recreation department. Others opened a quality daycare program to meet the needs of the working families in the community. One rural church farmed their property and utilized the proceeds to assist with the expenses of the church. A few churches sold candles each year while one of my favorites was a hymn-a-thon that raised substantial resources. Another set up an ongoing swap shop on the third Saturday of each month and all of the proceeds went to the church's needs. In one church that was in need of refurbishment of the facilities they sold engraved bricks for the patio which was the most visible portion of the remodel. In one church in the rural north central states area a group of ladies from the church developed a community decoration service team which would for a fee decorate the various banks, and community institutions within a one-hundred-mile radius. The team started small but eventually grew to be a group of men and women that massed to over fifty volunteers with ten teams of five members each on a team. In a rural Georgia area one church hosted a classic car show annually which drew attenders from all over each contributing a mere five dollars to attend the event. Food was also sold as a means to assist the church during the event. One church hosted a battle of the bands annually out on the lawn of their country church. Schools paid a small fee but attendees would enjoy the food offered up by the ladies' ministry of the church. Some of the small historic communities have murals and in one rural Florida community a church has gathered all of their artisans and hire themselves out to paint the historic murals for the community patrons and businesses. Many rural churches host annually a carnival on their property and the proceeds go towards some project the church has dedicated the receipts towards. In one old rural community a church sponsored an evening where there was a balloon lantern release night. Since they were in the country it was dark until the skies were alive with these balloon lanterns. There red floating lanterns were so beautiful and they lit up the shy. One church packaged their own coffee and sold it to the resident of the rural community. There are rural communities where you can apply for a rural grant to do some fixing-up of one's property. I liked the church that was dog friendly that hosted a Saturday evening event in which they called Yappy Hour. They helped raise money for the pet shelters. This same church hosted a pet picture day as they sold the photos to their guests after taking their pets pictures. I might suggest from my experience that you have two pet picture days, one for dogs and one for cats, since my experience was comical to say the lease. There are hundreds of ideas if you and your church are willing and creative.

Young Children and Middle School Youth are a Vital Niche

There are many things your church can do to draw families with children and youth. Just because your church has few children and a diminishing number of youth, does not mean you can't draw them to your church. Both children and youth seek adventure so put your thinking caps on and develop ways for your church to draw in the younger groups in your community. One church I know of would have a children's game night each Friday during football season so the parents could drop off their children and then go to the game. While the parents were often there at the game for an older child, the younger ones were being cared for and entertained in the family life center with all types of games, movies, food, and a brief message from the youth pastor. Then once the 10:30 pick-up took place, the youth gathered for a fifth quarter event. Remember there are not a lot of things to do in rural areas and the church which creatively addresses such a need will draw large numbers of the available demographic to these events.

Most High School Youth Will Be Working to Make Ends Meet Within the Home

You must be selective in ministering to the youth of rural areas. Many a high school youth will be working a job in order to resource the things they need for school and life. Therefore, you must be willing to look outside of the norms such as Sunday School and Wednesday night. Finding ways to be part of their lives is important and it usually does not take much money if any. One rural church sought to take the youth of the area to a summer camp and spent most of the year raising money in order for these youths to go free.

Nurals Will Be Returning or Retiring as They Close Out Their Working Careers

When the nurals return to the rural landscape remember that most of these who return home have grown accustom to activity and community. They want a church that does things like going out for a week day lunch. They like excursions and fun events. These who are returning to the rural landscape have retirement incomes and want to be about enjoying all that they can in their retirement years. Rural churches which have had gyms sit around unused might find that there is a growing niche for a men's early morning basketball league. Others will want to walk in the gym of take a craft class so you should be thinking about ways to attract the nurals which are returning to your community and your church. Nurals have money to expend so they will desire an active church. Because these who are returning to a rural landscape have worked out in the business world and have gathered a solid retirement income, they want to be doers of the word.

Rural Church Revitalizers Will Serve as Pastor, Shepherd, Moral Compass, Lighthouse, Evangelist, Watcher, and Prophet for the Community

There is more to pastoring a rural church than preaching. The rural church revitalizer will serve as the pastor preacher most certainly. Yet he will often operate as the one who is the moral voice and compass to a community that might be a little adrift. He will be the lighthouse for all of those who are heavy laden and a shining voice for those who seek something more than existence. He will often be the evangelist regionally. He will operate at times as the watcher on the wall as he cautions residents about the evils which could be draining the community of its children. Generally, such a church revitalizer often functions in the rural landscape as the community prophet like prophets of old. His voice is a clarion call for the community to come to Jesus, return to the church, and be drawn to the altar seeking forgiveness.

Well Established Family Networks in these Churches Must Embrace New Inhabitants

Even though some of the old family tree will not like it, you must speak openly to them about becoming more inclusive to those who are residing in the area. Nurals will be coming back to their roots and if you will not embrace them as a church, they will start a new church and leave you sitting on the side of the road as their church grows and your church dies. I have seen that in every state here I studied the rural communities. If a church turned inward, the gospel was still being delivered but instead of their church being blessed with a renewed influx, it was a new church plant that was more inclusive and not exclusive. You must teach these family networks to become more open and seek to include not exclude these new potential members. Here me when I say: if existing rural churches will not welcome the newbies, there will arise a wave of new church plants that compel the young and further push the declining rural church into closure.

Nurals are Technology Savvy So Blandness in Worship Will Not Do

As these nurals return to the rural context they will bring with them a savviness for technology. They will desire a visual presentation on a screen in the front. They like songs on the screen over signing from a hymn book. They feel more in tune with the preacher when he has a visual presentation that goes with his sermon each week. They seek fun and playfulness with a sense of humor. They want powerful preaching but they are more in tuned with a preacher which has the ability to be a strong orator and bold communicator. You must go bold if you are going to gather the nurals.

Near Urban Fringe Rural Churches Will Draw from the Suburbs

If you are revitalizing a church that is on the outskirts of a suburban fringe population center, you will draw from those fringe communities so be ready to adjust your preferences to some of the things in which these prospects are interested. These near-vile individuals want the best of both communities so you will need to be selective. Their ideas might have more to do with where they live over what you think would be best. It takes much prayer and communication for these individuals and about these individuals as you seek to draw them into an existing church.

Health and Dental Units Will Be an Advantage to Rural Communities if You Can Find a Church Partner in the Urban Context with to Partner

Develop relationships with your urban pastors and Christian agencies which could help you care for your rural families. Often an urban church would like to do mission ministries just a little bit away from their homes. It could be a great win-win situation if you met with pastors and shared your vision and see if the Lord might open up an avenue for your rural residents to be blessed by the larger urban church and its mission outreach.

Allow Your Facilities to be Used by the Community as Regularity Will Give You Influence

In your area having a meeting place is a solid asset so don't be shy about offering it to groups to meet. Often there are all types of events and groups which need a meeting place one hour a month and cannot find one. Become known as a place what is welcoming. If you have a large fellowship hall, offer it to youth sports leagues for their end of the seasons banquets. There are so many groups which need a meeting place that would be so appreciative of your churches willingness to be used as a blessing for these groups.

The Majority of Your High School Graduates Will Move Away Never to Return, Minister to those Who Stay

It is commonly known that presently most high school graduates will move away from the rural landscape as they seek to further their education. Most will never return. As a church revitalizer it is important that you minister to those who stay and begin incorporating them into the leadership fabric of the church. These young adults deserve a church which loves them and cares for them. They deserve to grow, learn to serve, and to become the future leaders of the church. A wise pastor will make it his goal to embrace, encourage, empower, and enlist these young adults for service within the church. Remember they have the energy which will help many a rural church so utilize it and advance it.

Avail Your Un-Used Facilities to Young Entrepreneurs' to Office and Network Out of by Providing Multiple Work Stations

Young entrepreneurs are trying to find their way within the rural landscape. Helping these men and women begin to develop a livelihood is honorable. Providing a place for them to dream and meet in regularly gives them a sense of advancement and accomplishment. Many entrepreneurs started down their particular career paths as preteens or teenagers. In fact, the nature of our child-labor laws within the United States, force most kids under the age of 15 who want to work, to work for themselves doing things such as mowing lawns, washing cars, babysitting, selling baked goods or any number of other age-appropriate activities. Those early ventures on the peripheral of the workforce may convince young entrepreneurs that they want to be self-employed for the rest of their lives but taking the next steps can be challenging. That's especially true if the kids don't have entrepreneurial family members or friends they can learn from, or if the adolescents don't really know what they want to do as a career. Honestly, there are many adults who are in the same boat.

As a church revitalizer, by providing a place for them to office and network out of it is a strong statement that you believe in them. Teach them some life lessons such as those I have included below. More and more, youth are turning to entrepreneurship as their career. Although often admired by peers, these young entrepreneurs are challenged by investors and even clients who are nervous about giving their cash to a 20-year-old with little experience. Don't let your youth get in your way of your success. As young entrepreneurs begin developing your reputation and take care of the few clients you have while pursuing new ones. Lead beyond your years. Teach them that one way to grow up faster as an entrepreneur is to surround themselves with older individuals who have already experienced success. Leverage your age. Although some young entrepreneurs may face occasional blatant disrespect due to their age and may be tempted to lie about their age in order to appear more competent, in some cases, their youth can give them a leg up. Starting a business is hard, and the difficulties often are compounded when you're a young person beginning the entrepreneurial journey. There are many moving parts and resources you need but may not have access to. Remind them they don't know everything. Young people, in general, struggle with a know-it-all complex. We may hear advice but too quickly dismiss it because we think we know what we should be doing. This can be a huge mistake. Not all advice is beneficial, but wisdom from those that have gone before us is invaluable. No one can go back in time but learning from other entrepreneur's mistakes is one way for us to avoid potential roadblocks. Be willing to at least listen and see if the advice can be beneficial for your business. Entrepreneurship offers you benefits that extend far beyond the material. The chance to live a life of freedom and make an impact in people's lives is priceless. The chance to live a life free of financial stress and to see the world is worth more than what you drive. Save your money and spend it on the things that you'll look back on later in life and smile about. Choose experience over stuff. Who you allow in your life will either help or hurt what you're trying to create. Negative people will feed into your doubt, fear, and self-limiting beliefs. Starting a business is hard enough without someone looking over your shoulder and pointing out what they think is "realistic." Surround yourself with people who will lift you up and be the support you need to push through failure. Many young entrepreneurs waste time, trying to be like someone they look up to. They conclude the key to their success is copying another successful entrepreneur. It's not. When someone wants to do business, they will hire or buy from the original, not the clone. People want to connect with you. They want to hear what you have to say and see how you can make a difference in their life. Embrace what makes you an entrepreneur. Dig deep and be honest.

Wrapping it Up!

There are tremendous being made today all across the rural landscape. Baby boomers are returning to their roots and making the choice of settling back into the rural climate they were raised. Often rural churches usually encapsulate themselves in a shell to hide from the things which they can't bear to accept, and that shell is nothing but the imaginary world in which they don't get hurt and don't have to accept the facts that church in the rural arena can choose to grow or it can choose to die. It can turn even further inward while some other rural church captures the heart of the community. I think rural church revitalization is all about acceptance and non-acceptance of the nineteen realities I have mentioned above. If you and your church is able to face these realities as they are then he not likely to be hurt by what the future in rural America throws at you. A rural church revitalizer and his members can certainly live in these new realities and embrace these opportunities they present with a smile. No rural church needs to live in an atmosphere of seclusion only to discover that the other rural churches which embraced opportunities and dealt with the challenges of trying to do more with less, have indeed impacted rural America while you and your choose to live in a cocoon and become a hermitic church that failed to reinvent itself for the good of the residents and for the Lord Jesus. You as the church revitalizer, your churches leadership, and those who call your church their church has a critical choice to make each and every day. Do you get out of bed and face the glorious challenges living for Christ in a rural community or do you give up and go back to bed never to make an impact that the Lord so willingly provided for those who will embrace and love the rural families all across their landscape.

Chapter 12
A Call for Rural Missionaries

"When you harvest your land, don't harvest right up to the edges of your field or gather the gleanings from the harvest. Don't strip your vineyard bare or go back and pick up the fallen grapes. Leave them for the poor and the foreigner. I am God, your God.[110]

In 2012 the Lord called me out of the city to pastor a church in rural northwest Missouri. My friends and colleagues in the city thought I was falling off the face in the earth. Folks at the new church assumed I, like they, couldn't wait to get out of the city. Both of them were wrong. My family and I loved where we were. But there was a new calling. A new community to know. A new people to love. A new pace of living life and doing ministry to embrace.

In many ways the move to rural northwest Missouri was a homecoming. During part of my elementary school years my dad pastored a church in an even smaller community a little more than an hour's drive from where I now live. After the dust settled from the move I went through some unexpected culture shock. Because I had lived in this "neck of the woods" before I was really taken back by my feelings. The first year was rough. We had a home in the city that would not sell. One of my children was having tremendous difficulty adjusting to the move. There were a few times that first year I thought, "Maybe I heard God wrong?"

I share that confession not from a sense of unhappiness or embittered spirit. I count it a privilege to pastor where I do. I love the people of my church and the community where my family and I live. I share my confession to prepare

---

[110] Eugene H. Peterson, *The Message: The Bible in Contemporary Language* (Colorado Springs, CO: NavPress, 2005), Le 19:9–10.

someone who is considering a call to a rural ministry to be prepared for some culture shock. I disclose my doubt to encourage someone who has just accepted the call to a rural pastorate. You are not alone.

I count it a joy to discuss rural ministry. More specifically to issue a call to be a rural missionary. In this chapter I want to add to the many definitions of "rural", discuss some of the challenges rural communities across America's heartland face, speak to some misnomers of rural ministry, and finally encourage some rural ministry practices. In the few years the Lord has allowed me to pastor in northwest Missouri I have come to understand that the call to renewal in the heartland is not just a call to pastor, or to revitalize. Renewal in the heartland is a calling to be a rural missionary. A calling to root yourself in a church and in a community for the sake of the gospel, the glory of God, and His good favor upon your life.

Defining Your Rural

The phrase "rural America" in the minds of many raises a certain nostalgia. Both those outside and inside rural America have stereotype of what rural America is. Type the phrase "rural America" in an image search on any internet search engine and you will retrieve photos of barns, fields, tractors, pickup trucks, gravel roads, and open spaces. For many, those images are all rural America is. For others rural America is tourist stop. Or the home of their favorite university. For others rural is a place that is lacking. Lacking jobs, education, and opportunities. There is not one single description that can capture all of rural areas in America. The first task then for the rural missionary is to define not just rural, but their rural.

A Fluid Definition

Defining what makes a community rural is challenging. Differing agencies of the Federal Government uses more than two dozen definitions to describe rural communities.[111] These definitions are based on population numbers, population density, land use, location to urban areas and other criteria. An article entitled "What is Rural?" on the web page for the United States Department of Agriculture offers this way to define rural:

> The use of different definitions of rural by Federal agencies reflects the multidimensional qualities of rural America. In this article one point brought out for defining rural is, "The choice of a rural definition should be based on the purpose of the activity." For example, when looking for funding, it is helpful to clarify the definition of rural with the lending agency or foundation to be sure of your eligibility.

In other words which definition of rural chosen depends upon whom researchers hope to secure funding from. The definition of rural, at least for the federal government, is fluid at best.

Commonly shared among most definitions of what is and is not rural are descriptions that focus on what is missing. A community that is not urban nor suburban must be rural. Rural communities then are often defined not by their own characteristics but by what they lack. Glen Daman illustrates,

---

111 John Cromartie and Shawn Bucholtz, "Defining the 'Rural' in Rural America," *United States Department of Agriculture: Economic Research Service*, June 2008, https://www.ers.usda.gov/amber-waves/2008/june/defining-the-rural-in-rural-america/.

"we do not know what rural is. We know only what it is not."[112]

Vivian Howard is a celebrity chef. Her award-winning show on PBS, *A Chef's Life,* depicts her passion for farm to the table seasonal cuisine. In its fifth season, Chef Howard takes her viewers to the farms of North Carolina to discover more about the produce or livestock that will become the centerpiece of her dish.

My wife and I were watching one episode in which Chef Howard spoke lovingly of her rural community. The thought crossed my mind, "How rural is her rural?" A quick internet search later I discovered that Kinston, North Carolina, where she is based, is a city of over twenty thousand people. The city is located in Lenoir County, North Carolina. A county of over fifty-six thousand people.[113] Compared to my own rural, the town of Kinston is over twice its size. To equal the population of Lenoir County I would need to add the population of the surrounding five counties together. We both live in rural areas, but her rural is very different than my rural.

My point is not to debate who is more rural than others but to highlight that defining a rural community is more than quantitative metrics. No two rural communities are alike. What my own town and county share with Chef Howard's though is a people whose lifestyle is directly tied to the landscape, its history, and its future. What makes a rural

---

112 Glenn Daman, *The Forgotten Church: Why Rural Ministry Matters for Every Church in America,* (Chicago: Moody Publishers, 2018), 32.

113 "Quick Facts: Lenoir county, North Carolina: Kinston, North Carolina: United States," *United States Census Bureau,* https://www.census.gov/quickfacts/fact/table/lenoircountynorthcarolina,kinstoncitynorthcarolina,US/PST045217.

community then is not the absence of all things urban but the people and their way of life.

The rural missionary then should be setting their focus not only on the place but also on the people who make up the rural community and the way they live. "People in rural areas do not merely work on a farm, in a mine, or in the woods. They *are* famers, miners, and loggers who see their work as their life and their life in their work."[114] The call to rural ministry then is not only to a place. It is a call to a people. A people whose lifestyle intimately ties them to the land, the community, and each other.

Challenges to Revitalization in Rural America

Driving through the countryside it is easy to be lulled into the notion that "this is the simple life." For many families across rural America life is far from simple. For many rural families daily life is overshadowed by poverty. In some cases persistent poverty. Many in rural America have difficulty finding gainful employment. They struggle with illnesses and substance abuse. The growing rural elderly are often isolated and lonely. Many farmers are weighed down with guilt, feeling like failures, because their children have gone to the city to work. The farm that had been handed down generation after generation, ends with them. Rural communities across America are plagued with outmigration. While each rural community is unique they each have some common challenges. Challenges that directly affect how the local church goes about its ministries. Not every rural family or town has these challenges, but these challenges are critical to know in the rural area to which you are called.

---

114 Daman, 33.

Cultural Christianity

One of the biggest challenges for the church in rural America is the practice of cultural Christianity. Too often rural citizens view their towns as "Christian communities", substituting respect for God and country as all that is necessary for faith and salvation. Many in the rural community view their town, and those they share it with as the faithful few who, unlike the prodigal son, have not gotten swept away with the sinful allure of city living.[115] Regardless of what happens on Saturday night, God always forgives Sunday morning.

Country music superstar Keith Urban's 2015 song entitled "John Cougar, John Deere, John 3:16" captures the impact cultural Christianity has on rural America. The chorus tagline "John Cougar, John Deere, John 3:16" succinctly expresses the triad of the rural culture, rural industry and the melding of religion through it all. The song's writer, Shane McNally, tells *Billboard* magazine, "John Cougar references all the sort of sexual tension of teenage angst all of us were growing up in. John Deere represents the way that our parents worked and what we saw living in the country, and of course [there's] the element of religion."[116] Art though often says more than the artist intended.

---

115 I have heard pastors in rural pulpits proclaim the son who stayed home as more holy because he remained on the farm. The focus of their message was the sin of city living not the embrace of the one who was lost and now found.

116 Robyn Jaymes. "Story Behind 'John Cougar, John Deere, John 3:16," *Robyn's Corner* (blog), February 25, 2016, *94.9 Star Country – WSLCI Warm & Fuzzy/Story Behind the Song,* https://robynnscorner.949starcountry.com/story-behind/february-25-2016-story-behind-john-cougar-john-deere-john-316-by-keith-urban/.

Across America's heartland that "element of religion" permeates the community creating a superficial, cultural Christianity which is wed into every fabric of rural society. The bar owner is "alright with God" because he put a cross up. The business owner attributes their recent slump as a sign they need to attend church to get God back on their side. Cultural Christianity convinces people that they are eternally set because they dropped a $20 in the offering plate. "John Cougar, John Deere, John 3:16."

Across the country church attendance is greatest in rural communities.[117] Southerners are more likely to attend church weekly than anyone else (36 percent). Their example is followed by Midwesterners (32 percent), those in the Northeast (29 percent) and finally the West (25 percent).[118] The influence of cultural Christianity flows well beyond regularly attending church. Andrew Murrow writes, "Small towns tend to be loaded with religious non-Christians. They may not go to the church very often, but they generally believe that God exists and the Bible probably has something to say about him."[119] There will be conversations in many places in rural America of faith and football, spirituality and soybeans, Christ and cattle.

Often one of the greatest challenges facing a rural missionary is convincing others that they were not born

---

117 Michelle Dillon & Sarah Savage, "Values and Religion in Rural America: Attitudes Towards Abortion and Same-Sex Relations," Fall 2006, *Carsey Institute*, https://scholars.unh.edu/cgi/viewcontent.cgi?referer=&httpsredir=1&article=1011&context=carsey.

118 Ibid.

119 Andrew Murrow, *Small Town Mission: A Guide for Mission-Driven Communities*, (GCD Books, 2016) 96, cited in Glen Daman, *The Forgotten Church: Why Rural Ministry Matters for Every Church in America*, (Chicago: Moody, 2018), 90.

Christian. That a life devoted to following Jesus Christ is more than the ethics of honesty and hard-work. To suggest that someone might not actually be believer is often perceived as an attack upon their character and cultural identity. The rural missionary pastor must graciously and clearly, each word seasoned with salt (Col 4:6), declare Christ (Col 4:3). Cultural Christianity may make for a superficially moral community but it blinds the hearts and minds of the lost to the gospel. One of the great blessings of living in a religious permeated culture is the freedom and ease in which matters of faith can be raised. Conversations can be directed towards Christ while shopping for a loaf of bread. The Lord can take a quick stop in the local library to be the right time to extend an invitation to attend church. In general, government offices and schools are not worried about reserving a public space for times of prayer and evangelistic calls. The same cultural Christianity that can be a barrier to the freedom found in the gospel cans also serve to create avenues by which salvation in Jesus, and Jesus alone, can be declared.

Challenges Many Rural People Face

Many rural communities across the heartland are riddled with issues once thought to be isolated to the urban core. Finding a job that can provide income to combat the generational poverty is difficult. Generational poverty has a noose around the poorest of the poor. Substance abuse, including opioids, and the ever-persistent outmigration of the best and the brightest plague communities across the heartland. Many will idyllically drive through the country side oblivious to the fractured families, social structures and persistent poverty that exists beneath the fresh air. The depth of problems prompted Osha Gray Davidson to identify rural America as the new ghetto. She writes:

The word 'ghetto' speaks of the rising poverty rates, the chronic unemployment, and the recent spread of low-wage, dead-end jobs. It speaks of relentless deterioration of health-care systems, schools, roads, buildings, and the emergence of homelessness, hunger, and poverty. It speaks, too, of the inevitable outmigration of the best and the brightest youth. Above all, the word 'ghetto' speaks of the better stew of resentment, anger, and despair that simmers silently in those left-behind. The hard and ugly truth is not only that we have failed to solve the problems of our urban ghettos, but that we have replicated them in miniature a thousand times across the American countryside."[120]

Many places in the heartland are being ravished. Little attention to the challenges of rural America cause many to see rural America as the forgotten America.[121] Policy makers focus their attention on the sway of voters in the metro areas whose sheer numbers determine the outcomes of elections. Some of the factors shaping the rural America include employment, poverty, drug abuse and outmigration.

Employment and Poverty

For some in rural America employment opportunities are a persistent challenge. Compared to 34 percent of urban dwellers, and 22 percent to suburban residents, 42 percent of those in rural communities say that the availability of jobs is a major problem.[122] The United States Department of

---

120 Osha Gray Davidson, *Broken Heartland: The Rise of America's Rural Ghetto*, (Iowa City: University of Iowa Press, 1996), 158.

121 Greg Jaffe and Juliet Eilperin, "Tom Vilsack's lonely fight for a 'forgotten' rural America," September 26, 2016, *The Washington Post*, https://www.washingtonpost.com/politics/tom-vilsacks-lonely-fight-for-a-forgotten-rural-america/2016/09/26/62d7ee64-7830-11e6-ac8e-cf8e0dd91dc7_story.html?utm_term=.2a56b9d10643.

122 Kim Paker, Juliana Menasche Horowitz, Anna Brown, Ricahrd Fry, D'Vera Cohn and Ruth Igielnik, "What Unites and Divides

Agriculture has determined that after six years of post-recession economic recovery rural employment remains limited.[123] Those in the rural community who are employed generally earn less than their urban counterparts. Between 2012 and 2016 those in urban regions earned slightly greater than $14,000 more than those in rural.[124]

Pew Research asked Americans if "they have enough income to lead the life they want." Researchers discovered that those in urban (68%), suburban (59%) and rural (62%) regions say they don't currently have enough income to lead the kind of life they want.[125] For many in our consumer driven, gather as much as you can culture, the response of "I don't have enough" is not surprising. What is interesting about this survey though is the follow up question of whether or not respondents believe they *will* have enough money in the future to live the kind of life they want. Nearly half of those in the urban (46 percent) and suburban (49 percent) areas believe that their future life will be better than their current one.[126]

In the rural community though, 63 percent of adults who do not presently have the enough income to lead the kind of

Urban, Suburban and Rural Communities," *Pew Research Center: Social and Demographic Trends,* May 22, 2018, http://www.pewsocialtrends.org/2018/05/22/what-unites-and-divides-urban-suburban-and-rural-communities/.

123 "Rural America at a Glance: 2017 Edition," *United States Department of Agriculture,* November 2017.

124 Ibid.

125 "What Unites and Divides Urban, Suburban and Rural Communities," *Pew Research Center: Social and Demographic Trends,* http://www.pewsocialtrends.org/2018/05/22/what-unites-and-divides-urban-suburban-and-rural-communities/

126 Ibid.

life they want, do not expect to have it in the future.[127] Many rural people do not see their lives getting any better. They did not see their parents' lives, or their grandparents' lives get better. Why should they expect that for theirs?

Accompanying low-wage jobs and poverty are the issues of persistent-poverty in rural America. The Economic Research Service of the United States Department of Agriculture defines persistent-poverty as those areas with 20 percent or more of the population living in poverty as indicated in the 1980, 1990, and 2000 census.[128] People who live in persistent poverty have lived that way for thirty years or more.

Neighborhood Works America states that 85 percent of persistent-poverty counties reside outside of metro areas.[129] The University of New Hampshire's Carsey School of Public Policy, cites research indicating that a rural child is more than twice as likely as an urban child to live in the vicinity of persistent poverty.[130] Children who live in communities plagued by persistent poverty "are less likely to have timely immunizations, have lower academic achievement, and

---

127 Ibid.

128 "Rural America at a Glance: 2017 Edition," November 2017, *United States Department of Agriculture: Economic Research Service*, 5.

129 Bill Bynum, Chrystel Cornelius, Jim King, Nick Mitchell-Bennett, "Turning the Tide on Persistent Rural Poverty: Blueprint for a Path Forward," April 9, 2017, *Neighborhood Works America*, http://www.neighborworks.org/Media-Center/Research/Turning-the-Tide-on-Persistent-Rural-Poverty-Blueprint-for-a-Path-Forward

130 https://carsey.unh.edu/publication/infographic/rural-child-poverty-higher.

generally less engaged in schools, and face higher delinquency rates in adolescent years."[131]

For decades much of the focus and resources to combat poverty have been attuned to the urban poor. Many programs, grants, and agencies who mission it is to combat poverty and the symptoms associated with poverty are not available to the rural community simply because they are not urban.

My wife oversees a food program that serves seven surrounding counties. The focus of her program is to provide food to children on the weekends during the school year. Each year she adds more and more children to the program. To help fund the program she applied for a grant from a corporation. Her grant request was denied on the basis that the corporation did not have any retail stores in the immediate area. The corporation wanted to direct their funding towards urban and suburban programs because of the greater likelihood that people in those areas would shop in their stores. I do not fault them for their focus. I simply want to illustrate that though nearly equal in need the rural poor do not receive similar attention as their urban counterparts.

The church in the rural towns across America must have some strategy to participate in alleviating the symptoms of poverty. Poverty this side of eternity will not be eliminated. Jesus said the poor will always be with us (Mt 14:7). As long as we live with the effects of the fall there will be suffering. The church cannot eliminate poverty. That is not her mission. But, to fulfill her mission of making disciples the church

---

131 Andrew Schaefer, Beth Mattingly, and Kenneth M. Johnson, "Child Poverty Higher and More Persistent in Rural America," February 23, 2016, *University of New Hampshire: Carsey School of Public Policy*, https://carsey.unh.edu/publication/rural-child-poverty-higher.

especially in rural America needs to have some strategy to feed the hungry, give water to the thirsty, clothe the naked, welcome the stranger, and visit the prisoner (Mt 25:35-36).

Healthcare

A second challenge facing the rural communities that will affect a church's ministries is the matter of healthcare. The Health and Policy Institute with Georgetown University report and Rural and Urban Heath states that while 20 percent of the U.S. population lives in rural areas fewer than 11 percent of physicians practice in rural areas. The shortage of medical professionals is attributed to "lower salaries, geographic isolation from peers and educational opportunities, and fewer amenities such as schools and recreation."[132] Again, many rural communities have great needs and few resources to address them.

The mission of the church is to make disciples not build hospitals. But a church may be called upon to help drive someone to a doctor's visit in a neighborhood town or closest city. Some of the dearest saints are those who give up their day to drive someone an hour-and-a-half one way for a chemo treatment. The church in rural America has some practical opportunities to love on people.

The effects of suicide in the rural community also directly affects a church's ministry. Julie Beck in *The Atlantic* highlights a 2015 study published in *JAMA Pediatrics* reporting that between 1996 and 2010 suicide rates among rural peoples between the ages of 10 to 24 were nearly twice that of urban areas.[133] More recently the Brookings Institute

---

132 "Rural and Urban Health: Data Profile Number 7," January 2003, *Georgetown University: Health Policy Institute*, *https://hpi.georgetown.edu/agingsociety/pubhtml/rural/rural.html*.

reported that suicide rates from 1999 to 2015 across America increased by less than thirty percent. But in the rural community suicide rates "surged over 40%, from just over 15 per 100,000 to roughly 22 per 100,000."[134] One death by suicide in any context is one too many.

One of the most frequently cited way to address suicide is through avenues of mental health. Unfortunately, many of those who live in rural communities do not have access to mental health care. Beck writes, that of there are nearly 4,000 areas in the U.S. designated as having shortages of mental-healthcare providers.

In the rural community often the only people with any level of counseling training are high school guidance counselors and pastors. A pastor may be called upon to speak to a crisis situation that is well beyond their training. A rural pastor should know their limitations, know their training, know where to find additional resources, and seek continued to advance their skills to care for those in their town.

The "Hallowing-out of Rural America"

Outmigration is perhaps the greatest challenge to rural America. Between 2010 and 2014 two out of three rural counties lost population.[135] The USDA estimates 462,000

133 Julie Beck. "The Growing Risk of Suicide in Rural America," *The Atlantic*, March 10, 2015, https://www.theatlantic.com/health/archive/2015/03/the-growing-risk-of-suicide-in-rural-america/387313/.

134 Alex Berezow, "Suicides In Rural America Increased more than 40% in 16 Years." *American Council on Science and Health*, March 16, 2017, https://www.acsh.org/news/2017/03/16/suicides-rural-america-increased-more-40-16-years-11010.

135 Andrew Amelinckx, "The State of Rural American in 2015," December 22, 2015, *Modern Farmer*, https://modernfarmer.com/2015/12/the-state-of-rural-america-2015/.

more people moved out of rural communities than moved in.[136] Many of the outmigrants are young people who leave for college, to join the military or better job opportunities. The USDA estimates that third or more of rural America High School graduates leave their towns and do not return.[137] The book *Hallowing out the Middle: The Rural Brain Drain and What It Means for America,* in which husband and wife sociologist team Patrick Carr and Maria Kefalas relay their observations of education in rural America. The couple spent a year and half in Ellis, Iowa interviewing and observing this rural community correlated their experiences to the whole of rural America. Carr and Kefalas' experiment led them to observe a paradox in rural life best summarized by an interview with a high school guidance counselor who said, "the best kids go while the ones with the biggest problems stay, and then we have to deal with their kids in the schools in the next generation."[138] The two write:

> Schools devote their energies to the most serious and committed students, and young people who are adrift get focus and maturity, not to mention, money, from work. Yet it is that compromise, which makes so much sense

---

136 John Cromartie, "Rural Areas Show Overall Population Decline and Shifting Regional Patterns of Population Change," September 5, 2017, *United States Department of Agriculture: Economic Research Service,* https://www.ers.usda.gov/amber-waves/2017/september/rural-areas-show-overall-population-decline-and-shifting-regional-patterns-of-population-change/.

137 John Comtrie, "Moving Back to Rural America: Why Some Return Home and What Difference it Makes," June 2, 2015, *U.S. Department of Agriculture: Research and Science,* *https://www.usda.gov/media/blog/2015/06/2/moving-back-rural-america-why-some-return-home-and-what-difference-it-makes.*

138 Patrick J. Carr and Maria J. Kefalas, "The Rural Brain Drain," September 21, 2009, *The Chronicle of Higher Education,* https://www.chronicle.com/article/The-Rural-Brain-Drain/48425.

during those high-school years, that ultimately comes back to betray the community and its young people.[139]

Article after article, some academic and others anecdotal, stress the struggles that communities in rural America share when the best and the brightest of their young people leave. Today the most valuable export from rural America are "young people, not hogs, steel, beef, corn or soybeans."[140] In many ways rural communities are cannibalizing their future. Outmigration impacts the local church in at least two ways.

First, outmigration hurts the sustainability of the local church. Corresponding to shrinking population is a decreasing economy. A reduction in a community's economic viability will ultimately impact a church's ability to pay their bills, offer programs, support missions, and hire a pastor. Those graduating from Bible college or seminary may be attracted to rural ministry but cannot support themselves, let alone a family on the salary offered by a rural church plagued by outmigration.

In an economically challenged area churches may need to creatively address their pastoral support. They may need to pulpit share in which a pastor serves two or more congregations. The church may only be able to support a bi-vocational pastor or seek assistance from the Association or denominational agency to develop and train lay pastors. All three are extremely viable options.

A church's expectations also need to be examined. A rural church with a lay or bi-vocational pastor should not have the same expectations as they would for a full-time pastor. I have tremendous respect and admiration for bi-

---

139 Ibid.

140 Ibid.

vocational pastors. I am greatly concerned though as to how many bi-vocational pastors after spending 40 to 50 hours a week at their job, raising their own families, and then giving another 20 or 30 hours each week to a church are running on fumes. Churches need to have honest conversations with themselves about what can realistically be expected.

Secondly, outmigration will continue to increase the social needs of the surrounding community, needs that a local church may not be able to adequately address. The church will need to choose what it will do, what it will not, and be okay with that.

Third, outmigration means that people, high school grads in particular, will move out of the community and many will never return. Pew Research has found that in the Midwest nearly half of the residents have spent their entire lives in their hometown[141] which means the other half do not, implying that rural communities will have people moving in and out the church and town.

There are not many things the church can do regarding outmigration, save one. The rural church needs to change its outlook on outmigration. The church must look at those who leave the community not through the lenses of loss but through the lenses of sent. Recognize that many of your high school graduates will leave your rural town and they will not return. Your church will have some young men and women who will stay. Invest yourself in those who stay. Disciple them to be rural missionaries alongside you. But for those who leave and may only return for holiday visits, intentionally send them out to be missionaries where they are going. If we truly believe that God appoints the times and boundaries of

---

141 D'Vera Cohn and Rich Morin, "Who Moves? Who Stays Put? Where's Home?" December 17, 2008, *Pew Research Center: Social & Demographic Trends*, http://www.pewsocialtrends.org/2008/12/17/who-moves-who-stays-put-wheres-home/.

men (Acts 17:26) then celebrate both his leading of people away and his keeping of people where they are.

Rural People Need the Gospel

Rural people need the gospel. That is not to say that urban and suburban people do not. To say rural people need the gospel is not only an affirmation that all people need the gospel, but it is also a declaration that those people in the places that feel forgotten need the gospel.

Much attention has been drawn to the people in the cities. Paul's missionary strategy seems to take him to the commercial centers of the major cities of the Roman empire to proclaim Christ. But Paul did not regulate his ministry to the cities alone. He traveled to the Galatian region and Phrygia as well (Acts 18:23). The word which "region" is translated from describes the space lying between places, the space around a city. It can even mean the land which is cultivated.[142] These definitions certainly sound descriptive of rural places. The cities are vital but not to the neglect of the rural.

I in no manner intend to add to the battle lines of rural or urban, agrarian or industrial, though my tone may have already have sketched those lines. My aim is simple; to identify some of the challenges rural people face and to help prepare the men and women who will be the feet of good news to the highways and the hedges. The rural church, and those denominational agencies who they are aligned with, cannot be guilty of ignoring the struggles that many rural mission fields face. They cannot be overwhelmed by them either. The rural church has been placed by God where and

---

142 "χώρα", *Thayers Definition*, https://www.studylight.org/desk/interlinear.cgi?t1=nas&q1=Acts+18%3 A23&x=0&y=0

when it is to love their first love (Reve 2:4-5) and make disciples (Mt 28:19, Acts 1:8). If they do not, our Lord Jesus, as He did in Ephesus, will remove the lampstand. Rural America desperately needs the lampstand of the church to burn bright.

Ministry in Rural America

After reading some of the challenges facing rural America, if you are not already ministering in rural setting, you may be thinking, "Why in the world would I want to go to a rural church, let alone a rural church in need of revitalization?" There are some great reasons to pastor in a rural community. First, I want to dispel three misnomers of rural ministry.

Misnomers of Rural Ministry

Just as the idyllic scene of rural America is not accurate, neither are the criticisms from afar. There are some misnomers of rural ministry. First, is that rural communities are resistant to change. Rural communities are continuously changing. Their change may not be as obvious as the change brought by a new shopping complex in suburbia, but rural communities are undergoing tremendous change. Fields once navigated by memory and eyesight are now mapped with GPS location. Broadband internet is penetrating many rural regions. A change that is welcomed with great optimism and hopes that highspeed internet will be a tool to help reshape the future of rural America. Churches in rural America are using tools that were once thought to be only available to the cutting edge ministries in the cities. Rural communities are not resistant to change. Rural communities are resistant to arrogance.

Many change agents who leave rural communities because "they just won't change" came into the community with the mission to cause change but never gave a convincing reason to change. Those pastors are often seen as using the rural church as a stepping stone to move on to bigger and what is supposedly better. Rural people may have been born at night, but it wasn't last night. Rural people, especially rural leaders, can quickly discern when a pastor is lovingly leading them and when he is using them to get to his next church. Rural churches do not need pastors who tell them to change for the sake of change. What they need, and what they are willing to accept, are pastors who loving lead change because they are more concerned about their future than the present. Secondly, rural communities are depicted as leery of outsiders, a misnomer that is reinforced by old sitcoms. As with change, rural people are not unaccepting of those who move into their community from the outside. What is interpreted as an unwillingness to embrace someone from outside the community is often from someone who moved into a rural community and instead of adjusting to their new culture they worked to make their new place just like the one they moved from.

Are some rural communities more difficult to be accepted in than others? Certainly. It will take longer to be accepted in a rural community than perhaps a suburban one. One reason it can take longer for someone outside the community to be accepted is because they are being tested. People who live in rural communities are committed to their town. Many have chosen to stay. Or return. Rural people want to see how committed you are to them.

One entrepreneur relocated to my own community. Their non-profit business idea was sound and met an unexplored need. But every time I heard this leader address a crowd he spoke poorly of the community and regularly compared where he was to where he had been. He easily let all who would listen know how much better other places where. The non-profit he began was reluctantly accepted but he was not. The agency board that he recruited, fired him and rebranded. Now that agency is making a positive impact in our community. The town was not leery of the outsider. They were tired of hearing how much better everyplace else was. When moving into a rural community do not expect to be immediately accepted as one of their own. Someone who has lived in that community their entire life will have more credibility than you do. Pave your acceptance by celebrating your new community. Avoid the temptation to compare where you are to where you've been. Buy and wear a t-shirt or a hat with the local school mascot on it. Make a conscious effort to celebrate what is good in your town. Many in the rural community know the problems they have. They don't need you to point them out.

A third misnomer of rural communities is that they are willing to accept the status quo. What I have found though is many, especially leaders in rural communities, are not so much willing to accept the status quo as they are slow to dismiss what is tried and true. An old beat up truck is held on to because it is reliable. What works and can be relied upon will always be chosen over what is new and untried.

When coming into a rural community take extra time to get to know the people. Create time for them to get to know you. It may take longer to accomplish something in a rural community than in a suburban one. You may find the efficiency of the rural community to be slower than what seems necessary. You may spend twice as much time in the checkout line at the store because the cashier is asking about a customer's family. You may have many conversations about the weather, how much rain fell, and deer hunting. That is okay. Those are some of the reasons people are moving to rural America.

Pastoring in Rural America

At the time of writing I have pastored in my rural community for over six years. Previous ministries included old suburbs located inside a city beltway, a university bedroom town and an exurban community. In the short time that I have been privileged to pastor in my rural community (yes, in a rural community six years is short) I have learned some important lessons in order to pastor well.

First, in rural America plan to pastor your community, not just your church. In rural America the title "pastor" still has clout that has been lost in the urban and suburban realms. Being a pastor in a county seat rural town can open relationships more easily than simply relocating for another job. But those relationships do not happen naturally. They must be developed. One way to develop community ties is to pastor the community.

Pastoring the community means showing up to community events. It is caring about others who are not a part of your church. Pastoring the community means that when you are out, you speak well of the community and of others. In a rural town you never know who is related to who. Be contagiously gracious. Even if that is not your personality. Spend time working to get to know the other pastors in your community. They are addressing some of the same problems you are. If someone from their church visits yours, don't chase them. Be kind, be gracious, but call their pastor. Let them know that one of their families visited your church. There may be a legitimate reason for their visit. You may find out that you want to pray they move on. You will not agree with every theological issue with the other pastors in the area, but you are not in competition but cooperation for the kingdom.

Pastoring your community means the being same pastor when you are at the grocery store in your shorts and flip-flops as you are inside the church sanctuary.[143] Be prepared to discuss spiritual matters when out. Going to the store for a gallon of milk can become a time to visit with one of your church members. Work hard to be a part of the community, not just the pastor at the church.

Second, move slow. People whose lifestyle is tied to the land know that it takes time to produce something of quality. That same sentiment is transferred to nearly every aspect of life. Decisions may take a little longer. What you may be able to accomplish in one year in a suburban church might take three in a rural. Take time to get to know your people. Let them get to know you.

Third, show that you care about the community as well as your church. Get involved in the community by serving with groups that make the town better. Serve on non-profit boards, attend chamber of commerce events, be a part of civic organizations. Help to organize a community service day with the other churches in town. In rural America you are there to create blessings not only receive them.

Finally, be prepared for loss. In a rural community you have those who are stable. Those who were born there, bred there and will die there. They see no reason to go anywhere else. Anywhere. For any reason. But you also have those who will only be there for a season.

I have observed that those who move out of the rural community and are not recent high school grads, are people who have had an impact in the community. They are at the teachers and school administrators who also serve on the

---

143 Yes, we still call it the "sanctuary." It's not the worship center or the auditorium. It is a sanctuary. A respite.

finance committee and the board of a local nonprofit. The rural movers are the professionals whose children have completed their high school education, now they have an empty nest, so they move for different career opportunities. While half the population of a rural community may never leave, the half that does had a real impact.

At the close of every school year I celebrate our high school graduates and then wait to see what families will be moving in the next six weeks. To pastor in rural America you need to be prepared for loss. As mentioned earlier one way to proactively prepare for loss is to change your thinking about those who move out of the area. Look at those high school graduates and families who leave not as those whom you lost but rather as those whom you sent.

Looking at those who leave changes the objective and raises the sense of urgency in your ministry. The objective of working with young people changes from ensuring they have something to do to training them to take the gospel to the ends of the earth. The Lord may let you influence a family for a short season so they can be leaders in another church in a different community. Your sense of urgency is raised because you may have them in your ministry for a short season. Send them, don't just lose them.

Conclusion

I am making a couple of assumptions about you the reader. Since you are reading a book on revitalizing the church in rural America, I am assuming that you are, in some form or fashion, a church leader from rural America. That whatever region or state in America is home for you your work, your play, and your life are rural. I am also assuming that you are well aware of the great challenges facing rural America. Challenges that at best feel ignored and at worst forgotten. Challenges of which you don't need to be reminded.

My approach to this chapter is from the perspective of what I had wished someone had told me before accepting a call not just to a rural pastorate but to be a rural missionary. To be a rural missionary you must define your unique rural community, know the people in your rural community, and immerse yourself within the community. A rural missionary is one, who by God's grace, will see a renewal in one corner the heartland. Renewal that can spread from sea to shining sea.

Chapter 13
The Top Ten Mistakes Churches Make in Rural Revitalization

Though the cherry trees don't blossom and the strawberries don't ripen,
Though the apples are worm-eaten and the wheat fields stunted, Though
the sheep pens are sheepless and the cattle barns empty, I'm singing joyful
praise to God. I'm turning cartwheels of joy to my Savior God.[144]

During my study sabbatical researching rural American churches, I wanted to get to the issues and challenges they were facing so I began reflecting long before my five trips to five states, about critical questions I might ask them about their individual communities and those who worshiped in their churches. It is estimated that there are more than 200,000 congregations serving rural America today! These churches have 7,153,937 congregants. For instance, within my denomination of Southern Baptist there are 20,227 rural churches as reported during the last Church Membership Survey (CMS). If you count all protestant denominations the total adherents are 31.5 million members which attend a rural church. Because every community has its own individual history it was important that I got to know about its past. Every church likewise has its own history. Some histories are good and some are bad. I asked each pastor simple questions about how the community came into being? I wanted to know if there was a predominant individual in which the community was named after. As I met with these pastors I asked if they knew what the focus of the communities' leaders were. To my surprise most were not even aware of the city council and various other community entities. You would do well to be aware of the focal symbol of one's rural community. In the rural church landscape many indigenous pastors are largely unnoticed. And when not overlooked, they

---

[144] Eugene H. Peterson, *The Message: The Bible in Contemporary Language* (Colorado Springs, CO: NavPress, 2005), Hab 3:17–18.

are made light of. In truth any effort to be of help to rural church life in America must understand and address these preachers. In many areas they are the dominant expression of ministry.

Doug Walrath took a last look at small church life, shortly before he retired in 1990 from Bangor Seminary, by doing a study of rural pastors in New England. He was critical of most of them at two points: (1) they were informed by Industrial Age thinking which stresses efficiency, standardization, tasks more than relationships, and the concept that there is "one best way to do things"; (2) many just passed through on their way to the city. Walrath, who played a key role in the resurgence of interest in small churches, contended that rural culture is not like urban Industrial Age culture. Rural folk tend the "make do" on the farm and in the church. Their explanation of "why things happen" is more "spiritual" and less "mechanistic" than that of modern society. He also asked pastors to stay with rural churches for the long haul, doing the work of the church in the local idiom. He told them to find satisfaction in impacting the lives of people deeply.145 (See Chapter 8, Carl Dudley, et al Carriers of Faith.)

There are numerous rural churches and pastors who fit Doug Walrath's description. They have stayed the course and been found faithful in a rural setting for a long time. These are the indigenous or homegrown preachers that one finds in the Made in America, rural churches particularly in the South. Yet, an argument can be made that some of them are often too entwined to the culture to speak a divinatory word, too much like their congregations in world view and in actions to lead them to a godlier journey; too tangled to their mutual pre-industrial culture to confront and contest its faults. Walrath is correct in his assessment that if the mainline

---

145 Carl Dudley, et al Carriers of Faith. See Chapter 8.

denominational pastors that he found in his study of New England, are in the ditch on one side of the road, in is a fair assessment to declare that many rural pastors in the south are in the ditch on the other side of the road. Both are flawed. Aren't we all? Yet, both have a role to play.

My parents rural area was a town square with a large clock in the park. Understanding the communities primary economic function is useful. My family tree has a rural ancestor who live near Valley Forge and was an honored Quaker in the Sons of the American Revolution. Are there any characters that provide a little bit of historical flavor to your area? Within your five-mile radius what is the ethnic make-up? Would you sense that your civic leaders feel like your area is on the upswing or the decline? Who are the young dreamers in your community? Being aware of these issues as well as any projects which are being utilized to bring about renewal could prove helpful for the rural church revitalizer. What are the top ten mistakes most often made in rural church revitalization efforts? Let's take a look.

Ten Mistakes Most Often Made in Rural Church Revitalization Efforts

Handcuffing the Church Through Feeble Prayer

The Lord is at work all around the nation through rural churches and town and country churches. Often churches which struggle to remain viable in the rural landscape have replaced prayer time with play times. Drawing together to seek the face of God has been replaced by feel good programs designed to cater to the self-interests of the remain few. Most churches are afraid to admit that they do not practice the spiritual discipline of prayer. Preachers preach on the need for abundant waves of prayer being offered up to the Lord on behalf of others and His church. Laymen discuss the importance of prayer and yet seldom are their deep times of prayer for the work of the Lord and His church. Prayerlessness prevails in most churches and that breaks the heart of God.146 The vast number of churches that are in trouble today and in need of revitalization or renewal are a display of either prayerlessness or at the very least possess a prayer focus centered around what we desire over what the Lord has planned for His church.

Not Taking Family Systems Seriously

Most rural churches are made up of five generational family trees. Yet most are found to consistently have active within the fellowship three generations. A family system is simply a small group system of tightly knitted together individuals which are related and will respond in a local church community as one fully aligned coalition. These family units are a viable force within rural churches and a wise pastor must not ignore such systems. In these rural churches there are usually great grandparents, grandparents, parents, children, and grandchildren which form a family group Each family in the family system is a small group in the rural church. Members are important stakeholders in the rural congregation as they believe they own their church. That is why it would be wise for the rural church revitalizer to embrace family systems and not antagonize them. Though most pastors see themselves as the leader, often within rural churches every participant regardless if they are a member or not are assigned an informal pecking order in the church. Unless the pastor has been there for a long time they are not seen as the influencing leader. That is saved for an older grandfather who has been instrumental in keeping the rural church afloat. In the rural church I restarted, I was warned to

---

146 More can be learned regarding feeble prayer and how it handcuffs the church from Chapter Two of *Slaying the Dragons of Church Revitalization: Dealing with the Critical Issues that are Hurting Your Church* by going to RenovateConference.org/bookstore or by going to Amazon Books!

stay away from two men in the church because they hated pastor. That was a lie. They loved pastors but they wanted them to be prepared and part of that was meeting with them regularly for counsel and advise. Granted you often will have gate keepers that have their own agendas. Yet, if your ego is intact you can handle shared leadership and allow the patriarch his due. It will only help you pastor in the renewing of a rural church. when these patriarch's we allowed to be involved, things where accomplished. When they were ignored, the family system kept anything from moving forward. I discovered that it was to the best interest of the church, and my ministry for that matter, to include these two godly men in the decision-making process. I choose to become a family member which meant I went to ball games and birthday parties. I attended family gatherings to which I was invited. By adapting to the family system and learning the ways of the families within that rural church, I became an effective rural servant of those dear people.147 To help you visualize it another way, by embracing the existing family systems within the rural church it could serve as one's survival kit for becoming an effective minister to the congregation and community.

The Church Revitalizer is Not Committed to the Call to Revitalize the Church

Has the Lord called you to be a church revitalizer of a rural church? If so realize that this is a unique calling today. You will be expected to anchor in and become part of everything that is taking place around your rural context. You are called then to lead your people and feed the people which the Lord has assigned to you. They need to know you and

---

147 The help you think through these concepts, Lewis A. Parks has sixteen thoughts on family systems in the local small church. You can find them at *Leading Ideas*, February 14, 2007 and it is titled: *Small Churches as Healthy Family Systems.*

grow with you. You must become a tender of your sheep. If you are going to revitalize a rural church it has a commitment to rural placed upon ones calling. During my study time with rural churches I noticed just how many rural pastors were absent from the rural landscape. They commuted into the area to do the work of ministry for a few hours weekly and then questioned why the Lord had not chosen to bless their efforts. Rural revitalization requires an all-in mentality. It is not a calling for the meek pastor. It is not a calling for the mean-spirited pastor. It is not for the petty pastor. Pastoring a rural church is not a calling for the impatient pastor. It is not a calling for the weak-willed pastor. It is a calling for one who chooses by divine call to love deeply and willfully give of one's self to a declining community that needs Jesus and an ambassador for the Lord Jesus. give you the opportunity to practice this skillset often. Without change nothing is going to happen. Remember that you were called to this ministry not hired!

Failure of the Revitalizer to Adequately Assess the Churches Ability to be Revitalized

Not every rural church pastor I met with desired to see their church renewed. One pastor told me during a break that he had a good thing going and if he brought up the subject of revitalization, it would require more than he was willing to give. He spoke of only desiring to preach on Sunday and wanted nothing more than a place to preach. I asked him if he had assessed the community's ability to be revitalized and he responded affirmatively that it was an area ripe with opportunity, but he was not the one to lead them. That would need to be done by the next pastor. If you are fortunate to be a rural community that has the chance for a church to be renewed then count that as a blessing. About one third of the churches I interviewed were lucky enough to be placed in such an area. Not stepping up to lead a church in such a community will usually result in a new church plant coming into the area and doing what the rural pastor refused to consider.

Not Developing Initially Sufficient Resources for the Effort and then the Process Stalls

It takes momentum for any church to begin to be renewed. That is certainly true in the rural portions of our land. Many who want to renew rural churches have not first taken the time to consider the resources in people and finances that will be necessary for revitalization. Taking the time to gain readiness for revitalization and not prematurely rushing the process is important. Many urban fringe churches are beginning to embrace the rural church landscape as a result of the nurals moving out of the city landscape preferring a simpler lifestyle as they move towards retirement. These churches are spending their mission money focused towards helping a rural church continue to minister to those living in either town and country or rural environments. In a day where so many denominations are all focused on the urban city landscape, it is refreshing to see churches putting their resources towards keeping the rural American church afloat. I know of a mission endeavor that has recently focused only on the city and is spending multiple millions of dollars on cities and yet all they can get out of their efforts annually is about 250 churches. That is a huge investment for such a small number of churches. We need to prayerfully embrace the rural communities all across America and work side by side with their pastors to minister to those who have chosen rural as a preferred lifestyle, less we hand over our rural heritage to cults.

Missing the Opportunity to Differentiate the Revitalization Effort with the Previous Functions of the Church

Many church revitalizers when working on a rural revitalization effort often struggle with weather or not they should close the rural church down for a season and then start it up again as something new. While it might help in most areas of our land, it is never wise to consider such a practice in the rural community unless the church is already closed and you are reopening it under a new name and focus. What is important to your effort is that you develop some distance between the previous functions which caused your church to decline and initiate new functions for the church that express opportunity over decline. Having the opportunity to say to the community we are trying something new can help. Disconnecting to the things that caused the church to decline and connecting to new values and ideals might be the thing to spark a new interest in the rural church. Consider why a church plant can come in to an area and see people drawn to something new. It provided an opportunity for those frustrated with the status quo to embrace the chance to reconnect with the community in a new way. Creating a time of transition can actually help the rural church and pastor prepare for the future of renewal.

Failure to Have a Revitalization Plan for Monday Through Saturday

For the rural church thinking one day a week is sufficient has past. Sunday is not enough! Make every day matter. Far too many rural pastors feel our work at church does not count. While our plates may seem full, our lives my not be. As a result, many choose to simply disengage to some degree. The result is that they are likely to become unproductive. Every morning makes a deposit of 86,400 seconds into one's life. You must live in the present on the deposit you are given. Remember the clock is running! The Psalmist reminds us when he declares: *Teach us to number our days carefully so that we may develop wisdom in our hearts* (Psalm 90:12). The Apostle Paul tells us to be ready for the coming of the day. Leon Morris says that we should live wholeheartedly for Christ. "Already" gives a touch of urgency to his exhortation; he is not speaking of some remote period for which they could make leisurely preparation but of imperative action now.148

All throughout the scripture we see that each day matters and not just the Lord's Day. We need to have a revitalization plan for Monday through Saturday if we are going to see renewal come to the rural church. In other portions of this book, I have shared how various churches created ways for other days to matter as they embraced their communities and culture. Don't drift through the day with no plan or idea of how you'll spend it. For the rural church revitalizer such a practice could actually set you up for failure because you become more of a drifter. You drift through the day, you allow distractions and interruptions to dictate how your day will go. Fill your day with intentions. Do not leave it up to chance. It's better to be pro-active than re-active. Success does not just occur one day in our lives. Every day of our life is preparation for the next. We need to make every day count in rural revitalization efforts.

Not Insuring You and Your Family are Healthy enough for the Tension Involved in Rural Renewal

There is a great deal of stress involved in rural revitalization if you are the newbie to the community. Some of it will be spiritually, psychologically, and physically. Often

---

148 Leon Morris, the *Epistle to the Romans*, The Pillar New Testament Commentary (Grand Rapids, MI; Leicester, England: W.B. Eerdmans; Inter-Varsity Press, 1988), 470 - 471.

revitalizers have a misconception that they will become an insider when in reality they will always be an outsider. Learn to live with it and press on. I work hard to embrace the membership of my rural church I pastored, but in the end, I was just the hired gun brought in to keep their church from closing and bring it back. Every time there was a push towards something outside of the norm, it was met with hesitation even though the church was being renewed. It is hard on the family of the church revitalizer so be sure they are up to the challenge. Remember you are in it for the long term. It is a long-term investment towards renewal and a minimal investment of 1000 days.

Stop Cloning and Start Connecting

There are many in the rural community which went to church in the past but for some reason have opted out. The rural church revitalizer would do well to understand that the unchurched and dechurched population needs the ministry of a pastor in the community. It is also urgent that you eliminate the cloning of what you did as a Church Revitalizer in a former revitalization effort. Failure to match a renewal strategy with specific church and community changes will eventually defeat any chances you have to turn around the church. Develop ways to connect with the community and the culture.

The Dreaded Reality of Rural Renewal

I was shocked when a spiritually mature church member came to me as the revitalizer and suggested that even though we were not fully renewed, it would be best to cease the process because it was getting good again. I mistakenly thought that because good things were happening in the church and people were getting saved and baptized, that we were well on our way towards renewal. The church could pay its bills. We were back giving to mission causes. Young people had returned to regular attendance and families were back making this their church home. As a seminary educated minister who has worked for about more than twenty years with rural area churches and now a leader of church revitalization all around North America. We have helped many rural church pastors and their churches. I have coached, held confidences, developed rural cohorts for these rural ministers. They are a blessing to the rural landscape but even more importantly they are part of the fabric of the American church. Rural churches are critical companions in the work of the Lord all across our four regions in North America. My misunderstanding was that when it begins to get good again, your people will want to quit the effort and go back to the status quo once more. Please do not blink at this defining moment. If you do that in about eighteen months your church will be back in trouble but this time their willingness to embrace such revitalization efforts will be removed because they tried it and it did not work. Lovingly keep the throttle on and ask the Lord to continue to renew His church.

Lessons I Learned from My Mistakes in Rural Revitalization

One of my church restart experiences was in a rural church and not everything I did in hindsight was correct. All of us make mistakes. I made mistakes as the leader and I miscalculated the memberships happiness with significant growth in membership and participation. Here are the fifteen mistakes (I know I probably made more than these certainly), I learned in rural revitalization.

I Tried to Do Too Much Alone

Because one often goes into a church needing renewal as the renewal expert, it is easy to become the one that is responsible for doing all of the work to bring about renewal.

It is not wise to allow your scheduled to become consumed with tasks that a willing laity could embrace.

I was Impatient

I am a driven individual and yet impatience can work against you in renewal of a rural setting. It can be seen as pushy. You might be labeled as thinking everything about the church is bad including the membership. Slow and steady wins out in revitalization. When I planted churches, it was the exact opposite. Go rapidly and reach as many as possible. Yet, that is not a best practice strategy for renewing a rural church. It takes time for the membership to trust you. Be patient, love your people and love your community.

Vision Comes First Not Second

I believed that the congregation would follow me as the leader before they embraced and claimed the vision. For the rural pastor, most rural churches have heard so many pastoral vision, which were never acted upon that they are numb towards the next one which is yours. Your delivery of your vision lies at the heart of the success or failure of the entire project. You may have great vision, but if you have not mastered how to communicate that vision, the renewal project is doomed to failure. Solomon wrote, "Where there is no vision, people perish" (Proverbs 29:18). And there is no vision if it is not a communicated vision. The Vision must be "caught" by other so they can "Run with it" (Habakkuk 2:3). Vision is the first step in revitalizing any congregation. Vision grips a person with a sense of authority. Vision is not about what a person wants to do. Instead, vision is about God helping a person draw a mental image, a picture, of what God expects His servant to do. Vision is the dream of the church revitalizer given by God yet, usually birthed in the pastor, but ultimately owned by the renewing congregation. It is the fire, flavor and fuel that drives your unique expression of the Great Commission. Andy Stanley writes regarding vision in *Visioneering*, "it is the course one follows to make dreams a reality. It is the process whereby ideas and convictions take on substance. Vision evokes emotion. There is no such thing as an emotionless vision."[149] He further continues later in the book, "Vision often begins with the inability to accept things the way they are. Over time that dissatisfaction matures into a clear picture of what could be. But a vision is more than that. Vision carries with it a sense of conviction."[150] Vision rarely requires immediate action. It always requires patience. A word of caution for the rural revitalizer here is to never force your vision in place of helping them discover their own!

Making Decisions on My Own

Even though I was given the positional authority to make decisions, often I made them too hastily. I made decisions without waiting for the congregation. Certainly, the runners who were with me were impressed that we were advancing, yet, there were significant individuals which in hindsight it would have been better to bring into the decision making process. There are things we learn along the way and for me it was to put it in neutral and allow for others to share their thoughts and ideas.

My Failure to Make the Time to Equip Others

In many churches pastors feel overwhelmed and believe they have little time for equipping and training of other. That was me during the initial five years of my ministry. I offered inadequate or no job training. In hindsight because I was not

---

149 Stanley, Andy. *Visioneering*. Sistera, Oregon: Multnomah Publishers, 1999, Pgs. 8-9.

150 Ibid, pg. 17.

engaged in a personal mentoring cohort myself, I did not think just how important, is such coaching really. Having now equipped pastors and laity for more than thirty years, I laughing wonder what I was thinking my initial few years of ministry.

Running Hard Put Up Wet

Another mistake I made in revitalization was the over working of the committed. There is a saying regarding horses that have been over worked which is: *Running Hard and Put Up Wet!* It signifies when you have pushed a horse further than was necessary. The same thing can happen in rural revitalization. Because you have a smaller number of willing individuals it is easy to over load them. I overworked the faithful few instead of reducing the pace or recruiting more widely. Far too often, I now realize that some of those who left the church did so they could get a rest. Slowing down the pace is much more preferred than pushing so hard that godly members think the only way to get some rest is by leaving the church.151

I Ignored Prayer and the Comfort it Brings

Having already written extensively about prayerlessness in the book *The Church Revitalizer as Change Agent*, I ignored prayer and replaced it with being busy. That has long since been corrected. Prayer is the beginning place, the middle place and the final place for revitalization.

---

151 In my book, *The Church Revitalizer as Change Agent*, there is a great chapter on pace in revitalization. Chapter Six which is entitled, "The Pace of Change in Church Revitalization." You can find this book on Amazon or go to: RenovateConference.org/bookstore.

I Failed to Pay Enough Attention to Visitation and Follow-up

If you do not pay attention on visitation and follow-up in a rural church no one else will either. It is interesting in a larger church the pastor is not the one who leads outreach and visitation, but in a rural church you are. You know what happens in rural churches if you do not focus on this area of ministry? What the outcome is there begins to be a sense of that someone else is taking care of it when actually no one is taking care of it. The pastor believes that the deacons and Sunday School organization is taking care of it. The deacons think the staff and Sunday school is leading in the effort. The Sunday Schools leadership believes that the pastor and deacons are taking care of the ministry of outreach and visitation and the resulting issue is that no one, is taking care of this critical portion of ministry in the rural church. It was not until my churches grew much larger that I was able to hand this off to another individual. In a small church you are going to be the one who must pay attention to outreach, visitation, and follow-up. I quickly learned that and began to be the point person for our weekly visitation program. So many pastors want to hand this off and that is good if it works. If it does not work it is still on you so step up and take the responsibility.

I Easily Took Offense

Because of my inexperience in ministry, initially I would often misunderstood the words and actions of key church members. Words offered as encouragements for a job well done I thought had ulterior motives. My inexperience led to cases of paranoia. There were times where I took other individuals anger personally when it was more a matter of their own frustration. In those cases, I allowed things to fester because I did not address problems or confront abusive people early enough. Taking offense is unwise as a church revitalizer. Remember this that even your biggest critic has a vested interest in you being successful. Once I learned that it was easier for me to lead turnaround efforts. If God has called you to revitalize a church there will be people who just will not like you because you are upsetting their status quo. Keep a short list of offenses realizing that the Lord is directing your path and He will lead you in that church or away from that church.

I Sought to Be a Peace Keeper Over a Leader

Early in my ministry I was more focused on trying to please everyone. Keeping peace was more important to me back then then leading them out of their doldrums. If we all could be one happy family life would be good. I learned that the Lord puts you in significant places to do significant things and you will not always have a peace until you have pushed through the abusive sin hurting the local church. Sadly, peace often in revitalization comes with a cost that is so high that it destroys any chances for renewal.

Wrapping it Up!

So, there you have it. The things I messed up and the mistakes I have made in my early days as a church revitalizer. Moving forward and making key decisions is risky! As you work under the Spirit's guidance, you will still face times where disagreements will emerge. Sometimes feelings will be hurt. Influence will begin to shift, as will possession of power. Both Pastor and laity will make mistakes! Take the time and make the time to get the proper training before you move forward in church revitalization! It is vital that you prepare the laity for the work of church revitalization as well as yourself. Communicate early and often with the church how the revitalization process will take place and how it will be implemented. Church revitalization is not about finding the magic pill or sure to succeed program. It is more about discovering God's vision for the church and practicing it.

Revitalization of churches is often very much similar from one church to another and yet it is often very much different in many ways! If your growth is to be measured in people becoming involved in various ministries inside and outside of the church, then ministry teams must become easy to join and able to make ministry simple not complicated. Hurting people are not healthy people. Unhealthy people make for an unhealthy church. We need to bring people to health before we can begin to renew the church. Most often we as pastors leave a pastorate too soon. Usually we mistake being tired for being all done! Far too often we as pastors allow a vocal minority to intimidate us into resigning. Restful vacations are good tiring vacations are no good. The best barometer to see if it is time to leave the church is to check out and see if you are still leading the church! Stop looking for plug and play solutions (programs) and start looking for ideas that will work in your setting. Leadership development is part and parcel for church revitalization. If you as the pastor are doing all of the work of ministry the church will never be revitalized! The rural church in the twenty-first century must develop new relationships and new ways of doing things to ensure a prosperous and socially healthy future. Tapping into the resourcefulness and creativity of the new rural (nu-rural) people will be essential in addressing this challenge. However, those returning to the rural landscape cannot do it alone. Those who have remained in the rural communities all of their lives must be open to ideas and opportunities to be a receptor of the new people coming to rural America. As the revitalization leader you must be willing to make the necessary changes in your ministry style in order to help the church revitalize. If you do not you might be packing and moving on while they seek someone who will make the necessary changes. In the area of church revitalization and renewal it is extremely important to realize that the goal is not to win the battles or wars, but to enable a congregation to move as united as possible into its own new future!

Chapter 14
This is Your Grandma's Church!

But you'll welcome us with open arms when we run for cover to you. Let the party last all night! Stand guard over our celebration.[152]

In the world of Revitalization and declining and dying churches, there are many obstacles and barriers that often prevent success. It is imperative that any course of action to revitalize a church take into consideration the full gambit of issues related to the community and the Church body. Upwards to 85-90% of all Churches in North America need some sort of revitalization action. A mistake would be to attempt a cart blanche process for all revitalizations.

Much has been made recently about the church declining and dying. When this topic comes up for discussion, often included is the shifting of the rural areas in America. Technology and industry have had its effect on the local farming and agricultural areas of America. The changing of the American cultural has been researched and documented sufficiently, that will not be the scope of this chapter. Instead, emphasis will be on the rural church and pastor in American life in the 21st century.

As the title of the chapter alludes to, there is a vast difference in the American church in America. Most congregations have fought through the "music wars" and use of screens during congregational worship. This is NOT necessarily the case with rural churches. While there has been a decline in the number of local farmers and their ability to plant, harvest and market crops, all the while staying afloat financially because of the large mega-farming conglomerate; the rural attitude has not died. This has been true of the Rural

---

[152] Eugene H. Peterson, *The Message: The Bible in Contemporary Language* (Colorado Springs, CO: NavPress, 2005), Ps 5:11.

mind-set in the local rural church. What may be outdated or obsolete in most other ministry environments, is still the order of the day for rural churches. It has been said that the "church is the slowest in changing" this can be no truer than in the Rural local church.

At the onset, I must ensure that rural gets a proper understanding. Rural is not country living. Country living by and large has to do with commuters who have chosen to move away from the rat race. A person living on a sprawling 20-30-acre plot does not make them rural. Rural doesn't mean animals necessarily, it can; but doesn't have to be included in the definition.

Also, very important to understand that rural in one locale does necessarily look like rural in another. For example, rural living in Nebraska is not the same in Georgia or West Virginia. The dynamics of culture clearly will define what rural living is in each geographical location. One could say that rurality is more about attitude than geography. There are two areas that have connecting effects on each other, and adverse effects on American culture and society; especially in rural America – the Church and the Community. I'll begin with the community.

In rural regions, Community identity and connection bears large on the cultural dynamic. One can think back a few years and visualize the community as it relates to its people. Most have been born and raised in the area. They have watched and engaged in the "normal" seasonal life that accompanies rural living. Time and seasons are the influence in the lives of the rural community. The seasons direct or prioritize the work and leisure of the rural community. I remember being in Presque Isle Maine during a fall trip in September. I saw fields filled with school aged children and wondered why they weren't in school. I was quickly informed that it was "potato harvest" and that all the children were released from school and in the fields until the crop was harvested.

In rural culture children/families learn early on about survival and life skills. A child in a rural community becomes a contributor to the overall community; pulling their weight and working in the respective community industry. In an urban or suburban culture, the children are not under compulsion to "learn the family or community business." Survival skills or life skills in a rural area far exceed any urban or suburban areas. Life has a different set of priorities in each culture. I can remember cannibalizing three bicycles to make one good one. I'm not sure that would be the case today for many of our children in urban and suburban areas. The commercial that depicts a young driver calling his dad, trying to reassure him that the boy has everything under control; then holds up a pipe of some sort and asks his friend if it was a lug wrench; gives credence to life skills development.

Years ago, community had connections with each other, they did life together, played together and died together. I remember that my neighbors had as much right to correct my behavior as my parents. Community has been fragmented by our mobility. I have people in my churches [very few] who have been born, raised and died in the same town. This is a struggle for me to understand in that I have moved some 17 times in my life via the military and ministry.

Rural communities stick together and are very wary of strangers or new people. A case in point was my second church in a rural community. I had a 16-year-old daughter with me when I started that pastorate. She experienced the "fear of strangers" rejection from the youth group. These youth had known each other all their lives, and the thought of a stranger in their midst caused them to become belligerent toward an outsider.

A rural community doesn't look at growth or enterprising the same way a city or town does. I live a few miles away from a town that really desires to keep small; and looks upon progress as an enemy. Bigger isn't always better; control and familiarity are huge in a local area. Everyone knows everyone and have a certain level of trust developed. I remember locking our house only once while growing up. The rest of the time, it was screen doors and open windows.

People living in rural communities are different. They have a different mindset and set of values and ethics they have adopted.153 Mostly I would say they are out of the "mainstream media" information chain. Interests are on hog and corn reports, not the latest fad or scandal. Folks in rural areas have been brought up in a "real faith" environment. The churches [usually only one or two] were the places everyone worshiped. Again, everyone knew everyone; their faults and their baggage. You can hear people being known by who their family was – There goes John Grant's boy! In a rural community, everyone reflects on everyone else. A town gets a reputation for who it is, what it does or doesn't do. Rural areas are protective areas. Our family had six kids; we would fight like no tomorrow; yet if someone tried to hurt one of us, we all ganged up on that person. In other words, rural people will fight, but be united if attacked by an outsider.

Rural living is identified by: Ranches, farming, livestock, fields, rustic living conditions and homes. Life is governed by crops and livestock reports, seasons of weather, agriculture, low population, close neighbor relationships and families.

---

153 McMullin, Stephen. How to Understand the Rural Mind-set. http://www.Christianitytoday.com/pastors/books/evangelismoutreach/1 clead03-11.html. Accessed via internet September 9, 2017.

Urban living is identified by: City/metroplex living, instant access to resources, social media, technology, concrete buildings, low income/poverty conditions, city dwellers, commuters and/or mass transit modes, traffic, crime, industry and over population.

Suburban living is identified by: Fringe population groups, soccer moms and sports/recreational activities, upper middle to upper class economics, country commuters avoiding traffic and people.

Now I know that many of the issues I have pointed out are generic and can be oversimplifications, but to do an in-depth comparison is beyond the scope of this chapter. The point I am trying to make is that there is a great disparity between geographical living locations. What is a must for life in one area is a luxury for another. When I titled this chapter "This is your Grandma's Church" it was meant to readily identify the stark difference between generations and geographical locations. If we look at "Grandma's church," we find several immediate differences. Many which if not observed and understood by a new or visiting pastor could be detrimental to tenure and reception of the members. The following is a brief list:

Hymns for music – not interested in the new songs or Praise Teams, or big screens, smoke machines or fancy lights.

Technology is a demon – most won't have a computer or smart phone; flip phones and cable TV are enough; can't spell internet and don't know what you mean by "Google it." They don't have Facebook or Twitter accounts, and Amazon is a river not a place to order on-line. They are not country commuters trying to avoid city traffic; they live in the Rural area, for that is where most have been born and raised. They are not interested in what the rest of the world thinks or does. News is only worthy if it affects them directly.

The church is family and neighbor run; a matriarch is probably the strongest/most influential person in what is approved or rejected.

Courtesy, compliments and respect are the order of the day. Expected is a behaving group of children; if not a direct reflection on the parents, oh and the "church community/family" has right to correct them if the parents aren't around.

New is not needed. Just because there is a new and improved, doesn't mean it is any better, and that it must be embraced.

Rural to them is more than a geographical location, it is an approach to life. People live outside of the "mainstream" of culture and politics. They are not interested in Wallstreet or Washington unless it directly affects them. Life in a true Rural culture is driven by the work on the farm or fields. Chores not allowances are the privilege and responsibility for all in the household to contribute to the success of the family. Children learn "life skills" while doing agricultural or livestock management. This philosophy of life is carried over into the Church community. Community is understood to be a place where all contribute and protect the whole, not just pursue individual or selfish goals. There is accountability to the community, likewise in the Church. Many times, the leaders of the Community have direct impact in the Church.

Another facet of Churches in Rural settings; the denominational separation is almost non-existence. I preached at a small rural church in Texas for several weeks; only to find out in the off weeks they met with the Methodist and Lutherans. There is in other words an ecumenical leaning that stems from the Community connections.
Any pastor, full-time or part-time, old or young seminary trained or not had better pay attention to the cultural dynamics of Grandma's church. If these are rejected and discounted as needing obvious change – the one changing

will be the minister in about a year to eighteen months! Oh, and do not make the mistake thinking that the Rural population doesn't matter – they assured George W. Bush a second term and in 2016 elected President Trump!

I have briefly described the demographic and social nuances of rurality in America. The focus of the chapter, however is How does a Pastor accomplish ministry in a Rural environment; taking into consideration the previous issues discussed. If a minister; pastor, music, youth or otherwise is entertaining a move to a rural area there are multiple shifts that will need to be done by the person, not thinking that the Church is the changing ingredient. One of the most important first steps is to know what you are getting into at the Church. I have talked with innumerable pastors who did not do their homework on the community and church before accepting a call.

Therefore, the hard work of doing cultural/community exegesis and church exegesis is a must. A minister/pastor is joining a local body of believers. It is a marriage. Too often a pastor has adopted a woman's perspective in that "she will change the man after they are married." This is a disaster waiting to happen. The Church [bride or groom] are who they are; accept them for who they are; and hold judgment until you have lived among them.

In Revitalization, there are three items the pastor must be able to influence and direct: Keys, Cash and Constitution. There can't be a fast timeline in trying to accomplish this. The Pastor must be the pastor. In other words, he must gain the respect and trust of the congregation. This will take time. Remember in most Rural churches, pastor rarely stay past a few growing seasons. *By having the keys*, the pastor has been given authority to lead the church. I remember being in deacon's meetings and never being asked what I thought. I didn't offer my thoughts, for I knew if they really were interested they would have asked me. Eventually, I had their trust and I became their voice on matters.

Secondly, is the cash. This might sound odd, but in Church life, especially in Rural congregations many feel that the money and ministry is theirs. By looking at the Budget reports you can tell if there are "pet projects" being funded by designated gifts. At one church I pastored there was over $120, 000 in designated giving, yet the Budget was short – yes $100,000. To accomplish Revitalization of a church, both the physical building and body of believers, the money must follow ministry, not pet projects. The giving must support the approved budget of the church, if it doesn't the plans, vision and mission of the church will be hijacked by the designated giving. A solution to designated giving is to only allow designated funds to be given to "church approved projects."

Third is the constitution of the church. This may take more time than you think. The reason for the constitution being key to Revitalization is it usually is the "that's not how we do things" argument. Sadly, most churches have a constitution, but they are so outdated and never followed except to stop necessary progress by someone other than the congregation.

In trying to address the three keys to successful pastoring and revitalization I have found that God knows His church and He will open and close doors of progress. The pastor cannot be a tyrant or bully; doing so will end the honeymoon phase quickly and alienate you from the people. Revitalization is as much "caught as it is taught." Take your time! Best estimates are Revitalization can take from 5-7 years; if it happens. This does not mean nothing is happening in the meantime – baby steps!

In continuing to talk about the Pastor; in rural churches there is another aspect of ministry that must be understood. Pastors of rural churches have shorter tenure than majority of other pastorates. Some of this could be with frustration in trying to move the church forward; it also could be that he was fired. Additional to short tenures is the Bi-vocational, second career, or what has been termed marketplace pastor. 154 Basically, this is someone who has other employment; works part-time or is retired and fills the pastor's position in a reduced role from full-time ministry.

There are different expectations for a bi-vocational or part-time pastor. Obvious is the tension of trying to balance both career and ministry. I have served in a bi-vocational position and found that there isn't such a thing. I was the pastor, secretary, youth minister, camp chaperone, lawn custodian and handyman. In pastoring a rural church, Jay Sanders identifies four mistakes to avoid. First, don't be lazy just because it is part-time or there is a small congregation. Expectations are high for a single staffed church. A rural church body is up usually before dawn taking care of livestock or getting into the fields; they will expect a pastor to be on duty early in the day.

Secondly, Pastors cannot use the comparison to other church mentality. Rural churches are not like other churches. The adage that the 'grass is always greener on the other side is a fallacy that must be avoided. Connected with this "comparison thought," the pastor cannot look for the church to be a stepping stone while waiting for something bigger to come along. The mind-set must be that God has called me to this church I am here until he moves me. By comparing the rural church to a mega or suburban church, then expecting to do the same things is unrealistic. Location, location, location – it makes all the difference in marketing a product as it does in programs and ministry possibilities.

154 Rainer, Thom. *Eight Characteristics of the New Bivocational.* http://thomrainer.com/2016/01/eight-characteristics-of-the-new-bivocational-pastor. Accessed via the internet August 21, 2017.

Third, Gossip will ruin a pastorate faster than most think. In a rural church there is the high probability that upwards to 75% of the congregation will be family connected -if they aren't they think they are. Gossip or rumors will move faster than the truth, while this is true in most churches, gossip moves at the speed of light!

Lastly, trying to build your own kingdom, not the Kingdom of God. I have witnessed this first hand. Bigger isn't always better, and in a rural area may not be sustainable. To build a rural church in hope of making a name for yourself will come at a great expense; mostly alienating the people.155

In some cases, a church will hire a part-time pastor or other minister because they don't want to pay full time salary, even when they can.156 In a lot of rural area churches, there has been significant decline both in population and economics and the church can't afford to pay anymore. A prospective pastor must consider how they will make ends meet; provide for their family and be willing to sacrifice a certain kind of lifestyle for the calling and service to the Lord and His church.

In continuing to describe the differences for pastors in rural ministry, Philip Nation discusses "Six Big Issues for Bivocational Pastor". Nation cites specifically the need for

---

155 Sanders, Jay. *Four Mistakes Rural Pastors Make (that all Pastors Need to Avoid).* http://www.lifway.com/pastors/2016/09/01/four-mistakes-rural-pastors-make. Accessed September 9, 2017 via the internet.

156 Dildine, Todd. *Death of the Church.* http://www.patheos.com/blog/jesuscreed/2018/04/18/the-death-of-the-church-2-the-ACF; accessed April 11, 2018. Note blog has four parts discussing the Death of the Church.

rest, building of relationships, quality study time, emotional frustration and a deep faith.157 The bottom-line ministry in Rural areas must be different than other geographical environments. Usually, time constraints are not observed. In his article "Smarter Rural Ministry," Marty Giese identifies how this "smarter Pastoring" takes shape. Some of the issues we have already identified but bear reemphasizing. Cultural dynamics must be observed. The ministry must take on a "practitioner approach, not a CEO, COO or CFO position. Servant -leader is another way of describing the pastor's work ethic.

There is a "Mom and Pop" order and structure within Rural congregations. Expectations and time-lines must be adjusted to the people's time schedule. Embrace excellence. It if is worth doing, do it right. Just because the church isn't a mega church doesn't mean ministry should be shoddy. Don't lower the bar for yourself or the people – "good enough" is not a standard!158

While pastoring a rural community church has its own nuances and problems, it also brings back to mind the days when life was much simpler. "Grandma's Church" isn't a bad church; it's its own local body with unique opportunities for family, community and Kingdom of God impact. Pastors cannot be in a hurry and must be called to the church, fully expecting people who are just a bit set in their own ways. The Pastor must intend to stay long enough to be included as part of the community family; and make the Church the center of

157 Nation, Philip. *6 Big Issues for This Bivocational Pastor.* http://www.biblestudytools.com/blogs/philip-nation/6-big-issues-for-this-bivocational-pastor.html. Accessed August 21, 2017 via internet.

158 Giese, Marty. *Smarter Rural Ministry.* Christianity Today Pastors. http://christianitytoday.com/pastors/2015/may-web-exclusives/smarter-rural-ministry.html. Accessed September 9, 2017 via internet.

all community life, for that is how Grandma remembers it growing up, and she isn't in any hurry to change this stabilizing variable in her life.

Chapter 15
Overcoming the Survival Mentality in Rural Revitalization

We're ready to study God, eager for God-knowledge. As sure as dawn breaks, so sure is his daily arrival. He comes as rain comes, as spring rain refreshing the ground."[159]

Church revitalization in rural America often struggles with the mindset of merely surviving as a church in a declining environment. Many a rural church is only interested in trying to keep it head above the water of decline. Survival is the most important trait in many of these churches. When you look at the demographic transformation going on in the rural corridors of our land it is no wonder why survival is a critical key rather than advancement in the local church. There is significant aging of the population found in most rural locales. The United States is on the cusp of an extensive and far-reaching demographic transformation as the senior population is expected to more than double in the next forty years. A rapidly aging population will significantly impact nearly all aspects of the nation's social, economic, and housing systems. With a median age of 40 years, rural America is "older" than the nation as a whole. And while approximately 13 percent of the U.S. population is age 65 or older, 16 percent of rural and small town residents are over the age of 65. In fact, more than one- quarter of all seniors live in rural and small town areas. Undoubtedly, the most influential age segment in rural and small town communities continues to be the Baby Boom generation, consisting of persons born between 1946 and 1965. Currently there are more than 18 million rural baby boomers, comprising nearly 28 percent of the rural population. The first of the baby boomers turned 65 in 2010 and millions more will follow in

---

[159] Eugene H. Peterson, *The Message: The Bible in Contemporary Language* (Colorado Springs, CO: NavPress, 2005), Ho 6:3.

the coming decade, reshaping rural society and communities. The age cohort directly behind the baby boomers, often characterized as the "Baby Bust" generation, makes up approximately 18 percent of rural people, and is relatively smaller than other age groups. The "Echo-Boom" generation (persons age 15 to 29 in 2010) outnumbers its preceding generation by more than one million persons and makes up 19 percent of the rural population. With the long-term pattern of outmigration in rural communities, however, it remains to be seen whether echo boomers will have the same impact in rural communities as they are projected to have nationally. There are just over 15 million children under the age of 18 in rural and small town communities, making up about 23 percent of the rural population.[160]

It is no wonder that there are big challenges in the rural landscape of America. Rural is an ever-changing environment which is being impacted by those leaving for the city and urban lifestyle while others are returning to a simpler style of

---

160 The information presented in this chapter, derives from HAC tabulations of various data sources. Most of the data comes from the U.S. Census Bureau's 2010 Census of Population and Housing, and American Community Survey (ACS) Five Year Estimates. The U.S. Census counts every resident and housing unit in the United States every 10 years. The decennial Census includes basic questions about age, sex, race, Hispanic origin, household relationship, and owner/ renter status. Additionally, the Census Bureau now conducts the American Community Survey (ACS), a nationwide survey designed to provide communities with detailed and timely demographic, social, economic, and housing data every year. Additional information in the report derives from HAC tabulations of other publically available data sources such as the Bureau of Labor Statistics Local Area Unemployment (LAUS) figures, FFIEC's Home Mortgage Disclosure Act (HMDA) data, U.S. Census Bureau's Small Area Income and Poverty Estimates (SAIPE),U.S. Department of Housing and Urban Development's American Housing Survey (AHS), U.S. Department of Labor's National Agricultural Workers Survey (NAWS), and various information from the U.S. Department of Agriculture's Economic Research Service (ERS) and others.

life and returning to the rural landscape. Rural environments have relatively few people living across a large geographic area. But rurality varies extensively based on proximity to a central place, community size, population density, total population, and various social and economic factors. The people of rural America make up roughly one-fifth of the U.S. population, but are located across 97 percent of the nation's landmass.[161] While rural America remains more racially and ethnically homogenous than the rest of the nation, rapid growth in the Hispanic population continues. With the continuing out-migration of working age residents, rural communities contain larger shares of older residents. These demographic drivers are important bellwethers of housing markets and demand. An older, more mobile, and diverse population will require housing options and solutions currently not available in many rural communities across the nation.

America has been largely a rural landscape in the past. The first U.S. census in 1790 revealed that 95 percent of the newly formed country's population resided in rural areas. Throughout the first century of post-colonial America, the populace remained vastly rural. But in the late nineteenth century, settlement patterns started to shift radically. The industrial revolution created a more urban-oriented economy. The United States became a predominately urban nation sometime in the 1920's. The 2010 U.S. Census counted a population of approximately 308 million people in the United States. Roughly 65 million, or 21 percent, reside in rural or small town America. If one thing our last presidential election taught us it was that the rural population wanted to make an impact on the election and that any candidate who ignored the rural landscapes of the United States, did so at their peril.

---

161 HAC Tabulations of 2010 Census of Population and Housing.

The church revitalizer serving in the rural communities must never down play the work God does and is doing in smaller churches in waning rural communities! God is doing many new things with churches willing to retool and respond to new needs that it had previously been unable or unwilling to consider. The fields are still white for harvest and God longs for new things. Rural church revitalizers must clearly understand the following questions relating to Church survival:

Who is sitting in your pews and how are they connected to the rural landscape?

Where are the church members that are keeping the organization strong?

Are these individuals New Rurals ("nurals") or have they been part of the landscape for a long time?

Is your congregation made up of church members who worn out and just want to belong?

Do you still have a significant number of rural church volunteers who are willing to do their portion of the ministry?

Do your rural churches show signs of members who no longer care about the community and the churches impact on community?

When the rural church gathers, who are those who are present?

Rural revitalizers build on the positive ones within their church! They accentuate the positive and eliminate the negative. Everyone in a rural church can find some degree of fault for the challenges or concentrate on past troubles and the current forecast from the naysayers. Rural renewal leaders must be eternal optimist in order to lead their people out of stuckness and into positive ministry. They must operate more as a community chaplain then as a single churches pastor. Daily they model concern for the membership and the masses in the community no matter how small those numbers might be. Rural revitalizers care for the entire rural locale not the few members in the congregation. Rural renewal pastors must demonstrate this long before your people will catch on. As you do the modeling of genuine caring and concern will begin to display for others how to reconnect with a community that believes you are unconnected. Rural communities need a pastor who assumes a servant's role. For you as the renewal pastor will often need to do things that others are not doing. Things like keeping the place clean, keeping things fresh will be asked of these leaders. Starting new ministries even if you have to lead them yourself for a while is part of the rural revitalizers responsibility.

Rural renewal leaders are busy people and adding new things to one's responsibilities takes commitment. Often you will need to begin new ministries yourself until you discover the apprentice you can equip and then give the work of that ministry over. One lesson I learned while serving as a rural pastor and church revitalizer was that I needed to be alright with accepting a maintenance ministry as a viable ministry, until the Lord brings about renewal and revitalization in His time. Rural renewal first and foremost begins with stabilizing the church that is hanging on. It is a viable challenge until God begins to lead it forward once again.

Prayer is a big key to this effort. The rural revitalizer needs to find his worth with ministering to the real needs of the people. There are needy people everywhere and for rural churches who desire to live out the biblical concept of meeting the needs of the community this can become a great opportunity to reach out in the name of Christ while leaving the results up to God. Here is a key lesson to be learned for the rural church pastor. Here it is: Every rural community needs what the local rural church has to offer. For the rural church revitalizer, it is critical that one work on becoming God's servant into the community and watch what the Lord can do through a church that really cares for the rural people who live there. Survival is not enough for rural church renewal.

The Storms of Rural Church Revitalization

In the gospel of Mark Jesus is reported to have declared to his faithful inner circle:

"And the same day, when the even was come, he saith unto them, let us pass over unto the other side. And when they had sent away the multitude, they took him even as he was in the ship. And there were also with him other little ships. And there arose a great storm of wind, and the waves beat into the ship, so that it was now full. And he was in the hinder part of the ship, asleep on a pillow: and they awake him, and say unto him, Master, carest thou not that we perish? And he arose, and rebuked the wind, and said unto the sea, Peace, be still. And the wind ceased, and there was a great calm. And he said unto them, why are ye so fearful? how is it that ye have no faith? And they feared exceedingly, and said one to another, what manner of man is this, that even the wind and the sea obey him?"[162]

It is clear that most rural church revitalizers are working too hard. They are putting in longer hours than most of them would prefer. Most are bi-vocational and work vocational jobs in order for their families to survive. These rural revitalizers are a little unsettled about their churches future. Individually and professionally, they are not sure about their personal roles and goals as they seek to bring about a transition within the rural local church. As rural pastors, we

---

162 C.f. Mark 4:35-41.

all work much too hard to wish for a survive only mentality. In talking to and surveying more than five hundred rural pastors during my one month sabbatical recently in Missouri, Kentucky, North Carolina, and Florida, I have discovered that these incredibly godly ministers long for seeing their church come out of the doldrums and begin to thrive and grow, not just get by. No rural church wants to become so extinct in its present function, but the reality is that the change required to bring about a transition is often very hard to be embraced by the current rural rank and file membership of a rural church in decline. Rural church survival is a brave step. But if one only seeks to maintain the status quo the question could be asked if the church is seeking to reach those within their ministry area. There are rural churches in North America that seek to just get by until a significant number of the membership passes away or moves out of the area. A rural church revitalizer serves as the spiritual leader of the rural community and is the ever-present hope for the community. Waiting for eventual extinction is not the goal of the real rural pastor. It is a heady calling and one that takes complete reliance upon the Lord. There is no magic pill for revitalizing your rural church, yet there are some principles and tools you can utilize to begin to bring about the change required to go beyond survival and embrace a new norm of growth. Change will be part of the process but it will be much slower than in urban churches. In many rural churches the membership wants to avoid any significant change which disrupts their comfort during their watch. Many would rather wait or ignore the opportunities until it is too late before they embrace the change required to bring about a new form, of growth. For the rural church revitalizer and the rural church, I see that there is a goal beyond mere survival and that it is discovering the joy of growing in a new norm and changing rural culture that surrounds your churches. I was amazed to see the number of healthy rural churches who were vibrant and though the challenges were many, they were actually making a difference in their locale for Jesus' sake. Some were locked in a time of turbulence but even this chaos was beginning to provide the very opportunities for their church to begin to become successful once more. The new rural revitalization paradigms presented will not be ones you have much experience with or you would not be in need of church revitalization and renewal. The mainstream of rural churches view change as a threat and survival as the only goal. Getting by or maintaining of status quo, is preferred over growing boldly and advancement. Yet, for the rural church change is not the threat but the opportunity. So, take the journey and see what God might do by challenging you to embrace a new rural norm and seek to revitalize your church.

Rural Church Revitalization Advancement Lessons

There are rural churches which are growing al over the country and yet there are also rural churches in decline. One of the big differences is how the growing rural church embraces change and new norms. Here are some rural church revitalization advancement lessons to consider:

Change is the new norm in a rural church regardless of your opinion about change.

If you are not open to change, even the small changes around you will defeat you. Comfort and stability is the bad news for the declining rural church, change is what is needed to succeed. Change allows you to embrace new opportunities and challenges. While there is a struggle to keep, the rural church moving there are churches growing in the rural landscape. Some of the things we are discovering for the healthy rural church is that usually they have a series of factors which help allow the church the best chance for stability and growth. Usually these churches are led by bivocational ministers who work out in the community and serve the church on Sunday's. Also, many have some form of alternative funding streams such as a school, community childcare program, or some form of community programs which utilize your churches facilities. Change is often the enemy of the current rank and file. The right change at the right time can lead to renewed growth and eventual turnaround success. Churches that change attract new prospects who want to change along with the church. Churches that operate in fear of change attract the status quo who live in fear of the new. Many lay people fear change so a strong Church Revitalizer is needed to lead them through the required changes necessary to keep the church live. Churches must understand that change equals opportunity for much needed growth. Rural congregations with a non-biblical view of pastoral leadership, often reject the very change the rural pastoral leader is called upon to consider. These status quo maintainers will work hard to defeat anything attached to change. If the rural church is going to reach the new makeup of one's community it will require positive voices proclaiming the need for change if success is going to happen. What I found in my one month sabbatical was that rural churches which innovate more easily change. They make the changes slowly but nevertheless they keep the rural church moving towards a change quotient. Most rural pastors and small town pastors realize that not all change is costly so they embrace the easy ones first that cost nothing and will not cause a conflict to brew in the church. Once there are a series of wins for the church with the changes that have been made it is easier to consider larger more dramatic changes for the good of the church and the rural community. Your churches stance on the changes taking place is much more important than the real changes you are making. Change is an asset not a liability. Rural churches which embrace change consistently and repeatedly grow gradually with new prospects.

Learn How to Work with the Five Types of Rural Church Member's

Rural churches can become more than survival churches. These rural congregations all over the North American landscape can experience renewal by discovering and embracing the followers, cultivators, visionaries, and the inventors in a church who can initiate change for the masses. There is one additional type found in rural churches which are not growing. Here are the five types of church members in most rural churches:

The Followers

The followers in rural churches are always ready to embrace the vision of their pastor leader. These are the ones within the rural church that are always extremely responsive to the rural church revitalizers leading and are willing to do whatever you challenge them and equip them to do. Followers are not known to create new norms of ministry yet they will follow obediently any direction the rural shepherd leads. The flip side of leadership is to have followers. It stands to reason that if leadership is important to performance, followership must have something to do with it too. In the rural church these individuals have the ability to take direction well, as they get behind a program, and to deliver on what is expected. Following is often unglamorous when compared to being the leader. Following matters in the rural church, it matters much. But there are no leaders without followers. The rural church is not only as good as the church revitalizer who leads but also as good as the followers who follow the trusted renewal leader.

The Cultivators

The cultivators in rural churches are always found working within the strategies of the church revitalizer which are designed to move the church forward and get it growing even if the pace towards growth is slow. These congregants work better within the structure of a strategy which is designed to win. One of the traits that the rural church revitalizer must understand is that the cultivators need acknowledgement and encouragement as to how well they are advancing and how well the ministries in which they lead are prospering. Cultivators are the ones who once they discover what is working they will continual to do more and more of these things and help the church grow. Cultivators seek repetitive improvement as they enjoy the ministry at church. Remember Aquila and Pricilla in the early church? They were cultivators. The early apostles were cultivators. They rural church members help the church advance by focusing on the positive rather than the negative, on what they can do to make a difference, not what they cannot do. Rural cultivators have a passion for leadership as they help others in the church to become leaders. Cultivators seek to get other involved. They are ambitious and often are found breaking the mold while redefining the rural community's cultural standards. Rural cultivators see two rural worlds. They see the rural world as it is and they perceive the rural world that they want to create. As an illustration of rural cultivators, they are perhaps more gardeners which are interested in spiritual cultivation then in outdated rules and regulations.

The Visionaries

The visionaries within rural churches are the great advancers of the health of the rural congregation and community in general. They are the great visionaries within the church. Rural visionaries are up on Jesus and the local church and not down on all of the challenges they must face.

They are infectious in their work for the Lord and others want to be just like them. They are always able to find the next new worker or the next new volunteer. They can take the existing strategy and keep tweaking it until it is functioning to the very best and drawing new and yet to be reached rural participants. Rural church visionaries usually see what something could be long before it actually happens. They have foresight and the ability to clearly present a plan for advancement that is practical and achievable.

The Inventors

The inventors in rural churches are always contemplating ideas which will help their pastor and church. These participants are the ones which design, develop, and deliver new ideas or systems into the local rural church. They present rural transformation at every juncture and often make it harder for those comfortable with the former things to continue to work in ways which bring about little or no change. These are the inventors in your church. Invention is the activity of investigating and finding a new method of achieving something and those in the rural church which do so are an incredible asset. Inventors introduce us to a new thing. Inventors in the rural church are the creatives which can work well in groups or if need be they can work alone until others come aboard. They take the mission in front of them and find solutions. Rural churches need to stop chasing the inventor away from their church. They have the ability to create something worthy for community and church. Inventors are sacrificial individuals which seek the best for the rural community and church.

The Dawdlers

There is one additional group found in so many of the rural declining churches and these are the dawdlers. The dawdlers in rural churches are in those who love to emphasize the past and seldom look towards the future. They are not unspiritual people but individuals who are not ready to do the work necessary to save their church. Those dawdlers towards change in rural congregations, will slow the church revitalizer down as they become a hindrance towards the necessary change required for advancing the rural church. Dawdlers are usually the last to embrace a new plan. They straggle on most ideas and appear to never be ready to do something to help the church. These characters are better left outside of your confidence group since they usually will hurt the effort. During my sabbatical study in 2017, what I discovered is that rural churches which are stuck in rapid decline are made up of a large number of these type of people, while in rural growing and advancing churches these individuals are either very few or non-existent. They are known for taking more time than necessary to align themselves towards a new idea. They often are found moving aimlessly or lackadaisically towards anything that requires the work of the laity.

Once you discover that little changes will not kill you or your rural church bigger changes can be considered. Little victories are the precursor to bigger victories. They prepare you for the eventual challenges you will face to bring about a new norm. Changing slowly wins out over a fast pace set of changes which are harder to embrace due to the jolt it sends to the rank and file member of the rural church. A church which struggles with change, is often made up of a larger portion of dawdlers. These faithful dawdlers can actually drag a church down because it is unable to move very quickly and by the time it does move most of the other members who were cultivators and inventors have moved on.

The rural landscape is changing and one of the proponents of rural America is Becky McCray who conducted a rural survey in 2017 of the challenges for small town residents. She led a research project for

SmallBizSurvival.com and *SaveYour.Town* as they joined forces to conduct an international rural survey of 250 rural residents during 2017. What was surprising in the study was that there apparently is a shift taking place in rural. She said that more rural people mentioned a lack of workers than mentioned a lack of jobs. More people were interested in market trends than manufacturing trends. She stated that more rural residents were focused on downtown issues than on recruiting outside businesses. While the survey was designed to identify rural challenges, people also answered with opportunities or solutions. Some included: taking advantage of the emerging trends in rural tourism and providing family friendly activities. So much of the media focus on rural America focuses upon employers or manufacturing moving away. This study stressed the discovery of rural entrepreneurs.

Choose Your Future

Consider this, if your rural church loses 12% of its longtime resident members every year due to transitions and you replace most of them, in six years you have a very different church since seventy percent of your congregants will be a new part of the church. the synergy of such an influx does wonders in a rural setting. I have seen churches all across the rural landscape who have been taught by their pastor how embrace the new residents coming to rural America and work at making them the new part of the churches culture. The result is that that rural does more than survive it flourishes. But it takes a pastor and a congregation desiring not to merely survive. How this takes place is up to the Church Revitalizer. For the rural churches that wait to embrace the new residents coming to their community, they are shocked when their church declines so far that all that is left in their church is the final 12%. Those that work on it have discovered in three years they have a new church flexible enough to make a difference in a new and bold way.

When the rural churches posture changes sufficiently the act of introducing new ideas and potential changes within the church no longer presents such a huge challenge for conflict. Because the act of eliminating ideas is no longer a big deal either. The end result for the local church working towards renewal is that now the number of new ideas for change that get initiated increases dramatically! The end result is that your rural church now has a greater chance for new growth and not mere survival.

Raising the Spiritual Temperature of the Rural Community

Do not believe for an instant that God is not already at work in our rural communities all across America! The Rural American church is a vital part of the rural landscape and while there are those who are faced with declining opportunities or prospects, many rural churches understand that they must make their own ways and find new opportunities to connect with the changing rural population. Many stalled or declining rural churches are comfortable with a spiritual temperature that requires little from those in their church and in their community. Growing rural churches seek to raise the spiritual temperature of their community. It is easy for the rural leadership of a church to grow comfortable with just "doing" Sunday. But when a church revitalizer is leading a rural group of believers towards growth and moving them off of a plateau or decline, there are some things one must achieve if you want to change the status quo and up the ante in the game of rural renewal. If you are the church revitalizer it is critical that you realize that you have more to do with the spiritual vitality and temperature of the church than anyone else. As the church revitalizer, you are called to continually reach out into the community, prepare and preach timely biblical messages, shepherd the immediate flock the Lord has given to you, and additionally pastor the rural community at large. To borrow a John Maxwell idiom, you are the lid. Every one of us as a rural pastor are the lid to some extent. Church Revitalizers are the primary thermostats when it comes to the spiritual temperature of the church. Getting the people of God to move away from passivity and apathy takes a pastor who is willing to remain in the trenches and do the work. In the Book of Exodus, Moses was leading a group of passive and apathetic people. Yet, he remained at the task and led his people. Correspondingly, if you are a rural pastor and you are the apathetic piece of the equation, your courageous and passionate members will not remain along your side for very long. They need you to be the "doer of the Word," not just the lip-syncer of the Word. Have you stopped to ask yourself why in the rural landscape new church plants are popping up everywhere? They are doing so because there are many courageous and passionate members who want something more out of church than the passive pastor is giving them and so they join a new vision with a new vibrancy that is compelling and it taking root in a rural community.

So, what should you do if you are the one who is leading a group of individuals that are passive while the community demands passion for the Lord? Here are some ideas that will work if you are serious about leading your rural church to better days and greener pastures.

Change the Game Plan

When you find yourself in a spot where you are leading a lukewarm body of people in a renewal effort that demands passion, there are a few things you must do to change the game. What you have been doing is probably not bringing anything more to your church than the status quo so change up your game plan and strategy. In rural radio I found a great lesson and it helped me as I developed free public service announcements for a local radio station. They were looking for something at the fourteen past the hour that was so different that it would keep the listeners thinking and engaged. This helped their ratings because they finished the first quarter hour strong and launched strong for the next quarter hour. So I would develop off the cuff radio spot that would make the listening audience reflect a little. I would reconnect them in the last portion of the quarter hour and reconnect them in the first part of the second quarter hour. The same is true for the rural pastor. Find new ways to reconnect with your rural landscape. There is comfort in certainty. Yet, not everyone in your community wants to do the same mundane things in church over and over again. In transitioning a rural church, one must plan the change and work the plan. But if we want to create a better future, one must let go of the stale things being done over and over bring no return. The Church Revitalizer needs to stretch himself and his church as they reach for the unknown. We need transformation. We adopt the most difficult and challenging strategy because leading is better than following and in a world of constant and frequent change survival is optional.

Do It Gods Way not Mans

Far too much declining church strategy is built around our desires and not the Lord's. As the scripture reminds us, "unless the Lord build the House those who labor, labor in vain." In rural surroundings, it is easy to build consensus on things that support the status quo. Church revitalizers in rural landscapes should continually strive to keep the emphases on the Lord Jesus Christ in all that they do. Nothing stimulates or rekindles passion within us like time with Jesus. As the leader of a rural church it is vital to gently remind the participants that Jesus Christ loves the church so much more than we do. Enough to give His life for it. None of us would be willing to do what only the Lord Jesus dis for the local church. Rural church revitalizers must remind themselves and their followers, that we must do it Gods way and not ours.

Jesus is the definitive source of passion for renewing rural ministry.

Find New Avenues to Partner

Finding new avenues to partner with a rural community is a must. During my sabbatical, one rural church I visited had a rather large parking lot smack in the middle of the county set community right on Main Street. Here was what they did to reconnect with the towns people. Every Thursday night they hosted a street fair right in the middle of downtown. Their musicians within the church, and eventually guests as well, played great music all night while the community enjoyed the street fair atmosphere. They allowed small rural entrepreneurs to set up pop up tents in their parking lot and sell their small business collectables, homemade baked goods, and crafts. These once a week temporary businesses came into being for the street fair and those who hit a niche actually developed a longer livelihood than once a week. By providing a place for short-term vendors setting up tents and booths at your street fair event provided all kinds of opportunities in a small rural town. Some of these small businesses which initially were launched at the churches weekly street fair become something larger by utilizing the venue and partnership with the churches street fair. In just about any rural landscape there are individuals who create crafts for sale, bakers who utilize the once a week opportunity to present a new business of catering for other events, and various artists who are given the chance to display their wares. Some of my favorites were those who turned high end ink pens on a lathe and sold them every week at the fair.

Another rural church utilized their parking lot in the middle of town for hosting a Wednesday lunch on the lawn of their church. This rural church allowed a few food trucks initially to park on property once a week and provide food truck faire. What started with only two trucks eventually became three then four then five and ended up when I was there with seven food trucks providing low cost lunches for the community. Some customers would pick it up and take it with them, but once the church put in picnic tables in the shaded lawn areas near the parking lot it became a gathering event for the church and the community. Mobile food trucks are hot anywhere because there is no need for a permeant facility to maintain. Rural areas have few rentable small buildings available for these beginning food entrepreneurs so having a food truck is a great way to launch a small business. One of the vendors told me she would take her food truck to three other small communities and do the same thing there at another church willing to find new avenues to partner with a rural community. Small towns are viable markets and church revitalizers who are willing to think outside the box are able to bless the church and the community at the same time.

Help People Start Tiny Shoes Size Businesses

Perhaps the coolest thing I have seen in the rural landscape was when a small rural church and its pastor allowed twelve tiny shoe box sized sheds to be placed along their property next to the main road leading into town and launched a Christmas Village occupied with extra-small businesses. These twelve brightly painted small sheds, which could be picked up at any local Lowes or Home Depot, provided a place for rural entrepreneurs to create a new business without having to pay for acreage. There was no electricity and they were not open once the sun went down. But this form of low risk allowed some rural community thinkers to launch a new business all because the church was open to doing a new thing. The result was that all the tiny shoebox businesses together drew a critical mass of visitors to the rural church. Such good will was immediately apparent as I walked around these neat little gift shops. Each one was run with a smart phone and a square credit card reader. When the phone got low it was recharged in the person's car. What the rural pastor understood was that the strategic aspect is to bring a number of these tiny shoebox businesses together. What the rural church also provide was a sense of community for these business owners. One along the side of a rural highway is a business that has little impact led by an individual which is lonely. But if you place a larger number of these together like that rural church did groups of tiny businesses are a draw and their owners are family. Individual crafters or artisans who could not fill an entire store get a chance to fill a tiny space. In the upper northeast, there are these types of spaces where business is selling maple syrup but while they cannot justify paying for a big building, they can utilize this rural strategy. A rural church which helps start tiny shoe box size businesses has a heart for the growth of the community. Rural churches are promoting and exploring businesses with new looks, shapes, new locations and new ways of doing things. They can be a vital part of the community's renewal impact and the community can be a large part of the churches renewal as well.

Utilize Your Empty Buildings During the Week

Unless your rural church has developed a partnership already with other small businesses in your community most of these churches have buildings which sit empty during the week. There are rooms which could be offered to individuals and businesses during the week for a reduced cost to them. It is usually cheaper to live in a small town than an urban or urban fringe area. There are individuals living in rural areas which need a small area to run their business out of. Freelancers and online marketers often need a small room to use for putting together promotion pieces. A church in rural Georgia just north of Atlanta, partners with a business each week to put together their inserts which will be going into various businesses all across the Atlanta business corridor. The business makes a specific contribution to the church and the church gathers some retirees to put the promotion pieces together. There are many companies which allow their people to work from anywhere as they deliver either digital or customer support services. If you have that type of space and you know of those individuals within your community perhaps a partnership could be developed. Rural resourcing is something to be considered for the rural church. These types of people include: web designers, writers, programmers, creative artists, marketers, consultants and virtual assistants. Fostering and tapping into a sense of place, is a great start for the rural revitalizing church.

Transforming the Rural Church

It is not only the rural church which needs to be making significant changes but just about every church in North America. But for the rural church transformation is motivated by existence, by the realization that everything needs to change or the body will die; that a significant breakthrough in mindset is needed in order to pursue new opportunities. The challenges to those church revitalizers who embark on and choose to lead a rural church transformation journey are many; they lead in a direction where the destination is not known. The challenge to those who travel with such rural revitalization leaders will be to trust and support the vision and the strategy. The church revitalizer must motivate congregants through a sense of urgency supported by the passion and drive of the church revitalizer to envision and create a new future. From either impetus, the entire mind-set and rural organization's paradigms are forced to shift.

Our Rural Traditional Thinking Has to Change

So, what does it take to transform a rural church? Simply stated, our thinking as its leaders and participants is has to change. If your rural church wants to hold on to the past, you will be asked to only make incremental process improvements and not rock the boat. In this manner we are content, complacent, arrogant, or unaware. If the rural world is changing in any significant way, it's only a matter of time before we will not survive as a church unless we do something about the decline. The timing of a rural churches irrelevance and eventual death depends upon the other rural churches around you. If they are doing nothing then you can get away with doing the same. But you just might want to be the lone exception in your community and watch how God will bless you and your fellowship by doing something significant for the Lord. Most rural churches, unless they have significant bank roles to support stagnancy, will not know if we have three months, three years, or 30 years to survive. Tradition is often the single ingredient which keeps most rural churches from being willing to try new things for advancement.

Rural Churches Must Move from Tradition to Transition

For the long time rural church, there is comfort in certainty. It is easy to remain in a traditional design and watch as the population base selects the more aggressive transitional churches along the rural landscape. In transition, the church revitalizer can plan the change and work the plan to bring about renewal. If we want to create a better future, we have to let go and reach for the unknown. Tradition holds on to the past glorying in what has already been accomplished. Transitional rural churches let go of the past glories and prepare for the changes it will need to make if it is going to move past a survival mentality.

Rural Churches Must Then Move from Transition to Transformation

But for the rural church that remains in a transitional mindset it is easy to find it back at the start locked even tighter in tradition. But for the process to be completed, rural churches must then mover further from transition to complete transformation. In my travels to more than three hundred rural churches the healthiest ones which were fully revitalized were those who moved completely toward transformation. We all need transformation. When rural churches adopt the more difficult and challenging strategy for renewal because leading is better than following and in a world of constant and frequent change something more than mere survival is its only optional. Rural revitalization is hard but it can be accomplished.[163] The way we respond to the storms in our life determines if we will stand or fall! It is not an accident or stroke of fate we have found that gets you beyond the problems of life. Remember Elijah? James reminded us that Elijah was a man subject to the same feelings and passions we have. The Bible says that Elijah plopped down under a Juniper tree, and asked God to kill him.[164] Think about this, this is the same man who, only hours earlier was calling down fire from heaven. What was the reason for his despair? A couple of things probably; fear, and just sheer weariness. We are told he had just run all the way from the summit of Mount Carmel to the Valley of Jezreel. When your body is tired, you are sometimes subject to depression. As the church revitalizer, there will be ups and downs as you lead the church. Will friends sometimes drop you, or shoot arrows through your heart? Yes, they will. Will there come tests of your faith when feelings have to be shunned and only your foundational faith will sustain you? You got it! How to be prepared for it? Well, I can tell you that the same God whom you worship in the light is the same God you reach for in the night. God is there with you at this moment, even though you are not aware of His presence. So, keep reaching and believing.

---

163 C.f. Luke 6:47-48.

164 C.f. 1King 19:4-5.

Wrapping It Up!

The way we respond to the storms in our life determines if we will stand or fall! All of us have challenges. Sometimes the Lord calms the storm; sometimes he lets the storm rage and calms the believer. A great scripture in the Bible is *"It came to pass,"* Praise God it did not come to stay. Someone has well written:

> "As you travel down life's pathway, may this ever be your goal: Keep your eye upon the doughnut, and not upon the hole!" The way we respond to the storms in our life determines if we will stand or fall! To realize the worth of the anchor we need to feel the storm."

When you face these types of storms everything we have talked about before is important. We need to Remember that God is in the Storm- you are not alone. Don't blow storms out of proportion. These are not weekly storms. Cast out the anchors to hold us. God's unchanging nature and purpose. Resist the temptation to give into fear. Fear makes terrible decisions. We need to find our refuge strong and mighty. Only God is sufficient. Find our strength in the river of God. Strength that comes from God inside. Listen to the direction and wisdom of God. Be still and know that I am God. There are a few lessons we can learn from the story in Mark 4, that we can apply to the life-threatening storm, or could I say faith-threatening storm. It is important for us to understand that this event in the boat took place after Jesus had just finished talking about faith. He told parables pertaining to faith as a seed. What good is a lesson with practical application? Sometimes to hearing it is one thing, but to live it is another. Three things about the story should have given the disciples confidence in the midst of the storm.

First, Jesus promised that they would go over to the other side. Sometimes all we can do is take God at his promises. Although God gives us his promises, he never promised an easy ride through life. *Second,* Jesus was with them (God in the flesh). They had already seen what he was capable of through his miracles and ministry. But some reason they just could equate his abilities into their circumstances. Sometimes, we have seen the abilities of God and yet are unable to convert them into our circumstances. *Third,* Jesus was perfectly at peace in the midst of the storm. While the storm was raging and waves were crashing, Jesus was asleep on a cushion. And if Jesus was fine with the situation, then they should have been fine with it. All three of these things should have calmed them down and their faith should have remained strong, but it didn't. As any human being, we have to go through tough times in order to find our faith flourish. A strong faith is a tested faith. James 1:3-4 tells us:

> *For you know that when your faith is tested, your endurance has a chance to grow. So let it grow, for when your endurance is fully developed, you will be perfect and complete, needing nothing.*

What do we learn from this story that will help us get through the storms of life as a rural church revitalizer? Well while you are being thrown into the middle of the mess it is important that you do not jump to conclusions about God. The disciples say those words that we tend to say at times to God, and even many today think this way about our God. They said: *"Teacher, don't you even care?"* Yet God knows and cares about what is going on in your life.[165] Also, the Lord knows how you feel even when revitalizing the church is difficult.[166] God want to work in your challenges and storms of renewal.[167]

---

165 C.f. Matthew 10:29-31.

166 C.f. Hebrews 4:15-16.

167 C.f. Matthew 23:37.

It is critical that we understand the power of God. The Disciples gave up. Jesus stands in the midst of the floundering boat and simply says to the wind and the waves: hush, be still. There is a force to the words that Jesus uses. It means "to put a muzzle on one's mouth." It as if He stands as says shut up and stop whining. The wonder is that the winds and the waves obey. As a church revitalizer please learn that God's power to still the storm is manifested in at least two different ways in life. Sometimes God stills the storm and sometimes God stills His people in the midst of the storm. There are a few key things I see in this story of Jesus in the boat with the disciples. There was a diversified pressure which contributed to the storm. Followed by a difficult period that contributed to the storm. A divine individual contributed to the storm. Lastly, a demanding place contributed to the storm. As a church revitalizer in a rural situation you must move through the storms that come your way. Your storms in renewal will help you and your church grow. You will become more grateful as a pastor and as a people. It is important that you overcome the survival mentality in rural revitalization.

Conclusion

While the rural landscape is ever changing, the rural church appears to be lagging behind in some cases. Tapping into the resourcefulness and creativity of the new rural (nurural) people will be essential in addressing this challenge. However, those returning to the rural landscape cannot do it alone. Those who have remained in the rural communities all of their lives must be open to ideas and opportunities to be a receptor of the new people coming to rural America. The rural church in America in the twenty-first century must develop new relationships and new ways of doing things to ensure prosperous and a socially healthy future. The lasting solutions to rural America's churches challenges will be found in rural America. The rural church, while distinct in its mission and character, is not separate from the social and economic life of rural America. But we should not delude ourselves into thinking that the rural American church has so many unique issues. In fact, most of the challenges facing the rural American church today, are often the same challenges for the declining rural, urban fringe, and extreme urban church seeking renewal and revitalization. Yet, while the challenges are similar, but the solutions are more unique. Granted the rural church is perhaps the most irrepressible organization in North America. It is often the meeting place for its residents on all types of matters. A church revitalizer would be wise in developing or continuing a sense of community with the church as partner. The Church Revitalizer operates as the social navigator of key community needs and issues and becomes the influencer for the betterment of the community. Renewal is focused on care of community residents, conversionism, social services, social issues of the community, and serving as a leadership voice into the community for the residents.

Often a challenge in the rural church is that patriarchal and matriarchal memberships begin to lower the bar towards core values and doctrine in an attempt to draw non-respondent prospects. When the rural church lowers its standard for living in things such as cohabitation, use of drugs, and addiction with alcohol, it damages the churches reputation and chances for drawing the returning nural into their church. There creeps in a wounded personality disorder feeling that the rural church is not able to meet the needs it should. I have found during my year-long study that in some places that was true and in other it was anything but true. Granted from talking to rural pastors I sense that for about one third of our rural churches this is indeed the case. But there are other churches working hard and are on the opposite end of the continuum. Some rural churches I discovered were greatly depressed because their pastors were that way. Others believed that God was up to something again in their church and looked forward to being part of the solution not the problem. These rural churches were churches where the nurals were returning to the landscape and there was a growth momentum beginning to take place. Change was the matter of the day for these congregations and even the most stiff-necked of members had to acknowledge that God was up to something. These nurals often are buying small farms to retire on. They are not seeking to become farmers but want a little land mass because many have been cooped up in urban centers for so long they rave the open landscape. One of the things I tried in my journey around the rural American landscape was to discover how many formerly rural pastors who went to the city to pastor for a long time were returning to pastor these churches as they either neared retirement of embraced retirement. It is acknowledged that some rural churches are led by the guy just out of seminary, but that I not a bad thing. If the rural church will love on him and his family they might just stay forever. I heard that so many times in my journey. One guy said, "I came thinking it was temporary until I learned how to minister, but instead I fell in love with the community, the church, and the people. It was a blessing of the Lord to stay here now for over thirty years." Another rural pastor told me about a ministry he had that he would go to city churches and raise funds so he could come back and pain the rural barns for his community where people could not afford to do so. Such an act of kindness gave him an open do for ministry. He also said he liked to paint and think as he ministered to these families. In rural it is not always about great growth but more about a continual effort to transform the people who live there into examples of Christ Jesus. I found that almost everywhere the rural pastor works much harder than the urban or suburbia pastor. Part of that is because they usually work two jobs. Rural congregations, I discovered, follow their pastor. That was so refreshing to see in a day where many urban churches want to fight their pastor.

Rural churches have a tremendous mindset that they will keep on keeping on and do the work of the Lord until no one it left or there is no longer any breath in its membership. Even in areas where finances were a challenge I hear members and ministers speak of keeping things tight so they could continue to minister to their community. Rural events in churches such as singing events are popular still I found. In reality is provides a place for the community to gather and sense togetherness. In one church I was preaching at I had told the music people that I was going to share a song I had written in the sermon that was going to be modeled after a song of Johnny Cash. They said "preacher we will stay up here and play the music for you while you sing your ditty!" It was wonderful. The rural church revealed something that I expected, but now I know, and that is it is much friendlier to guests then urban churches. In urban churches you need to go there awhile before they embrace you while in rural churches you are welcomed almost immediately. To some degree there is an instant connection. Granted you are not asked to lead the women's union of the men's group but you are genuinely welcomed and embraced. Almost every rural pastor I interviewed taught me something that was unexpected. They were so much better at doing weddings and funerals because that was often when most of the community showed up. They made it count and it served them well.

Rural churches are found everywhere and not just in southern rural states anymore. You can find them on the fringes of a town or city. These collar communities are far enough away not to become annexed into the expanding urban landscape but close enough to go to town when it is needed. Rural churches are still found near agriculture communities or forestry towns. You can find them near mining areas. In West Virginia where I once pastored, these communities make up the majority of the state's landmass. Rural churches still exist in what we call small hamlets of the north east. We have joyfully found rural churches around recreational centers while we vacationed. These churches were thriving. Some were near fishing areas. Others were near various water sports environments such as beaches and lakes. There are many rural churches near a college town. As I visited my research states, I discovered how many were near our military bases. Interesting to me at least was that rural pastors who were revitalizing their churches spoke of their renewal efforts being pushed from a six-mile focus to a thirty-mile focus. That was a key concept for me.

It has been just a little over a year since I completed my study sabbatical focusing on rural church revitalization. Our research revealed three profound types of churches among the rural landscape. The first type were those churches which were *benign*. These benign churches were 118 (33.71%) out of the 350 rural churches surveyed. *Benign* churches are the churches which have primarily a maintenance mindset which is displayed by very little effort and very low expectations. The second type we discovered were the *bewildered* churches in the rural landscape. *Bewildered* churches are those which are so frustrated that they are all but ready to jump off the proverbial bridge. These churches were 117 (33.43%) out of the 350 churches interviewed and surveyed. They were not only doing nothing, they had no desire to seek renewal or life. They are the ones which have the mantra that the last one left alive remember to turn the lights off. The third type of rural church our research and interviews revealed are those who are the *bold*. These *bold* churches among the rural landscape have leaders which operate more as a community watcher and chaplain for the entire region not just a few church members. These churches were 115 (32.86%) of the 350 churches surveyed and interviewed. Without a doubt these were the healthiest of all three types. They had a forward focus and were willing to try almost anything to reach their tiny population for Christ Jesus. Those churches were led by leaders who were strong voices for righteousness in their rural communities. They were not only participants with community leaders but they were partners in projects for the good of the area. The *bold* churches were most interested in connecting with the community. They sought ways to think outside of the box for the betterment of community not just the church. They emphasized newness over deadness. I am extremely encouraged at what I have seen and the pastors who are giving it their all for the sake of Christ in these rural areas. What a wonderful experience and what wonderful people. As a rural church revitalizer, you cannot settle for just doing a little. You must give it your all if you are going to revitalize a rural church. Successful rural revitalizers stay out front and on the edge. Dying rural churches are more focused on relaxing in a recliner. There have been many who I met that could barely make ends meet and yet their daily walk and Christian experienced makes ours pale in compare. There was such joy and intimacy in these congregations. The pace was much slower and so much more relaxed. These rural churches affirmed the membership and accepted everyone. Pastors of these rural churches were known in these small communities. They were making a difference. Thank you each and every one of you who allowed me to speak with you. Thank you for your openness. This will be the most challenging ministry assignment you will ever face! Might I make one more parting observation? While so many in denominational life are focusing on a small number of urban centers for their future hopes, perhaps such short sightedness will be the cause for us to lose the rest of America. What a sad day that will be. Our Lord Jesus loves the little communities just as much as He does the big ones. Hold on and keep on. Hold on Rural Church Revitalizer. Hold on!

ABOUT THE AUTHORS
Dr. Tom Cheyney
Founder & Directional Leader
Renovate National Church Revitalization Conference
RenovateConference.org
ChurchRevitalizer.guru
tom@renovateconference.org

Tom is the founder and directional leader of the RENOVATE National Church Revitalization Conference, Executive Editor of *the Church Revitalizer Magazine*, and leader of the RENOVATE Church Revitalization Virtual Coaching Network where he mentors pastors, churches, and denominational leaders in Church Revitalization and Renewal all across North America. He serves as the National Host of the weekly **Church Revitalization and Renewal Podcast.** Dr. Cheyney has written over 5,000 print, audio resources, guides, or books for church revitalizer's, pastors, church planters, and lay leaders. His most recent books include: **The Nuts and Bolts of church Revitalization (along with Terry Rials)**; **Thirty Eight Church Revitalization Models for the Twenty First Century, The Church Revitalizer as Change Agent, The Seven Pillars for Church Revitalization and Renewal, Practical Tools for Reinventing the Dying Church, and Preaching Towards Church Revitalization and Renewal(along with Larry Wynn).** Cheyney has written along with his friend Rodney Harrison **Spin-Off Churches** (B&H Publishers). Tom is a nationally recognized conference speaker and a frequent writer on church revitalization, church planting, new church health, and leadership development. Others have label Tom as the *Father of the Church Revitalization Movement* as his influence has stretched across multiple denominations and countries.

Dr. John Kimball

John Kimball learned the ropes of church revitalization as a rural pastor in southeastern Virginia and has been helping local congregations reengage with their mission since 1992. He now works nationally in church revitalization with the Praxis Center for Church Development (Manchester, New Hampshire) and as Director of Church Development with his denomination, the Conservative Congregational Christian Conference (St. Paul, Minnesota). John is the Lead Pastor of Palmwood Church in Oviedo, Florida.

Dr. Chris Irving
Lead Pastor, First Baptist Church of Gonzales, TX
Rural Revitalization Specialist

Chris served as a youth pastor in several churches throughout Texas and has pastored two other churches in the rural settings of Texas. He led a small rural church to revitalization and is currently involved in the revitalization process of First Baptist Gonzales. He earned his doctorate at Midwestern Baptist Theological Seminary in leadership studies and seeks to help pastors equip the lay leadership of the church. He has been married for 15 years and they have 6 children.

Rev. Rob Hurtgen
Pastor, First Baptist Church, Chillicothe Missouri
Rural Revitalization Specialist

Rob Hurtgen serves as the pastor First Baptist Church, Chillicothe Missouri. He is completing a D.Min. in Church Revitalization from Midwestern Baptist Theological Seminary in Kansas City, Missouri. He and his wife Shawn, married in 1995, have five children. Rob is a featured writer for the Church Revitalizer Magazine, the only magazine totally focused on church revitalization and renewal.

Dr. Jim Grant
Lead Pastor of Heartland Baptist Church
Alton, Illinois
North Central States Consultant

Jim Grant is a seasoned pastor of 20 years. His ministry has been exclusively in the revitalization of declining churches. He is a 25 years Air Force veteran. His travels have equipped him to speak distinctively to various church models and ministries. He received his doctorate in Church Revitalization from Midwestern Baptist Theological Seminary. Jim Grant also served three churches in Texas. He is an Air Force veteran, retiring with 25 years of service. His extensive travels while in the military allowed him the unique ability to have served in the full gambit of churches styles and health. He has been married to his wife Kathy for 39 years; they have two daughters and six grandchildren. Dr. Grant is a conference speaker and innovator of church revitalization practices; sharing in United States and Canada. You can follow Jim's blog at: preachbetweenthelines.com

Church Revitalization in Rural America

57465663R00163

Made in the USA
Columbia, SC
11 May 2019